WHERE
TWO WORLDS
TOUCH

WHERE TWO WORLDS TOUCH

Spiritual Rites of Passage

GLORIA D. KARPINSKI

Ballantine Books • New York

Grateful acknowledgment is made to the following for permission to reprint previously published material:

W.W. NORTON & COMPANY, INC., AND HOGARTH PRESS: Excerpt from Letters to a Young Poet by Rainer Maria Rilke, translated by M.D. Herter Norton. Copyright 1934 by W.W. Norton & Company, Inc. Copyright renewed 1962 by M.D. Herter Norton. Revised edition copyright 1954 by W.W. Norton & Company, Inc. Copyright renewed 1982 by M.D. Herter Norton. Reprinted by permission of W.W. Norton & Company, Inc., the Estate of Rainer Maria Rilke, St. John's College, Oxford, and Hogarth Press.

THRESHOLD BOOKS: Excerpt from *Open Secrets: Versions of Rumi* translated by John Moyne and Coleman Barks. Reprinted by permission of Threshold Books, RD 4, Box 600, Putney, VT 05346.

Library of Congress Catalog Card Number: 89-91499
ISBN: 0-345-35331-5

Text design by Holly Johnson
Cover design by Janet Dudar
Cover photograph: The Image Bank/© 1985 Don Carroll

Manufactured in the United States of America

First Edition: July 1990

10 9 8 7 6 5 4 3 2 1

This book is lovingly dedicated to Elizabeth H. Gilmore,
my mother and my friend,
in gratitude for her intuitive understanding of my choices
and her unconditional support of them.

The breeze at dawn has secrets to tell you.
                    Don't go back to sleep.
You must ask for what you really want.
                    Don't go back to sleep.
People are going back and forth across the doorsill
                    where two worlds touch.
The door is round and open.
                    Don't go back to sleep.

—Jelaluddin Rumi
Thirteenth Century

Contents

Exercises

Acknowledgments

This book is offered as an expression of gratitude:

To God for life and opportunity;

To Spirit for remembrance and revelation;

To the Masters for their spiritual legacies.

To thank all of the individual people who have contributed to my writing this book would require another volume. It would have to include every group that has invited me to lecture and all of the people who have attended my workshops and opened their personal worlds to me as a counselor. These individuals have been and continue to be my teachers.

The support, intimacy, and unconditional love of my family and friends are written into these pages. I thank each one of them for their constant encouragement of my work through the years and their continued support of this project.

Specifically I want to thank my editor, Cheryl Woodruff, for sharing her extraordinary skills, her perceptive guidance, and her "tough love" that would accept nothing less than the best I could do. I also thank Barbara Shor for her careful and sensitive editing; Everett Susco for his patient retyping of the manuscript; and Judith Puckett for her many readings of the manuscript as it developed over the months, her thoughtful feedback, and her careful attention to the bibliography.

I have been deeply impressed with the unwavering support and commitment to excellence demonstrated by every department of Ballantine Books. I am honored to have this book published by them.

WHERE
TWO WORLDS
TOUCH

Introduction

Change challenges, relieves, frustrates, threatens, saddens, or exhilarates us. Mainly it forces us to grow. It is the mechanism through which nature ensures evolution and the way God calls us home. It scares away our illusions about ourselves and others. Angel of mercy or Saturnian disciplinarian, change is constantly tailoring us to become all that we are meant to be. It molds us as surely as winds sculpt a tree or flowing waters reshape the hardest rock. Through change we are initiated into higher and higher states of consciousness. Our consciousness is our total awareness, a synthesis of heart and mind that enables us to act.

Change invites us to stretch and risk. It offers new births in consciousness to the degree that we are willing to die to the old. When change is only stoically endured or loudly protested, nothing is learned and the inevitable is delayed. Yet when change is accepted—no, more than that, embraced—it catalyzes our lives, expands our understanding, and shifts our perspective from one of fear to one that affirms life. For life is change.

There are ways of dealing with change creatively and without fear. One of them is by understanding the dynamics of change itself. Caught in the drama of a sudden personal crisis, it is often challenging to be able to see any purpose in it. But change is always a matter of process, even when it comes suddenly. Change often seems to be chaotic and threatening, with no intelligent direction. The key word here is *seems*. From a larger perspective or in retrospect, in change we see the workings of personal or planetary evolution.

THE RHYTHMS OF CHANGE

There is a rhythm in the way change occurs. I gradually became aware of this rhythm through years of being privileged to share the "classrooms" of hundreds of people as they met their challenges, even though the arenas and specifics were as different as the people themselves.

As I attuned myself to the rhythm of change, I realized that many of the people who came to me for counseling for the first time were either twenty-one, twenty-eight, thirty-five, forty-two, forty-nine, fifty-six, or sixty-three. In time I realized that this meant that they were in the first part of a seven-year cycle.

I came to see that the major turnings in their lives that heralded profound changes—marriages, divorces, deaths, births, career moves—all clustered around the actual year of a cycle change or a few months going into it or coming out of it. In case I missed the point, I would occasionally have clients who would insist that I see their teenagers, who were, like as not, age fourteen.

At first I casually assumed that this occurrence was in sync with the biological and psychological developmental tasks of the various ages. And I do think there is some correlation there, certain broad strokes that have to do with the desire to marry, likely times for career promotions, our own aging, and the aging and deaths of our parents.

However, it stretches credibility pretty far to make all the changes I was observing fit the scientific models. And this point of view made no sense at all when a man experienced a car wreck that crippled his body and changed his life exactly when he was thirty-five; or when a young woman's mother would suddenly die when she was twenty-eight. Why not twenty-six or thirty? Why did the divorce occur precisely at forty-two? The lawsuit at fifty-six?

Many cosmologists from around the world suggest that creation takes place in cycles of seven. In the biblical account, God created for six days and rested on the seventh. Metaphysicians would say that cycle symbolizes seven great epochs of time and would point to corresponding versions in Zoroastrian beliefs and in Japanese Shintoism, in Hinduism, and in the myths of a number of other world cultures.

From sunspots and economic crashes to the spawning of fish and changes in fashion, all life moves in cycles. Good astrologers are rarely surprised by predictable cycles of activity. They look at the horoscope of an individual person or an entire country, plot the cyclical paths of the planets through the symbolic signs of the zodiac as they overlap, oppose, or complement each other, and indicate the likely times and intent of upcoming changes. They don't know what specifically will happen, but they can successfully indicate that something profound is going to happen.

The universe is just that—a universe—and we are in rhythm with the energy that holds it all together. We affect and are affected by all that happens.

Whether we're working through a deeply ingrained pattern, in which the dance of change might last a lifetime, or addressing a more superficial pattern in which the stages of change might be worked through from beginning to end within a few weeks or months—we are always in process with many changes at one time. Our lives are made up of cycles within cycles—some turning over rapidly, others moving slowly.

THE 7 STEPS OF
CONSCIOUS CHANGE

How we perceive change begins with our understanding of who we think we are. The collection of habits, attitudes, and beliefs we gather around ourselves tell us who we think we are. Events might come and go, but there is no real change in us until one of those events actually challenges our perception of who we are. It's quite possible to simply endure with the same mind-set until the next big event. But once a deeply held belief about ourselves is really challenged, then the dance of change begins. We may resist, or we may join the dance—usually the former before the latter—but we'll eventually resolve the conflict between the status quo and the challenge, commit to a new direction, endure the necessary purging of the old habits, and finally surrender fully to the new.

It is this journey, through these seven stages of conscious change, that is the focus of this book.

1. The first step is the FORM. This is the basic belief we hold about ourselves on any subject. It defines the boundaries of our perception, dictates our opinions, and, most importantly, establishes our personal reality. This is the point at which all change begins.

2. A sense of movement in the process of change begins with the second step, the CHALLENGE. Some event happens, or we are exposed to something or someone that disturbs the status quo, and our original Form no longer works.

3. RESISTANCE, the third, and usually quite uncomfortable, cycle of change, when our old way of being and our new perception lock horns in a battle of ambivalence and indecision. Logic, conditioning, and history argue for the past, yet the strongest pull is toward the new.

4. Eventually we're rescued by the fourth stage—the AWAKENING. This is the exhilarating part of the cycle in which a break-

through occurs in the previous struggle. At this point we make the critical shift from indecision to the new viewpoint.

5. Next comes COMMITMENT. This is the point in the cycle when we put all our resources—time, money, energy—into the new direction. This stage presents us with a series of choices that help us bring our new goal into manifestation.

6. PURIFICATION is the inevitable next step—one that takes us totally by surprise. This is the time the actual transformation takes place. And it is often painful. Old hurts and fears repressed during earlier parts of the process rise up to be acknowledged and, ultimately, transformed. It is a time of dying to the old; a time that tests our faith in the new.

7. Finally we reach the last stage—SURRENDER. This is the point in the process of change when we actually become the new belief. It is characterized by synthesis and integration. The new becomes one with the whole being, and the old form is but a memory.

When events in the outer world challenge our beliefs—our form—we have the option of refusing to change. We can deny the new, defend the old, and cling tenaciously to our existing understanding. Or we can stop, pay attention, and ask, "What can I learn from this challenge? How can I become really conscious with this?"

We're always making choices about our inner world, whether consciously or unconsciously. These choices create patterns that attract certain kinds of future experiences. When we choose to use the challenges that force us to confront our ideas about ourselves, when we choose to use events as stepping-stones toward greater understanding, then we opt for *conscious change.*

A MUTUAL CONTRACT

There is an expression from Iceland that says "I won't sell it to you more expensive than I bought it." That's my contract with you. The ideas about the dynamics of conscious change that I'm sharing with you in this book have emerged from my personal laboratory of over fifteen years of healing, teaching, and counseling. I will report events and experiences honestly and interpret them as clearly as my understanding and skill allow.

As for your part of the contract, I ask that you read with an open mind and listen between the words. At best, words catch only a thimbleful of meaning. When we attempt to describe the nonmaterial in concrete terms, we find ourselves instantly on tricky ground. It's like using a net to catch flowing water. Spirit is everywhere and in all life. To pull any one thing out of Spirit and name it is immediately limiting. The whole can't be made specific. But we can understand more about the whole by studying its parts.

If a story or a phrase stirs you into remembering a bit more clearly who you are, I will be grateful. If the thoughts in this book help you to go through your changes with more understanding, my intention will have been fulfilled.

And if this book should not be for you, then I ask that you gently lay it aside and make neither of us wrong. Our conflict-ridden world needs us to celebrate, not argue about our diversity. There are endless prisms through which the Light breaks—one Light, many colors. I infuse my words with the prayer that, above all, you may find the color that is yours and live it and that both of us may grow in our understanding of the many colors within the one Light.

As I write and you read, our worlds do indeed touch. They touch like the smile that says "Don't I know you from somewhere?"

PART I

Initiation

Changes

Change: Reassuring in its cycles. The annual promise of spring flowers emerging from the snow, reminding us that the seeds of new growth are germinating.

Change: Arriving less gently. Exploding reality like a careening car, shattering our carefully ordered world in microseconds.

Change: A welcomed birth. A new life whose first breath rearranges all our priorities and relationships—restructuring money, time, and loyalties.

Change: Teasing us with safety. The long-awaited victory that goes flat because we no longer want what we thought we wanted.

Change is inevitable. No one would argue about something so obvious. Yet we're nearly always surprised when it happens.

We know that our children might well grow up differently than our program for them. But because we don't really believe they will, we agonize when they do. We know that our parents will grow old one day, and so will we. Yet we panic at the first signs of frailty. We'll even admit that no job is 100 percent secure and that relationships need to be in a constant state of redefinition or they'll die. Yet when we tell a loved one "You've changed," it is more an accusation than an acknowledgment of a natural and inevitable process.

We may attempt to protect ourselves against the reality of change, but the primal self knows. We observe and entrain with the cyclic rhythm of the seasons, celebrating ancient seasonal rites of planting, gestation, and harvest. But the self, concerned with survival and dependent on the earth, watches warily. It remembers the year the land withheld its fruit, the day the still mountain suddenly belched fire, or the time the life-giving waters went on a deadly rampage of destruction, when the Good Mother, abundant and fruitful, unpredictably became the Terrible Mother, jolting us out of all conceits of manipulation and permanence.

Change announces itself with a birth, a death, a firing, a hiring, a success or failure, with aggressive headlines informing us the world turned while we were innocently sleeping. Without warning, the reliable plot of our life script, in which all the actors know their lines, dissolves into an unfamiliar drama. What happened to the hero? Who's the villain? What's my next line?

Everything we observe in the universe demonstrates that change is the one constant of life. From the rapid turnover of cells to the life cycle of stars, all nature is in a continual process of birthing and dying. We may grasp for reassurance by repeating the old homily "The more things change, the more they stay the same," but all this means is that we're focusing on the slower processes of evolution.

We deceive ourselves when we try to capture life and lock it into permanence. We might as well try to catch the wind in a sieve. For life is movement. Whatever we see today is already in the process of dying. We live in yesterday's dream made manifest, and tomorrow we will see the results of what we dream today. No matter how much we manipulate, measure, and analyze, life remains wonderfully, terrifyingly mysterious.

To resist change is no doubt very human. Stubborn resistance—the I've-made-up-my-mind-don't-confuse-me-with-anything-new variety—is rooted in fear of the unknown, and it has caused a lot of pain, both personally and collectively. Wars are fought in every arena of human life when the beliefs of the past are challenged by changes in the present.

We have a history of killing off the messengers of change. We don't like our myths to be challenged. Yet innovators in every area of human accomplishment—scientific, educational, political, religious—have lived in sync with the mystery of change. They look to what is and ask what it can become. Unfortunately resistance to the change they herald often results in their being ignored, ridiculed, even killed, only to be resurrected from infamy years later to become the heroes of new legends. The process starts all over.

Whenever we build a citadel to defend a known truth instead of leaving it open-ended for further inquiry, we crystallize life into dogma. Yet just as soon as we think we have it all figured out, evolution steps in, throws open the doors and windows and all the dust of the past is tossed around, and we have to change yet again.

In the meantime we cope with the present, often discovering within ourselves unimagined capacities for courage and endurance. Century after century humans pick themselves up from splintered dreams and build anew. We persist, three steps forward and two back, through the slow, grinding discipline of experience. We are driven toward a higher perfection as surely as the sun pulls the life in the seed toward its light. We are propelled by the promise of a potential not yet realized.

To those who fear change, evolution is the enemy. But to those who respond consciously to the steady beat of evolution, it is the essence of life summoning us to become all that we can be. It stirs our longings, makes us discontent with injustice, disease, pollution, and war. It plants in our hearts a sureness that life need not be as it is. Evolution nudges, encourages, and hurls us toward change.

As a "Funky Winkerbean" cartoon puts it, "Evolution may not be getting any better, but it's certainly getting faster!" From where I stand, it also seems to be getting better in spite of outer appearances. And this is because we're gradually waking up to the fact that we're all in this together. We're totally interdependent upon each other and all the other life-forms that share our world.

MARKING THE TURNINGS

Self-knowledge is the primary step in spiritual realization. Helping people confront and integrate their own personal fears and limitations makes it possible for us to deal with these problems on racial, national, and planetary levels.

Counselors, therapists, and teachers are in a good position to observe personal transformation, possibly because people rarely seek their services when life is rolling along. Usually it's a trauma of some sort that compels us to reach out for help. It might be an obvious crisis, such as a loved one walking out on us, discovering that our child is on drugs, the sudden death of a friend, the diagnosis of a life-threatening illness, a debilitating depression—any of the hundreds of triggers that suddenly and unequivocally rearrange the world we had so carefully planned.

People also seek out those in the helping professions when they are moving through changes in their spiritual lives. Shifts that arise from the deepest levels of self only appear to be less violent than an immediate and demanding crisis in our outer lives. Soul changes tend to be evolutionary rather than revolutionary. But at major turnings any change can erupt with all the

fierceness of a crisis, for there is nothing in our life that is sep-
arable from Spirit.

The word *crisis* originates in the Greek word *krines*, meaning
"the parting of the ways." That says it all. In the wake of a
major crisis we nearly always part ways with our past view of
reality—whether we do it willingly or kicking and screaming.
The Chinese have two words for crisis; one means "danger,"
the other "opportunity." From a spiritual perspective what appears to be dangerous often offers us great opportunities for
growth.

Many times we can sense a major shift approaching. It may
not have expressed itself yet in the physical world, but we feel
its energy at work, disturbing the status quo. Before a great
storm there is often a very tense silence, almost as if the air itself
were holding its breath. We find ourselves in the middle of this
tense silence, sensing the approaching "birthquake," as a friend
puts it. Turning points announce themselves through a variety
of vague symptoms: deep restlessness, a yearning with no name,
inexplicable boredom, the feeling of being stuck.

Life-altering changes often occur as if a time-release capsule
had been dissolved inside the psyche. However, the event itself
is often less important than the learning opportunities encapsu-
lated within it. If it is time to learn a specific lesson, then events
will happen that set up the perfect opportunity. However, if
events haven't unfolded to provide the lesson needed, or if the
lesson isn't heeded, then another set of events will occur that
offer the same lesson.

Suppose the capsule is time-released for John, age twenty-
one, to learn about forgiveness. The classroom might be his job,
and the boss he seems unable to please becomes his teacher. The
event that occurs is that John gets fired from his job. If he for-
gives the boss, he is free to move on. He doesn't have to repeat
the lesson. But if he refuses to learn about forgiveness, then he
gets a new classroom and a new teacher—but the lesson stays
the same: forgiveness.

John might find himself with a new job—this time he is threatening the ego of a colleague, who retaliates by taking credit for his work. Or he might become friends with someone who makes off with his girlfriend. Or his car might be stolen. He is still going to have to learn the lesson of forgiveness. If he doesn't forgive the boss, perhaps he'll be able to forgive the co-worker, or the friend, or the robber.

The changes John is experiencing are really about changing consciousness. To put this in context with his other cycles, let's suppose that his soul's intent is to learn several major lessons so that he can ultimately use his talents in helping others. Perhaps if we could see him two cycles later, we'd discover that he's become a physical therapist rehabilitating people who have work-related injuries. He isn't going to do this work until he is thirty-five and maybe has no idea at twenty-one or twenty-eight that such work will appeal to him. But his soul knows. This purpose is part of his seed pattern from birth as surely as is the color of his eyes.

So, from the time John is born until he grows into this work, he will unconsciously draw to himself all the lessons he needs to clear himself and to prepare him to help others through their blocks and challenges. Some of the lessons might be quite tough. For example he might have a serious accident when he's twenty-eight that seems like a senseless interruption of his life at that point. If we try to understand that painful change at the point when it happened, we are not likely to succeed. But as John goes through months of struggle and therapy to regain his health, he will learn to reach deep inside and tap his will. He will learn about discipline and patience, and about compassion for others. Levels of awareness will open up to him that were outside his conscious awareness before the accident.

We'll assume that John eventually learns his forgiveness lesson, since he couldn't teach his patients much about it if he hasn't learned it himself. So by thirty-five, when he's ready to move into his life's work, he has graduated from the classrooms that taught him what he needed to know to do his work well. For-giveness, self-discipline, and compassion have been synthesized in his consciousness.

THINGS AREN'T NECESSARILY
WHAT THEY APPEAR

I recall once working with a teenager who was brought to me for some minor physical problem. But his parents' real concern was his endless carelessness. He was forever creating pesky problems and then having to face up to what he'd done. He was the kind of kid who'd jump up without looking and always break something. He'd cut five minutes of study hall like lots of other kids, but he'd be the one to get caught. He'd drive to the store but forget his license at home, and then get pulled over by the police.

As I worked with him, I was told in Spirit: This young man has important work to do in the future. However there is a carelessness in his use of energy that must be disciplined. So he is bringing to himself one situation after another that will allow him to learn this. Tell the parents not to be concerned. *It is the soul tailoring the personality for its own purposes.*

I often think of this advice when I see people rerunning the same lesson over and over. Once we come to realize that our souls are methodically holding us in the same classroom until the lessons are learned, our impatience and our judgments of ourselves and others are eased and softened.

Most of the time we have no idea what that lesson may be for other people. But we begin to understand that a hard time, even a tragedy, is very likely an important and necessary lesson in their lives. At this point we become aware that things are not what they seem, and that "Ain't it awful?" ain't necessarily so!

It took me quite a while to learn that things are not always what they seem. I recall working with a brilliant woman who kept finding herself in the role of promoting other people's work. She has several degrees, including a Ph.D. in psychology, and was fully capable of doing the level of work that would have gained her much attention and plaudits. Yet she was very comfortable in this role, and that was not the reason she sought counseling. Her pattern of remaining in the background began at birth. She was born into a large family, where financial pressures prevented her from going to college as a young woman. So she went to work to support her younger siblings and put them through college first. At the age of thirty-five she finally finished her undergraduate work with honors. She pursued her graduate work with a very famous man and then devoted herself to supporting his work. When we first met, she was in her sixties and was hard at work compiling the writings of her mentor. She had also served as therapist to several students who later became well known in the field.

As we looked at the broader scope of her life plan, it became clear that she had incarnated to work on the process of soul initiation that could be defined as "laying down your life for others." This kind of soul work doesn't necessarily mean that one has to die for another physically. Laying down one's life has more to do with putting aside the lower ego in order to use our talents to serve others. It's definitely Ph.D. work at the soul level and is not to be confused with psychologically sabotaging one's own talents.

False martyrdom leaves one resentful and unfulfilled. You won't see much joy in such a person. However, willingly acquiescing in the lesson of sacrificing fame and fortune to support the growth of others generates great joy—much to the puzzlement of those who are still looking after number one. Interestingly enough, before we are asked to devote ourselves to this kind of lesson, we first have to learn how to do a good job of looking after number one. I guess we have to have had something worth giving up before we can do it well and with joy.

Another example of someone working on laying down his or her life for another might be a person who had been famous in a previous lifetime for his voice and has chosen, from the soul level, in this lifetime to be a great voice teacher. That person's genius is used to help others reach their potential. A great writer might become a great editor for others. Another, fully capable of accomplishing many things for her own glorification but deciding to work on this particular lesson, might choose to be full-time mother to several children.

Each of these people, using his or her own resources to promote the talents of others, discovers that sacrifice only seems like giving up something when seen through the eyes of the younger student. It is, in fact, about gaining. Like all soul lessons, it can't be faked: the inner self knows whether we are acting out a pathology, a programmed family myth, or growing in understanding.

Faith in one's soul purpose is not very compatible with a value system that wants an instant payoff. From that point of view changes constitute a steady source of frustration, often devastating and embittering. Once we begin to perceive ourselves and others holistically, in our total lifewalk, we will recognize change as the dynamic force behind the unfolding of the soul's plan.

Most of us could look back and see that a difficult change that made no sense at one point in our lives prepared us to fulfill later an important task. Madeleine L'Engle, in her book *The Irrational Season*, speaks of the no that often precedes the yes. She points out that it was the no of Gethsemane that made the yes of Resurrection possible.

In the face of a disappointment or a radical change we dislike, it is a challenge to trust that there is purpose. To accept this is one of the first lessons in living changes gracefully. How many times have we tried to manipulate the world into something we wanted, and failed? The timing was simply not right, even if we didn't know it. Later the same doors we wanted so desperately to force open earlier, fling themselves open to an unexpected opportunity, and we sail through, seemingly without effort. The timing is right. Like a clay pot that has to be repeatedly fired in order to withstand the pressure of what it is to hold, so are we tempered in preparation for the future.

THE DIFFERENCE BETWEEN QUOTING AND KNOWING

Sooner or later even the most materialistic person will ask, "What is the point of my life? Why am I here going through all these changes?" The very cry of the heart to know is an affirmation that there are answers, however veiled they may seem at any given moment. We tend to believe—or at least hope—that there will be some authorities around who can answer the mystery of our changing lives. The advice given by the oracle at Delphi was "Man, know thyself"—not "seek an expert."

A Sufi story warns us about experts. It seems there was a man presumed dead who suddenly began banging on his coffin. The people raised the coffin lid, and the man said, "What are you doing? I am not dead." After a bit of silence one of the crowd said, "The doctors and the priests have declared that you are dead. So dead you are." And he was promptly buried!

I once read that the difference between mysticism and religion is that religion is believing in someone else's experience of God, whereas mysticism is believing in your own.

It is inspirational, encouraging, and comforting to study someone else's journey into enlightenment. All of us would have a much harder time stumbling around in the dark density of materialism if we didn't have the illuminations of enlightened ones who have gone before us. Their radiance, lighting up the treacherous twists and turns of the path toward self-awareness, is a gift, for when we focus on the wisdom of an enlightened person, we have that same potential within us quickened.

But it is so much easier to acquire stories about enlightened ones than it is to follow their lead. In *Song of the Bird*, Anthony de Mello tells the story of an explorer who went to the Amazon. As he enjoyed the richness of the country he thought to himself, how will I ever be able to tell the people back home what it feels like to paddle the canoe over the waterfalls? How can I describe the riotous colors of the flowers, the exotic sounds, the rich fragrances? So he decided to make them a map. When he returned home the people were thrilled by his stories. They pinned the map on the town hall. Some people memorized every turning of the river. Some became map experts. But none of them journeyed to the Amazon themselves. The Jain teacher Gurudev Chitrabhanu tells of his first meeting with the man who was to become his guru. Chitrabhanu had been traveling all over India learning to "talk the talk" with many wise ones, and he thought he knew a lot. But the first thing his guru told him was "You don't know anything. You're just a good parrot." He says that was the true beginning of his learning.

Most of us quote a truth a long time before we own it. We talk of oneness even as we fight for ego territory. We speak of God's love at the same time that we are backing away from Grace. The fact that a truth is recognized does not mean that the old, programmed self abdicates the crown of ego willingly. But in time, and with commitment to our search, it does.

When the mystery of self begins to yield its secrets, it makes no difference how universal a revelation is, because it has all the awesome joy we feel at the birth of a new child. It is said that the hope of our species is born anew with every infant. The same is true with every spiritual birth.

"Seek and you shall find" is the master key. It is not just the promise to believers in any one system, nor is it a romantic notion. It is a tough, working law of energy. The dynamic of this law of energy is attraction. The desire to understand sets in motion powerful forces, and the answers begin to come slowly, a bit at a time. The right book, the sudden intuitive knowingness, the person with a piece of the puzzle—they all seem to appear as if by magic. What we used to think was coincidence is in fact directed by an unseen intelligence. I've always liked the expression "Coincidence is God's way of staying anonymous."

Is it supernatural? No. Naturally super? Oh, yes. The fact is, we've just been working it unconsciously, unaware of the powerful, unrelenting law of attraction. We have been creating our own reality all along. Now we can make it intentional.

FROM COPING TO CO-CREATING

"You create your own reality" can read a bit like New Age hype that has nothing to do with the real world of money, power, politics, the homeless, AIDS, or your personal life. Not understood, such a statement seems like an empty cliché at best, often guilt producing, insulting, and totally irrelevant at worst. "What did I have to do with a world at war, a birth defect, an out-of-control economy?" And, more personally, "What did I have to do with what I started out with in this life—my family, gender, race, country, or economic status?"

These are not easy questions. Rely on appearances to evaluate existing "hard data" and it's likely to seem totally chaotic, the "roll of the dice." The trouble is that hard data are constantly changing as yesterday's absolute truths give way to today's absolute truths—and tomorrow's.

It's little wonder that intelligent people sometimes opt for skepticism. It's a useful transitional energy. It questions and probes for the counterfeit, but it is still open to learning. Sri Aurobindo, who was both mystic and intellectual, once said, "First of all I believed that nothing was impossible, and at the same time I could question everything."

However, cynicism, as opposed to skepticism, is a dead end in the search for understanding. I was once told in Spirit, "A cynic is someone who has attempted to make God over in his own image and failed." The cynic is likely to say there's no cause, no guiding intelligence, transcendent or otherwise.

The keepers of some of our myths tell us that an anthropomorphic deity made all the decisions for us, assigning us the role we are playing. If you were born a blind Vietnamese female who died in a napalm raid at the age of four, well, that's just the way this deity called it. It's not for us to know why, it's just the mystery.

Yet down through the centuries ancient teachings from all over the world tell us that reality is not something done *to* us; we create it. Perhaps the word *we* should be underlined, for many of the realities we experience are those we have made together. As we look at the enormous challenges of our lives and times, it is worth serious investigation into the possibility that we are indeed creators. It might result in some sobering confrontations with our egos on first consideration, but just imagine the implications for creating the future.

There is danger in oversimplification when discussing how we create our own realities. But be patient while I explore that for a moment, and then we'll look at some of the principles involved.

First of all, we didn't just begin with this life. The you that is beyond personality, the real you, has always existed. There never was a time you were not; there never will be a time you won't be. If you can accept that, from some higher level of be-ingness, you chose to be in the life you're experiencing because it was going to allow you maximum opportunities to grow and contribute, you will see that all those fixed realities you started with had purpose. That you were born a Jewish male in Manhattan rather than an Islamic female in Tehran represents the first major bit of reality creation in anyone's life. No matter how you think you came to be born, it was purposeful. Many realities were created by that birth choice.

For example I know a young woman who was born in abject

poverty in a Third World country. She was one of those big-eyed children you see on televised relief programs. She lived under these conditions until she was ten, when the next, seemingly unlikely, phase of her journey opened: being adopted by a family in the United States who could give her the opportunities she needed. She arrived speaking no English. Ten years later this girl was in graduate school on an academic scholarship, majoring in political science and committed to improving conditions in Third World countries. This young woman incarnated with a brilliant intelligence. Her soul purpose was to use this life for world service. In preparation for the life she intended to grow into, she imprinted her awareness in the early years with devastating poverty, and when that was done, it was time to train the intellect. If she had been born into privilege from the beginning, she might not have cared enough to commit her talents to world service. As it was, she was on fire for reform from the soul level and was given the opportunity to do just that through education. She might well have to work through her personal rage at the world's injustice, learning to transform frustrations and pain from her early years. But that is part of preparing an effective instrument for service.

I also know of an infant who was rescued from a garbage can by a man who started and operates an orphanage for street children in Brazil. That orphan grew up to become a medical doctor who now serves the orphanage.

LIVING WITH MULTIPLE REALITIES

Once we arrive on the earth plane, each of us lives within many realities, and we create within all of them. First of all we experience ourselves as individuals who are making choices based on predispositions, personal needs, preferences, and unconscious motives. Those choices create our realities. If I trash my body with junk food, refuse to exercise, and continually poison myself with negative thinking, I will create a personal reality that will give me back the results of these choices within a matter of weeks or years.

Secondly we also live in realities in which we play only a part. You and I are part of families that provided us with not only our genetic inheritance but also our ideas of family values. We in turn contribute to our family's story from the moment we are born. Even if we were to run away, our rejection would affect everyone and become part of the family story.

Our genders help shape our realities too. At the moment of birth we inherit all the prevailing attitudes of gender—all the myths, prohibitions, and expectations. While we cannot single-handedly change the world's perceptions of masculine and feminine, the choices we make as we live our lives as men or women do *influence* the whole.

Lastly we're influenced by, and participate in creating, the reality of our species. We are thinking cells in the one mind of humanity. Our attitudes and beliefs, our visions and our terrors, pour into the collective sea in which we all swim.

THE ONENESS OF ALL LIFE

The myth that we are separate and apart, that we are each a closed system, is now dissolving into the greater truth that we each affect what we see.

Since the 1920s, when Werner Heisenberg developed the uncertainty principle, science has been showing us that there is no such thing as purely objective analysis. Our observation of a thing is part of its reality—and our own.

In David Peat's book *Synchronicity: The Bridge Between Matter and Mind*, physicist John Wheeler is quoted as saying, "We had this old idea that there was a universe out there, and here is man, the observer, safely protected from the universe by a six-inch slab of plate glass. Now we learn from the quantum world that even to observe so minuscule an object as an electron we have to shatter that plate glass; we have to reach in there. . . . So the old word *observer* simply has to be crossed off the books, and we must put in the word *participator*. In this way we've come to realize that the universe is a participatory universe."

Quantum physics teaches us that nothing exists in isolation. All of matter, from subatomic particles to galaxies, is part of an intricate web of relationship within a unified whole.

The work of physicist David Bohm on subatomic particles and the quantum potential led him to conclude that while physical entities seem to be separate in space and time, they are actually linked or unified in an implicit or unifying fashion. Beneath the explicit realm of separate things or events lies an implicit realm of individual wholeness, and this implicit whole connects all things.

An ancient Sanskrit teaching tells us that in the Heavens of Indra there is a network of pearls so arranged that if you look at one, you see all the others reflected in it. In the same way, each object in the world is not merely itself but involves every other object and in fact is every other object. Today we recognize the reality of Indra's net in the amazing multidimensionality of the hologram.

Holograms can best be grasped by illustration. If you take a holographic image of a dog and enlarge only one section of it, say its head, you will get more than a picture of the dog's head, you will get the whole dog. The head of the dog is a part of the whole, and the whole is present in each of its parts. Stanford neurophysiologist Karl Pribram speculates that the hologram may be a model of the human brain and, even further, that it may reflect the structure of our whole universe.

Personal experience has brought me to the same conclusions. The healing work I have been privileged to participate in for many years often involves clients who may be hundreds or even thousands of miles away. Healing energy and information are transmitted through the unifying medium that connects all life—Bohm's implicit order—and that medium is beyond the time and space we normally perceive. We are inseparable from all of nature. We can no more upset the balance of nature and expect to be unaffected than we can upset our personal lives and expect our families to remain unaffected.

The book *Resettling America: Energy, Ecology, and Community* by Gary Coates reported a story that underlines what happens when we refuse to honor nature's complex system of interdependence. The World Health Organization (WHO) sprayed tribal villages in Borneo with DDT in an attempt to eradicate malaria. The villages consisted of low, thatched "long houses" where up to five hundred people lived in a single dwelling, so it was a simple matter to spray the huts with the chemical. The short-term effect was a dramatic drop in the incidence of malaria.

However it didn't take long before the villages were invaded by rats from the forest carrying fleas in their fur. This was a matter of some concern, since the fleas were carriers of plague.

As it turned out, a number of creatures had lived in the thatched huts. There were cockroaches, small lizards, and cats. The DDT was absorbed by the cockroaches, who were eaten by the lizards. The lizards in turn were food for the cats. But because DDT becomes increasingly concentrated as it moves up the food chain, it was the cats who all died of DDT poisoning. With the demise of the village cats the way was clear for the marauding rats. To deal with this, WHO had to parachute cats into the villages.

This was not the only side effect. Small caterpillars had also lived in the thatched huts. When the DDT killed a smaller organism that preyed on the insects, the caterpillar population suddenly soared. Unfortunately what the caterpillars fed on were the thatched roofs. It didn't take long for entire villages to come tumbling down.

We *do* create all of our realities, but we don't necessarily create them entirely by ourselves. We are "co-creators" with other people and with nature. We create personal worlds with instant feedback as well as long-term personal realities that take many lives to manifest. We also help to create family, racial, sexual, species, and planetary realities. We are participants in—not victims of—a world we influence by every choice we make.

Every time we wantonly kill off a life-form, we dishonor all life. Whenever we buy products from manufacturers who exploit people, we contribute to the total reality of abuse. Whenever we pollute the environment—even with so small an act as tossing a soda can out a car window—we set in motion a domino effect in nature. With every disregard for the physical environment, we help create spaces for virulent new viruses to incubate. Whenever we fill the sea of our unified consciousness with violence and fear, we are contributing to the moment when that violence and fear will erupt in our own personal lives.

And conversely, every time we are the instruments of an act of justice, no matter how small, we add one more bit of justice to the whole world. Every time we clean up one bit of fear within ourselves, we do it for everyone. When we love, forgive, respect all life, and interact with harmlessness, we contribute toward these values becoming a reality for all of us.

When we look at the child enduring devastating poverty, the freedom fighter languishing in a political prison, the young man whose life is cut short with AIDS, we say, "There but for the grace of God go I." Perhaps we need also to send them a strong thank-you. Their nightmare is also a sacrifice that allows you and me to understand more clearly what needs to be cleaned up for all of us. We are all so interconnected that, as a botanist once said, "Pick a flower, disturb a star."

THE LAW OF ATTRACTION

The principle of attraction—in which we magnetically pull to ourselves what we seek—is a law of energy and, like any other law, is activated through natural processes. The world was round, after all, even when we insisted it was flat. But before we discovered the truth of roundness, we created a host of demons and monsters that guarded the edge of the world.

How could something that never truly existed have the capacity to create such fear and limitation? Because our belief in them was so powerful, we breathed power into them. Such is the power of our minds.

The law of attraction—like attracts like—is one of the master keys to reality creation. "Seek and ye shall find" is at work when attractions are pulled in from fear magnets and the narrow demands of the ego. The law is equally at work when we seek to be aligned with our deepest spiritual self and we pull into our world all that is needed for creating from the highest in us.

We have only to look around at our world to see what we have collectively created from our blind egos—wars; dangerous pollutions; social, racial, and economic injustices; knowledge so untempered by wisdom that we teeter on the edge of self-annihilation.

We have brought ourselves collectively to planetary crisis, and we don't have the luxury of delaying much longer. We are in a time of profound choosing. We must realize that our destiny is one with all people and all life. Not only are we co-creators with each other, we are also in partnership with the Divine. Evolution pushes us either willingly or by means of hardship into accepting that.

Each of us is a magnet that pulls into our world whatever we hold in mind. Mind is much more than just the brain. Mind embraces our consistently fueled intentions, thoughts, actions, words, and images. Mind establishes and sustains the fire of consciousness.

THE WILL—UNIVERSAL
CREATIVE FORCE

The single most potent force you have is your will. For most of us it is the least understood. Yet everything we see around us, from social conditions to personal relationships, has been willed into existence. As we move through the intense changes of the new decade, we are going to hear more and more about the will. What is it really and what is the difference between God's will and human will? How do we know when we are in accord with God's will?

When the term *God's will* comes for us in our daily lives, it's likely to be used to cover anything from a natural disaster to a child's death to the winning or loss of a war. If we can't explain it, it must be "God's will."

When the image of a deity "out there" lingers in the collective mind, it's not too far removed from the old mountain and river gods. The will of such a deity carries dread. Sooner or later we fear that "it" will demand sacrifices. We suspect that "it" is taking notes and that any minute all our faults will be revealed and punished. How do we live so that "it" will reward us, or maybe not even notice us?

Many loving and intelligent people choose to dismiss the whole idea of a transcendent divine will as wishful thinking or pure superstition. It's little wonder, then, that they find that the concept "God is love" simply doesn't compute with that of "God's will," which seems so indifferent to human suffering.

It's never likely to compute as long as we think God's will is done *to* us rather than *through* us. We will have difficulty accepting that there really is a loving God behind all the chaos we see.

Is there a transcendent plan, a blueprint for planet Earth? During times of intense acceleration, such as now, many people catch symbolic glimpses of what appears to be an unfolding plan through dreams, visions, intuition.

I experienced such a vision a few years ago—one that spoke of a "new world" born. I was in prayer for the planet, holding before me the image of a whole Earth. Suddenly it blew up, shattering into a thousand pieces. But then, out of all this destruction, there emerged a luminescent planet, like the old Earth, but clearer, brighter, lighter. I did not feel this was prophecy of a nuclear holocaust. Rather it was an encouraging image of the world that is to be when we finish with the purifications that will seem to blow apart the world as we know it. I was guided to understand that we are in the process of co-creating this new world, and that it is to be a world "without harm"— characterized by creativity—unmarred by violence. But to get there from here, we first have to live through the blowups.

Spirit then proceeded to underline this vision for me so that I wouldn't think I'd just made it up. The week following the vision, I went to Jackson, Mississippi, to conduct a workshop. I told no one of this vision, as I tend to keep such experiences to myself until I feel I've integrated them. After the workshop a group of us went to the planetarium. While we were there, someone in the group bought me a present at the souvenir counter: a paperweight with two Earths etched on it. Not two hemispheres of the Earth, but two Earths exactly alike, side by side.

Many people are having similar impressions of the world that is to come out of the dark and dangerous passage we are experiencing now. The message in all of them is to hold tight to a vision of our world in ecological, racial, economic, social, and political balance.

How this new world will come into being is through us. While we cannot know the whole plan, each of us can know our place in it. It is not a secret that someone else can unlock for us. We carry it inside us. The divine gene that carries our cosmic DNA includes our plan for this lifetime. All it really takes to activate it is what an anonymous fourteenth-century writer called "the lively longing for God." The whole journey of transformation is really about rediscovering our true identity and will.

SURRENDERING TO
THE HIGHER WILL

Most of us feel some confusion when we hear such expressions as "Surrender your will to God." Of course this is what we ultimately do when we wake up to who we are. But we also know intuitively that the will is important to survival, and *surrender* sounds a lot like annihilation.

On the surface, surrender does look like death to the ego. But in fact surrendering to the Higher will restores our true identity. Try substituting the phrase *Higher will* for *God's will*. The concept of surrender of will takes on new color when we feel we're giving up a little self to a bigger self—one that is connected with God.

In many of the self-help programs for addiction, such as Alcoholics Anonymous and Adult Children of Alcoholics, the road to recovery begins with admitting that we are powerless over the addiction, and that we must surrender to a higher power for help. We release the rigid ego controls of the lower will when we acknowledge that it is limited in conquering our addictions. It is the Higher will within that holds the power to transform an addiction. This is as true of an emotional addiction as it is of a chemical one. The Higher will acts as a conduit to and from God. When the rigid controls of the ego are surrendered, the true power takes over.

We are made in the image of God, and the Higher will is very close to its essence. The gift of will makes us creators. As we continue to speak, desire, image, and think a thing, we reinforce the scaffolding for the blueprint to take shape on the physical plane.

We really are a funny lot. We use this divine birthright to create from our will. But when real things begin to manifest, we stand around complaining, "Who made this mess?"

SWIMMING IN THE RIVER OF ENERGY

Things don't just happen; they are willed into being either consciously or unconsciously, either by individuals, by groups, or by the whole species—even by our species interacting with the will of other realms of nature. We know that everything in the universe is vibrating. All of those trillions of cells that make up our individual biospheres are in a constant state of motion. For all its material appearance, nothing is solid. Track even the densest materials back to their molecular parts, and there they are, dancing to an unseen beat.

The space between all the atoms in your body is a hologram of the spaces between the stars—all of it connected, all of it in a state of constant readiness. For that connecting space is the medium through which any living, vibrating thing, from a planet to a thought, sends its message to the whole universe.

Moving in, around, over, under, and through all space is a cosmic river of flowing energy. That energy has been recognized and called by many names in many languages. *Chi* in Chinese; *ki* in Japanese; *prana* in Sanskrit; *rauch* in Hebrew; and *mana* in Polynesian, to mention just a few. In the West, of course, it has been given very scientific-sounding names such as "odic force" and "orgone energy." It's all the same energizing stuff of life.

This river of energy can be harnessed to enliven anything at any frequency. It can give life to a thought, a feeling, a physical body. However the blueprint is signed, this energy will bring it into being. And once the design is no longer needed, or has fulfilled itself and dies, the energy flows back into the river. This energy can be gathered, harnessed, shaped, expanded, or contracted, but it cannot be destroyed.

If the blueprint of a body, thought, or desire is clear and unblocked, this energy will flow through it unimpeded, and the intention will come to full fruition. However if the blueprint is blocked, compromised, or ambivalent, then the energy will amplify the distortion. We get to choose what we'll do with it, and we're equally responsible for what we bring to life with it.

Once we get through the shock of realizing we've been carefully building our own world—and participating in the building of our joint world—the next realization is that the power for creating in new ways is unlimited.

THE WILL TO BE

What force diverts the energy from the river into tree cells, or liver cells, or the molecular structure of rocks? What motivates them to come into existence in the first place? A seed, a pattern? Yes, of course. But there's more.

There is the will to be. Without this will the energy is released back into the universal flow. Withdraw the will out of anything and it's dead. This is as true of an emotion as it is of a physical body. Choose to withdraw the will out of hating, resenting, and fearing, and those emotions will die a natural death for lack of energy to support them.

The key word is *choice*. And we make these choices all the time. Dr. Viktor E. Frankl, a Jewish psychiatrist and philosopher, was imprisoned by the Nazis during World War II. In his book *Man's Search for Meaning* he observed that even in that most degrading of all possible conditions, a Nazi concentration camp, robbed of even the simplest dignity and unable to change the events, people continued to make choices. Enduring the unendurable, some people rose to nobility, sharing and caring about others, finding an inner peace in the midst of madness. They couldn't change what was happening, but they could choose how they would react to it.

We cannot just freeze and say we will do, think, or feel nothing in a given situation. That is itself a choice that energizes our fear.

We can always choose to will the status quo. But if we do, the wars, poverty, and injustices that were "good enough for dear old Dad" will be good enough for us too. However, we can also choose to design new blueprints, birth new desires, think new thoughts, utter new words. History will repeat itself as long as we continue to create out of the lower will of separation from God and from each other. The Inquisition, the Holocaust, Hiroshima, the Christian persecutions—all of the horrors of our history are variations of the theme of the alienation of humankind from its Spirit origins.

When we create out of the lower will only in order to satisfy greed, our finest productions fall before time as easily as sand castles give way to the sea. But when we listen to our deepest impulses from our highest will, we create from a blueprint that seems much larger than our own. We become co-creators with the universe, bringing into the physical realm new sounds, symbols, social concepts, discoveries, and inventions that enrich us all. Such creations are beautiful, and they endure because they provide for the good of all.

Grandpa put it well in Forrest Carter's *The Education of Little Tree*: "It is so with people who store and fat themselves with more than their share. They will have it taken from them. And there will be wars over it . . . and they will make long talks, trying to hold more than their share. They will say a flag stands for their right to do this . . . and men will die because of the words and the flag . . . but they will not change the rules of the Way."

Masters throughout time, regardless of culture and religion, have taught us the Way. They tell us that if we want to understand divine will, we must look within, that we are divine in origin and quite literally made in the image of God.

But we tend to get nervous if anybody takes that too seriously. The biblical injunction "Ye are gods" seems to be direct. Many people have experienced persecution throughout the centuries because they found that truth and spoke it. In the old days it was called blasphemy. Depending on the reality model today, accusations range from self-delusion and arrogance to ego inflation, and even that old bugaboo—demonic possession.

I suspect we are terrified of the responsibility inherent in living up to our divine potential. It's easier to blame events on forces outside ourselves or, in frustration, to assume that nothing intelligent is running the show. This allows us to perpetuate the illusion that we have nothing to do with the chaos of our personal lives, nothing to do with all the changes, and even less to do with planetary madness. However, when we are aligned with the One Will, we act as a grounding agent for that will on Earth.

The will is our sacred birthright. As the sunbeam is to the sun, so are we to the Source of all life. The light of the Source is within each of us, regardless of how dim it seems at times. There never was a time when we were not in existence as part of the whole. Nor will there ever be a time when we will not be part of the whole.

We lose that sense of wholeness when we give authority to the lower will, and we return to wholeness when we shift that authority to the Higher will. We carry both of them within us at all times. It's not a matter of denying, repressing, and conquering the lower will. It's a matter of choosing which will be in charge of our lives. The Higher will embraces and works through the lower will, not the other way around.

The Higher will within us chose the circumstances of our birth. It is interested in the growth of the soul and its return to oneness. Pain and disappointment are seen as being as great an opportunity for growth as success and pleasure. The lower will often makes choices that are good for the ego and sees pain and disappointment as mere failure. The lower will tends to see a universe of limitation. It looks to outer symbols of success to validate itself. It feels the need to control. God is perceived as being apart from self—an entity that has to be appealed to, invoked, even begged for favors. If the lower self doesn't get what it wants, it believes that its prayers weren't answered; it lives in fear.

The Higher will sees a universe of unlimited abundance, one in which there are plenty of resources for everyone. Living in oneness with God, it draws to itself all that is needed. It does not perceive the universe as a reluctant supplier; rather it uses knowledge as the instrument of wisdom, living in faith that all is unfolding in perfect order. It experiences life fully, making choices from inner rather than outer direction. It lives in love.

A person living under the domination of the lower will is neither good nor bad, just asleep and young in understanding. But before we can begin to surrender the lower will to the Higher, we have to know we have a will to create in the first place. The gift of free will allows us to explore our abilities to create, and when we are ready to give up the lower for the higher, we do so as fully conscious beings, not as sleepwalkers.

There was a time when we were aware of being totally at one in the Source. Our myths remember that time for us—we call it paradise, home. In the story of the Fall the ego usurped the will and used it for its own vehicle of validation. Sadly, as we became more civilized, we deepened the split, and Spirit became the enemy of the flesh. We both loved the Earth and at the same time struggled with it as the prison of our spirits.

REALIZING WHO WE ARE

Dr. Dianne Connelly entitled her book on traditional Chinese acupuncture *All Sickness Is Homesickness*—a brilliant title that defines our problem in one phrase. We're homesick for inner wholeness, homesick for unity with both the mother and the father aspects of God, homesick for our creative will to be at one with its source.

The divine gene is our wellness gene. It travels with us, no matter how many lives or experiences it takes for us to wake up. It guarantees that one day we will be sick and tired of using our wills to create dramas that leave us unfulfilled. We will want to get well. And the coding in this gene carries all the information we need to do that.

Planet Earth is the training ground for will-in-training. But we can become so identified with all that we are creating that we forget who we are. We get to make up all kinds of movies here, anything that suits our fancy—melodramas, comedies, romances. The trick is to realize that we are the creators, not the movies we have created. Until we understand the difference, we keep making lots of sequels with the same characters and similar plot lines.

The degree to which we think we're the part we're playing is the degree to which we're likely to suffer, for other people—other creators—are also participating, and even our best-laid plot lines are going to change.

Before my work opened up, I was feeling anxious about what I should do. I knew I was at a turning point, but the new direction had not yet emerged. "What am I supposed to be doing?" is usually the first question a lot of people bring to any counselor. In the West we are deeply conditioned to "do something." Doing, not being, is often the focus.

Then a beloved teacher said to me in Spirit, "The point is not to do anything. The point is to realize who you are. And when you realize and then become who you are, you will literally change the vibrations of everything in your environment."

The doing grows naturally out of the being. To seek to do before we seek to know is to create another false identity. To think that who I am is a spiritual counselor or teacher is as false an identity as to think I am any other role I'm playing. Who I am—who we all are—is a being made in the image of God, seeking to remember that by participating in the Earth drama.

We are indestructible. While our form may change, our true identity does not. We are not our careers, our money, our relationships, our successes, or our failures. Roles come and go. We create them because they offer us perfect settings in which to explore ourselves and learn. To further our process we magnetically attract all the supporting players we need for the drama. And our enemies are as important to the story as are our friends. In a sense our enemies are the pivotal players because they mirror for us the enemies within.

There are always perfect players available for whatever drama we create. People working on the same issues find each other. Rescuers will always find plenty of people sending out signals to be rescued. Victims will always find abusers. Love finds love. And the student who desires to learn attracts the teacher with the same urgency that the teacher attracts the student.

It is not easy to withdraw the desires that magnetize us to others. It's as if we're on a Ferris wheel: We get the rush of the lift and what seems like a higher view from the top, but then there's the swift descent, and suddenly we're back at the starting point. Yet when we decide to get off the wheel, we often discover that we actually miss all those addictive ups and downs.

We must be very gentle with ourselves and with each other as we take the courageous step, otherwise we can't support ourselves and each other when the resistance to change comes up. And it will. The ego has ruled the personality so long that when we decide to claim our true self, the illusionary self fights back.

It is not an accident that the way home to wholeness—the

path toward fusing our will with the divine will—is described in so many sacred texts as a kind of death. Gandhi told his followers, "I walk the edge of a sword daily." To give up our individual will to a Higher will, no matter how badly we want to, is a death.

It is also a birth. And this is what initiation is all about.

INITIATION

Yesterday, Today, Tomorrow

*I*nitiations are passages that mark both a birth and a death. There is a giving up in order to gain. Every major change we undergo—from leaving home for kindergarten to getting married, from hormonal shifts at puberty to others at midlife—represents a passage that gives us the opportunity to be initiated into new levels of awareness.

Krishna taught that the self must die for the Self to be born; in the *Tao Te Ching*, the Chinese sage Lao-Tzu tells us that the student learns by daily loss; Jesus told us we must lose our life in order to gain it. At this point we must remember that the mythic bird the phoenix also rises from its own ashes. To give up ego control we take a courageous step, otherwise we can't support ourselves and each other when the resistance to change comes up. And it will.

We have a need to mark our rites of passage with ritual. A yearly pilgrimage; Christmas, Easter, Ramadan, or Yom Kippur; spring or fall equinox services—each of these cyclically affirms our truths through ceremony. The weddings, funerals, christenings, confirmations, and bar mitzvahs all stop time for a moment to say, "Pay attention. Something significant is happening here."

Whether we are taking solemn vows or mastering a difficult

41

course of instruction, we are entering the new, and we take note of it. A choice is made, followed by a period of preparation, of testing, and then of acceptance—each one is a step in an initiation into new experience.

Even in our most mundane activities we obey an inner need to mark change in our lives. If a formal ceremony isn't built in, we unconsciously create a ritual that punctuates the passage. We move, buy a car, clean out the closets, have a garage sale—something that says, "There, that's finished. I'm making way for the new."

A girl, identified only as Elizabeth, reported her healing of a rape experience in a *Reader's Digest* article (February 1988). She and her friends performed a cleansing ritual at the scene of the rape. It was her way of finishing it. "Rituals are a wonderful way of drawing a box around something so you can begin to let go of it," she said.

Rituals bring things to a conclusion or announce a beginning. We are always participating in a process of completions and new beginnings. Step by step, we experience ordinary life in order to reveal the Divine. Everyday life might not always look like it has anything to do with the Divine because we've been programmed to see the two as separate. But even the most mundane experience is a spiritual exercise. That's the agenda on schoolhouse Earth. Even when we're living out our darker sides, we're being given the chance to learn more about who we are and who we are not. Every time we take a conscious step forward, we are bringing Spirit into the physical. That conscious step is part of the eternal process of initiation. It marks the point at which inner awareness is brought into outer expression, when body, mind, and Spirit come together in clear integration. When you are being initiated into something, you are becoming it.

BECOMING WHAT WE BELIEVE

It's not hard to become intellectually facile with concepts, whether they're spiritual, psychological, or scientific. But it's quite another thing to become a living statement of those principles. We long for a truth, discover it, weigh it, try it on for size, are confronted with everything within us that it is not, resist the change it demands, and purify ourselves of any remaining dross. At that point there is no more struggle, no more ambivalence. It is who we are.

To be initiated, then, is to become what we believe. And there's no faking it. We may fool each other, even agree to fool each other—"I'll believe your hypocrisy if you'll believe mine"— but what we are is what we vibrate into the world.

Actually there is a great relief in recognizing the futility of pretending to believe a truth we haven't made our own. Pretenses weigh a lot, and they take a great deal of effort to carry around. Letting the pretenses go allows us to look with more clarity at what's really going on; otherwise we invest them with so much fervor that we begin to believe them ourselves.

All of us yearn for a truth long before we become it. Desire is the first step, however. Just remember the old wisdom "Be careful what you ask for, you'll get it in time." In the meantime we generally have to confront a lot of mirrors reflecting how what we desire is lacking in our life. If we pray for patience, it doesn't arrive like a bouquet of roses. Instead we run into situation after situation that allows us to practice patience. If we pray for peace, all our own inner wars will be declared so that we can learn to be peaceful.

I know a woman who left a successful profession as a therapist, in which she was highly regarded for her insights and skills, in order to devote herself to her spiritual life for a few years. She wanted to become the love she believed in. She went to an ashram in India, where she was promptly put to work cleaning bathrooms. Superficially it would seem that this was not a good use of her education and skills. But the job mirrored perfectly for her the tyranny of the ego that clouded love with judgment and exclusivity. As she scrubbed toilets and floors for others in the ashram for a few months, she learned to bring love to that task. She became that which she asked to be taught. This humble assignment became her initiatory teacher.

A ROOM WITH A VIEW

Initiations are the portals through which we pass from one room into another, and then another, each bringing us closer to our own center, the Holy of Holies. Each room holds challenges for us; its size, contents, the people in it are perfectly designed for our growth at that point. We always have the choice of deciding whether we'll go farther. We have the privilege of saying at any point, "Thanks, but I'll get off here." Some rooms hold glamorous enticements to linger: "Forget the whole thing. Have a good time." And we can choose to stay in those rooms, like guests at a banquet, bejeweled and well fed, assuring each other that this is the best possible place to be.

Some of the rooms hold terrifying images of our shadows which seem to guard the next portal like the fierce gargoyles on old temples. If we want to get through these places, we have to accept, master, and integrate the shadow monsters of our own psyches.

A few years after my work started, I got stuck in such a room, and I stayed there for a couple of years. I had been doing the healing ministry and personal consultations happily. But whenever I should even think of teaching or lecturing publicly, I would feel cold fear. That didn't make any rational sense to me, as I had done a lot of public speaking and had been pretty visible through a wide variety of activities since childhood. I knew I had a deep resistance to going public, but I wasn't in touch with why.

Finally I got tired of dancing with my shadows. That's usually what triggers a shift. As my wise aunt says, "People get well when they get sick and tired of being sick and tired." I began praying for insights into the fear. They took a full year to come.

At last I had a vision in which I experienced being a young Christian girl sometime in the early centuries after Christ. I entered the story at the point where I was being led to a stake to be burned because of my religion. As my hands were being tied to the wooden stake by a soldier, I looked into his eyes. He was silent, but his expression tried to tell me he was only doing his job. I saw him light the fire and smelled the first smoke. Then suddenly I was no longer in my body, and I heard a loving voice say quite clearly and gently, "Now, was that something to be afraid of? All you did was die."

And I got it. In one moment the fear disappeared. I had been carrying a fear in my consciousness that if I went public with my beliefs, I would be persecuted and put to death. Of course that was illogical, but fears are not based on logic. Although the fear we feel is real, the source of it is in the mind. The next day I was willing to talk publicly to anyone who would listen to me.

People who are familiar with the therapeutic process know that one aha! experience doesn't usually make a fear disappear. It is usually followed by months of integration. Yet this *aha!* went straight to the heart of the fear and discharged its hold on me. Part of the cleanup was to forgive everyone involved in what I perceived to be my persecution, then to bless the experience and release it.

It hardly matters whether one wants to interpret this as a

recalled past life, an archetypal experience, a symbol, or a racial memory. A fear is still a fear. Until that energy is freed, it is still a magnet attracting similar situations. If you fear something, you set yourself up to experience it again and again. As Job said, "What I have feared has come upon me."

Our initiations come day by day through living our lives in the here and now. Through our willingness to honor our own classrooms and to be fully present with our pain and grief, our loves and discoveries, our light and our shadow, we transform all that is no longer needed. And transformation is the goal of initiation. The prefix *trans-* means "to go through"; it can also mean "to go beyond." What it doesn't mean is "to avoid."

We can spend many years moving through a wide variety of experiences to learn the lessons on any initiatory step. We can even spend many lifetimes. But each step that we master represents a spiritual initiation. The less burdened we are with the luggage of our preconceived ideas about ourselves, all of which are temporary, the closer we come to what is real and lasting.

I once asked Spirit to help me understand the difference between the Real and the unreal, and this was the answer:

The unreal perceives separation. The Real knows there is none.
The unreal despairs, is lonely, worries; the Real sees challenge, creates solutions, knows.
The unreal produces more and more confusion.
The Real empowers.

All of our dramas have the purpose of teaching us the Real, one plot at a time. Each takes us closer to being initiated into another level of understanding. What seems real to us at any one moment is relative to our understanding and perspective. Looking at an experience in process, and what you see is only the experience, and we say it is good or bad based on whether it gives pain or pleasure. Viewed from the perspective of years or better yet, from spiritual insight, and the experience is seen in an altogether different Light.

I once knew a man who was totally unconcerned with anything but his immediate and self-centered goals. He broke his back and ended up in a hospital totally incapacitated for a year. That seems bad. But after that year he opened a camp for physically handicapped children. From a larger perspective his "lost" year was the one in which he found himself.

The broader the vision is, the more inclusive it is, the greater the ability to say yes-yes to things that *seem* paradoxical instead of insisting on yes or no.

I was once told in Spirit that a paradox exists "when the mind has not expanded enough to embrace seeming opposites." If we are dedicated to a search for the Real we can live comfortably in the world and not just tolerate or attack that which seems paradoxical. It becomes part of the delight in exploring the unfolding mysteries.

Multiple realities coexist; they don't cancel each other out. Perhaps you've seen the picture of the vase that becomes two profiles facing each other when you shift perception. Once you get it, you can easily switch from one perception to the other. But until you perceive that, it is one or the other.

To climb a ladder, one needs every rung. No one rung is more important than another, but you can't be on a higher rung unless you first climb the ones before. However, each step higher affords a broader view. Our perspective from the lower rungs cannot conceive of the vistas afforded by the higher views. However, the vantage point from the higher rungs does not invalidate all the graduated steps. The first rung of the ladder is real; so is the tenth. The difference is that the tenth includes the first.

I once gave a consultation for a young social worker very

committed to serving "New Thought." But he was puzzled by having to work in what seemed to him to be a plodding, bureaucratic system. As we looked at his deeper intentions, it seemed that his mission in this life was to work within existing institutions, in a conventional job, as a stabilizer during the upheavals of the changes we are experiencing.

In order to help him grasp the importance of this, I referred to the deeper significance of the story of Noah. I was told in Spirit that during any major age change there are those whose task it is to preserve the creative seeds of what we have accomplished as a species thus far and to carry them into the new age. When it is time for us to move through an initiation as a people, we go through the dying process that seems to involve massive upheaval and destruction. But what we have evolved to thus far is not lost. The creative seeds—the two by two of the creatures preserved by the ark—are taken with us through the portal of initiation into higher understanding.

The fruits of each incarnation and the wisdom we have learned are preserved in consciousness between successive lives and carried into new incarnations. Again and again in counseling sessions I have seen that the talents a person has today draw upon accomplishments he or she "stored in heaven" in the past—*heaven* meaning "an indestructible state of consciousness." Those developed gifts are not lost after a single incarnation; but those things "stored on earth"—that is, strictly serving the ego and nothing else—die with the person and are no more. It seems we *can* take some things with us.

GUARDING THE
SACRED KNOWLEDGE:
THE MYSTERY SCHOOLS

Instruction on the human relationship with the Divine has always followed two distinct courses: the outer, exoteric religion, with its emphasis on obeying church dogma and structure; and the esoteric, hidden teaching. Each major religion has its inner core of mystical teachings, Sufism in Islam, Kabbalah in Judaism, Gnosticism in Christianity, Zen in Japanese Buddhism, and the Tantric path in both Hinduism and Tibetan Buddhism, to mention a few.

It would require a full library to introduce the hundreds of secret schools and societies that have existed since recorded time and beyond. But we would miss a major point in our understanding of change—and initiation—if we did not remind ourselves of the continuity of the teachings of spiritual rebirth.

Basically the point of these teachings is to free the God within each of us from entrapment in matter. The Secret Doctrine, or the Mysteries, as the teachings were often called, offered the straight and narrow road to self-realization. While the slow movement of evolution will eventually reconnect us all with our Source, there is a shorter path by which we can take charge of our journey. It is much harder and more intense, but the Way has been shown—and lived—by enlightened teachers and avatars throughout time. This is the path of initiation.

The teaching of the Mysteries has always been given in private to highly trained individuals as preparation for taking major initiations, major steps in spiritual development. This information was never given to an untrained public. Knowledge is neither good nor bad; it just is. But knowledge is also power. It can be dangerous in the wrong hands. So the esoteric branches protected this body of knowledge by burying it in codes, symbols, languages, and sciences known only to those who had been taught to see the hidden meanings. Initiates, as these practitioners were called, were sworn to secrecy, often forfeiting their lives if they revealed the teachings. If they fell into the temptation of exploiting the knowledge for their own ends, they were unable to complete the full initiations when the techniques and skills that had been conceived to show progress in the spiritual journey were corrupted and reduced to tools of sorcery and divination. Typically, when a civilization began to collapse from its own weaknesses, the pure teachings would become increasingly veiled in order to protect the sacred from the profane.

When candidates in the Mystery schools passed all the tests and temptations, they became initiates and eventually highly trained adepts who preserved the knowledge. Their knowledge sowed the seeds of all that we see taught today in universities— chemistry, mathematics, astronomy, medicine, architecture, philosophy—as well as the sciences of Spirit. Ignorance was definitely not equated with piety. In the larger world the Mystery teachings were often perceived as threats to the powerful religious institutions of their various cultures. Adepts often endured terrible persecution in order to preserve the knowledge.

Robert Macoy, a 33-degree Mason, pays tribute to these ancient Mystery schools in his *General History of Freemasonry*: "It appears that all the perfection of civilization, and all the advancement made in philosophy, science and art among the ancients are due to these institutions which under the veil of mystery sought to illustrate the sublimest truths of religion, morality and virtue and impress them on the hearts of their disciples. Their chief object was to teach the doctrine of one God, the resurrection of man to eternal life, the dignity of the human soul and to lead the people to see the shadow of the deity in the beauty, magnificence and splendor of the universe."

Ancient religions whose names are all but forgotten had their counterparts in Mystery schools all over the world. Many names we think of as mythic were possibly symbolic concepts that formed the core of a Mystery school: Isis, Dionysius, and Orpheus, Gaia, or Apollo, for example. The colorful stories in which gods and goddesses displayed all the conflicts, foibles, and ambitions of humans seem, to our modern reading, mere fancies of superstition. But given the symbolic code of the initiates, each of the deities and each of the stories embodied teachings of the steps toward self-mastery and reunion.

THE BIRTH OF THE SELF

Preparing an individual to enter the "gateway to the Eternal" was always—as it is today—the mission of the Mystery teachings. Whether it was taught in the disciplines of Hermeticism, alchemy, Rosicrucianism, Freemasonry, or Theosophy, or through the secret societies of Isis and the monasteries of Tibet, the object was essentially the same.

Entrance into the Mystery schools was very difficult. It is said that Pythagoras, the great mathematician and philosopher who founded a large Mystery school in ancient Greece, required years of silence from candidates before they were even considered. Through precise training of the mind, body, emotions, and Spirit, students were prepared for the body "death" that would allow them to be reborn into the ritual, initiatory fullness of their true nature.

The journey from the death of a limited, ego-centered view of self to birth in the fullness of the Self was classically marked by degrees of understanding. As the initiatory candidates progressed in their symbolic dying to their former selves and fascinations, they moved from the role of student to that of aspirant, where the serious work of opening the self began. With persistence aspirants proved their dedication through a period of probation, then discipleship, becoming in time full initiates, and then adepts. As they attained each step, more and more of the Mystery teachings were given to the student.

Regardless of the outer mythology and ritual practices, the

inner teachings around the world taught essentially the same path of self-knowledge and self-responsibility. The path of conscious initiation is the path of responsibility for self. It is different from the random path of the uninitiated seeker who may have ecstatic moments with Spirit but returns from them to a life in chaos. The initiatory path may also have its moments of ecstasy, but it is also necessary that the initiate learn how to participate fully in the daily affairs of life while retaining the wider perspective of the teachings.

Aspirants were taught techniques for purifying the body to enable it to handle more and finer vibrations of universal energies. This regimen included changes in diet, fasting, meditation, and required the steady mastery of sensual appetites. This doesn't mean that they were necessarily required to give up sex. What aspirants needed to learn, rather, was how not to be pulled this way and that by momentary impulses and how to choose carefully what to do with their sexual energy and with whom. They were also trained in techniques for converting sexual energy into spiritual energy.

Just as aspirants were taught how to clean up the aspects of their physical lives that were still unconscious, they were also taught how to clean up their emotional and mental confusions and distortions. They gradually emptied themselves of the past in order to approach each new initiatory step carrying less and less baggage. The goal was to be in touch with pure love—not the love that binds others to self but a love marked by its inclusiveness.

All of the training was carefully designed to prepare the student to experience the first major initiation, the birth of the Divine within. This was—and is today—the most significant spiritual step we could take since we first buried ourselves in forgetfulness. The initiatory teachings, whether taught outright or through metaphor, describe the new life of the awakened soul as it begins to live divine consciousness in human form. The ancient stories lay out the path and warn of its dangers and temptations, its joys and opportunities for service.

THE DIVINE FEMININE

In the true Mystery schools the feminine was not superceded by the masculine nor vice versa. Indeed progression was only possible when one understood and worked with both energies within the self.

As beings made in the image of God, we hold within us all the characteristics of wholeness. Wholeness encompasses both masculine and feminine energies as creative forces within Spirit. Even as we incarnate as male or female in order to fulfill the laws of creativity on the physical plane, we are in essence both. Saint Paul says, "In Christ there is no male or female." Gender is only the physical expression of polarity; energies are masculine or feminine at many nonvisible levels, such as thinking and feeling. But in our most awakened state—the level of the Christ consciousness—we are poised beyond duality and able to use both masculine and feminine energies at will.

The Taoists describe the movements within wholeness as *yin* (feminine) and *yang* (masculine). The one is always in process of becoming the other. We are not one or the other; rather we are both. Yin and yang are movements of energy, not identities. I might be emotionally yin in a relationship with one person or situation and very yang in a relationship with someone else. My body might be yin, but other aspects of my personality might be very yang.

We get severely imbalanced when we attempt to polarize the free movement of these energies into permanence. We do this when we say, "This is a woman and therefore yin and passive," or "This is a man and therefore yang and assertive." The whole person is both passive and assertive, inclusive and specific, receiving and giving.

At conception each of us begins to reenact the whole evolutionary drama of our species. Eons ago we drifted in a primordial paradise experiencing no duality, no individualized selfhood, no separation from the Source. With the gift of divine will we willed ourselves into the Earth plane and individualized. We ate of the Tree of Good and Evil and learned duality and separation.

We reexperience the primordial oneness during the first few weeks following conception. It is not until the fifth week, when the hormones kick in, that sexual differentiation appears in the zygote. Prior to that all zygotes are "feminine." The split from wholeness, the separation of the masculine and feminine within ourselves, begins in the womb. We long for the other half of ourselves. We long for the spiritual connection, the Christ consciousness, that will restore wholeness beyond duality.

Until we restore that inner connection, we project that longing outward, into our societies, giving authority first to one polarity, then to the other. When we were a matriarchal people, we lived in the tribal consciousness of unity and connectedness to the Earth. This was the epoch of the Great Mother Goddess, the connecting, synthesizing principle.

The next step in our psychospiritual evolution was to learn more about our uniqueness as individuals, so we began to explore the masculine principle. Like the growing baby who comes to recognize that he or she is a unique being, separate from the mother, we began to see ourselves and the world as made up of distinct and separate things. We learned to identify, catalog, examine. Our sciences and industries have grown out of our masculine focus.

But in the development of our masculine drive we as a species lost the sense of what these individualized "things" had to do with each other. We lost the sense of relatedness. While the masculine is busy identifying and cataloguing, the feminine is preoccupied with wanting to know how it all relates. The masculine brings knowledge to the world, but without the wisdom of the feminine to guide the uses of that knowledge it becomes dangerous and unrelated to the good of the whole.

As the masculine aspects of our natures began to dominate, they were accompanied by a growing fear of the feminine. Perhaps some of the fear was because of a primal threat to individuality, the fear of being absorbed back into the womb. Many of our global myths of the past three thousand years reflect this fear of the feminine, and they have been acted out in human sexual terms. In the early years of the organized Christian church, which built on its Judaic foundations, the feminine aspect of God was practically ignored. It was not until the fifth century A.D. that the Virgin Mary was given a position of honor in the hierarchy of the Church. It's likely that there was a good deal of pressure building within the populace and it became necessary to externalize and balance the energies of the inner Divine Mother. People were starting to drift back to the temples of the earlier goddesses. So the Church stripped away the icons, temples, and titles of the earlier "pagan" goddesses and gave them to Mary, often with nothing changed but the name.

In the earliest times we perceived the Earth as our Mother. But as our scientific knowledge increased, we naively began to think that we could conquer Her for our own ends. This imbalanced patriarchal consciousness perceived the Great Mother as the force that kept our spirits trapped in the flesh, separating us from God the Father. We blamed Her for the Fall, and Her physical daughters on Earth began to be viewed as potentially dangerous traps for the masculine Spirit seeking reunion with the heavenly Father.

The struggle to balance our dual nature of flesh and Spirit has been told in myths and allegories all over the world. These myths are really about one person—Everyman, Everywoman. The battles and conquests tell us about the struggles of the inner man and inner woman, first to discover our own identities, then to overcome the enemy of inner illusions, and finally to celebrate the marriage of these dual energies. Unfortunately by the time these allegorical lessons were popularized, the universal principles they taught had been either lost or distorted.

Inner guidance once told me that "only a virgin can birth the Christ"—a statement that would leave most of us arriving a bit too late if this dictum were to be taken literally. But when we understand that the soul has classically been portrayed in world symbologies as feminine, the statement takes on new meaning. It is the feminine soul within us all, the receptive principle, that must be made pure in its desire to receive before it can be filled with the Universal Christ.

Theologies based on the literal interpretation of allegories were elaborately rationalized and programmed into a priesthood who in turn held them up to the people as God's holy word. Case in point: Adam and Eve.

A woman attending a course I was teaching on the feminine arrived for class one evening so upset that it took her several minutes to become coherent enough to tell the following story. She and her husband had been having serious marital problems, for which she had consulted her pastor, a minister in a very large and prosperous mainstream Christian church. His final comment to her was that she was "sharing the burden of the guilt of Eve."

Such a story would hardly be worth the telling if it wasn't repeated so often in one form or another. Many symbols of the old allegories—such as the serpent, which has a deep and profound symbolic meaning having to do with wisdom and healing in the personal journey of transformation—have been similarly distorted, and these distortions have been repeated so often that they end up masquerading as powerful truths in the collective unconscious.

The serpent still shows up in perfume and lingerie advertising, subtly reinforcing the old image of woman as temptress; but this image stands for more than just sexual temptation. To patriarchal eyes, woman represents the urge to abandon heaven for earthly sensation. She is the archetypal temptress luring man away from his spiritual search. She is sister to Odysseus' sirens, the Blue Angel, the Russian Rusaka who draws unwary men down to her watery home, and hundreds of similar stories from around the world.

Young virginal girls with "dangerous" psychic connections to natural forces are periodically dragged out of the collective unconscious for movie plots. For example, there was Carrie and her power with fire; Jennifer and her ability to conjure up snakes if you made her mad; and the possessed Regan in *The Exorcist*. These archetypes are not far removed from medieval counterparts, for it was not just folklore that said that women were subject to demonic possession; it was the teaching of the Church. And this led to the witch-hunting mania of the fourteenth to sixteenth centuries, during which time thousands upon thousands of women were put to death.

It is far too complex a subject for this book to discuss the many indications of the end of the exclusive reign of the patriarchy. There are many excellent books on the subject that I would encourage any spiritual student to read, several of which I have included in the bibliography at the end of this book. But I do want to share one insight I received in Spirit.

I was shown that in the physical, emotional, and mental realms we have collectively created very dense and dark thought forms that prohibit a soul in a feminine body from seeking self-realization. Naturally there are those who have escaped those thought forms, but the majority have not. When a soul in a female body longed for reunion within the totality of self, she would be permitted to go just so far but no farther. When she encountered those dark, all-pervasive prohibitions—which extend far beyond mere rules and regulations, they're part of the very air we breathe—she was likely to give up in frustration. Often she chose to attach herself to a man, for men do have permission to experience the Christed state. Perhaps she might snatch a vicarious taste of spiritual wholeness.

The message went on to say that these thought forms must now be dissolved, for as long as they remain intact, we cannot enter the next stage of our evolution. I was also told that thousands of souls who have had a great deal of spiritual training in previous incarnations are choosing to incarnate now in feminine bodies, particularly in the West. They're doing this not only to pursue their own development but to participate in cracking up the old thought forms for us all.

As women (the earth-plane symbol for the Mother) are not only permitted but encouraged to be self-realized, as they are accepted as teachers and leaders side by side with men, we will have new models for wholeness that will help free us of the tyranny of polarization. However we cannot swing totally in the opposite direction either, for our ultimate goal is wholeness. To polarize to the Mother to the exclusion of the Father is as off the mark as when it was the other way around. But before we can synthesize and integrate wholeness, we have to reclaim and heal that which has been lost. This healing is one of the most important initiations we will make collectively in the next few decades.

The repression of the Divine Mother over the past three thousand years has led to a divided self and a divided world. All life emerges out of the Mother's womb, and all life returns to Her to be recycled. It is She who shows us our connection with life in all forms. And She it is also who is the disciplinarian who shows us the price of our arrogance in attempting to conquer nature and abuse the life-forms of Earth. Not only is it not nice to fool Mother Nature, it is deadly.

Heaven and Earth can only meet in Spirit, which unites the Divine Mother and the Divine Father. When we do not honor both, we are totally off-balance and lonely for the other half of ourselves. Repression, hate, resentment, and fear of the "other" are rooted in the fear we feel for the other within ourselves. Fear becomes trapped in culs-de-sac in the body, in the emotions, and in the mind. Psychospiritual training is about cleaning out those culs-de-sac so that our energies can follow their natural course toward union.

We experience the inner wedding, the "mystic marriage," when the feminine and masculine energies within us are first claimed, then purified of all distortions, and finally fused back into wholeness. Yogic texts, the Kaballah, the Bible, the Bhagavad Gita, the I Ching, and the Tarot—all are teaching methods for helping us to bring our divided selves into balance.

The Universal Christ is born of that union.

THE UNIVERSAL CHRIST

The Universal Christ is not represented only by the historical figure we call Jesus, for many of us perceive of him as the supreme expression of wholeness—of God made manifest. The Universal Christ is not confined to any one religion. Rather it is to be understood as the ultimate potential that exists in all beings. But it only comes into flower in one who has become fully self-realized.

Great masters, those self-realized beings who live as manifestations of the Universal Christ, have appeared in many different traditions throughout history. They have demonstrated by their total beingness and their teachings the way to bridge humanness and Godness. That potential is present in every being. The Universal Christ is the means through which we reconnect with the Source. It is the saving grace that leads us out of ignorance and bondage on the wheel of rebirth. It is the Light of the world, which transforms lead into gold through the alchemy of pure love.

The full mystery of the Universal Christ is surely beyond human comprehension. But as this cosmic energy descends into human affairs, the Christ pattern is poured into the mythic vessels of all cultures. Building on the foundations of the mores and history of various peoples, using the cultural materials on hand, the One Story of the soul's journey toward reunion with the Source has been told throughout time.

Whenever and wherever darkness seems to blind people, whenever the purpose of human existence is lost in its own mire, a great illumined being comes again to bring the truth. Some legends say they come from the heavens as an act of grace. Others perceive their enlightenment as the flowering of the best of our species. But however they arrive, they come when they are needed and instruct us according to the level of our understanding at the time, leaving us a legacy of teachings that continue to advance our evolution. Woven into the actual facts of a great teacher's human life is a story that transcends any one life, for it belongs to the pattern of the Universal Christ.

The universality of the One Story may be challenging to face when one has been raised to believe that the truths of one's own religion exclude all others. But it is one of the gifts of our time to have the scholarship and global communications that allow us to research and share the many variations of the story across the globe.

It would be a grave loss to dismiss a story because we discover it has counterparts in different cultures. The power and truth of these many stories of the Universal Christ lie in their universality, not in their exclusivity. We keep telling the stories generation after generation and from culture to culture because we deeply resonate with their truths about our nature and the way in which we can reconcile humanness and Godness. Through them we find guidance on confronting our shadows and on facing the trials and temptations, dangers and sacrifices, in living Christ consciousness.

We do not return to wholeness through any one religion; we return through the Universal Christ. The Mysteries taught initiates that we first enter the path, then we follow the path, then we become the path.

In Revelation it is written, "To he who overcomes [masters] I will make a pillar [a cosmic power] in the temple of God, and he shall go out [incarnate] no more."

As long as we live out the Adam-and-Eve story, we will continue to die again and again. When we live the Christ within, the Buddha within, when we are infused with the Holy Spirit, then, as Krishna said, we are saved from the "endless wheel of death and rebirth." And, as Jesus said, we gain "eternal life."

This is the path of initiation.

INITIATION TODAY

So whatever does all this bigger-than-life drama have to do with paying bills, raising children, pursuing a career, and surviving on planet Earth in the late twentieth century?

Everything. Initiation from darkness into light is why we are all here in the first place. There is no such thing as an ordinary life. The raw material for spiritual initiation exists as much in a small apartment and a nine-to-five job as it does in the dramatic setting of an ancient tale. The battle between the hero and the dragon is waged daily in offices, in hospitals, in laundry rooms. Every moment, every interaction, every relationship, every success or failure gives us an opportunity to learn more about who we are and why we're here.

Life is about initiation. Just as any mythic figure, we willed ourselves into physicality and we're working our way through all the density and challenge of this dimension to remember that you, that I, that all of us are Beings of Light—nothing less. The process of gradually remembering takes us through portal after portal of insights. The persons and events in our life are the means through which we learn. They are our teachers as surely as if we sat at their feet.

As we win the inner battles—fought in the arena of human affairs—we move through various initiations. Each piece of self-mastery over cruelty, selfishness, and indifference peels away our illusion of separateness a bit more. The loving sacrifices made by parents to educate a child; the battle for integrity won in business; the courage to face hardships without bitterness—this is the stuff of initiation. By living authentically in the here and now, our Godness infuses our humanness, and the two become one.

Chances are you are not in a Mystery school. Maybe you haven't learned the esoteric codes. But you have incarnated at a time when the esoteric Mysteries are being made public. "Look for the water bearer," said the incarnated Christ. The water bearer is symbol for the astrological sign Aquarius, which sig-nifies the great outpouring of the waters for all. Aquarius heralds the beginning of an epoch such as has never before been realized on planet Earth.

The first step is to prepare the way. Our inner John the Baptist says, "Clean up your act. Make ready for the Universal Christ, who will be born in hearts around the world. Make ready, for the entire planet is about to be lifted into a new fre-quency."

THE SHORTER ROUTE

Just to put some perspective on the subject of initiation, the education you have acquired since childhood was once taught only in the Mystery schools. Reading, writing, even the physical-fitness education that emphasizes stronger bodies through cleaner diets and exercise, have always been part of the preparation for handling higher frequencies of energy and bringing them into the physical body in a way the nervous system can handle.

While moral codes and ethics have been taught in other religions, what has been missing in our spiritual education is the direct teaching of the sciences of bridging the spiritual and the physical: the universal laws and principles of light and energy, the understanding of subtle bodies, and the use of the breath. The sciences of Spirit are now readily available through thousands of books, teachers, organizations, magazines, and video and audio cassettes that offer helpful techniques and information. Worldwide communication and transportation systems have expanded our realities to embrace all the world's knowledge.

A word of warning, however: We must practice discrimination in picking through the spiritual smorgasbord available today. For everything that is real there is also a counterfeit.

In the sense that I am using the term initiation, it does not necessarily take place at the feet of another human. A person of great clarity may very well have the ability to catalyze our energy when one is ready to make the leap. Such a person may serve as teacher, guide, disciplinarian or model. Many times we don't know how it feels to be stress-free until we are in the energy of someone who is. A being who lives the love that he/she is affects our entire energy field. The love in us resonates and stretches to respond to love. Very high beings have the ability to channel powerful energies to assist our choice to grow—the operative phrase there is "our choice."

The maxim "When the student is ready, the teacher appears" is certainly true; guidance comes exactly when we need it. But there's another way to understand that maxim: The teacher may not show up in glowing robes. Sometimes the role of divine teacher is played by our boss, our next-door neighbor, our spouse. When we're really ready to learn patience, all things requiring patience show up. When we need to learn forgiveness, there they are, everyone and everything that pushes our buttons, perfect teachers of forgiveness. Our classrooms are not easy, but through them we discover a courage we never knew we had.

The story is told of a master who was trying to explain to a king that it did little good to force things upon people. Lasting change was only possible when you changed consciousness. The king resisted the point, still believing you could force people to change. The master told him to put the palace butcher into a large hole in the ground. He was not to have anything in the hole with him. After several days they removed the butcher and discovered he had spent his time fashioning animals out of the dirt and then destroying them. No matter what was imposed on him from the outside, his consciousness was to butcher. Just surviving being put in a hole doesn't change one's consciousness.

Given enough of the same kind of "holes," one does eventually learn. But that's the slow, grinding way of evolution. However when we surrender to the hole, we can then say, "Okay, what's this about? I don't like it, but what can I learn from it?" Then we master the hole. This is the shorter route offered by initiation. Conscious initiation is the direct route home.

THE WORST OF TIMES, THE BEST OF TIMES

You and I have elected to be present during this chaotic time on planet Earth, although sometimes we may wonder if we should have thought the contract over before we signed on. Actually it's the best possible time. As a Chinese delegate to the United Nations said a few years back, "Conditions are excellent; the world is a terrible mess."

Destruction is the first step in conscious change. The old dies so that the new might be born. This is true whether it involves individuals, societies, or the whole species. It would be lovely if we allowed change to happen gracefully. But our unconscious fear of change often brings on labor pains. Yet the more we relax into the contractions, the less pain we feel. If we completely surrender to the process, even ecstasy is possible.

Just as we have an individual purpose for being here, and a destiny we are moving toward, so does our planet. An ancient Greek name for Earth was Gaia, the Mother Goddess. Gaia is a living, breathing entity, and each of us is a cell in her body—as are all other life-forms. Many cultures that have been mislabeled "primitive" knew the Earth was a sacred living being, and they lived in respectful harmony with her. In forgetting this we have come dangerously close to destroying ourselves. Interestingly it has been our scientists who have been our alarm clocks, waking us up to ignorance, neglect, and arrogance. The most advanced theories in all the sciences, from astrophysics to zoology, now tells us we must see every system on earth in terms of its inter-connectedness with the whole.

We are the agents through which Gaia's initiation will be brought about. Some of us come with the task of cracking up the old models of reality. Others have the job of preserving the best of what we've learned thus far. Others are bridge builders, teaching us how to get from the old to the new. Then there are the true visionaries, who see the new world. Many of our children are in this group, with the blueprint for a new world stamped in their cells. Many of them already know what we're just figuring out. They're a willful bunch and will no doubt be a challenge to raise. But they have to have powerful wills in order to carry the vision through its birth. They will be our teachers.

Waiting out a delay at an airport, I recently had a lengthy conversation with a four-year-old charmer. Daniel is black, with huge, shining eyes, an infectious laugh, and a precocious vocabulary. At one point I asked him what he liked to do. Without a second's hesitation he announced, "I like to baptize myself!"

THE SPIRALING LIGHT

The turning points in our initiations, both individually and as a species, are often depicted graphically as an upward spiral. Perhaps the spiral is a design which originates in our cell structure, since nature does so love that form, using it in everything from the patterning of our DNA to the shape of our galaxy. It is the connecting interface where the formless comes into form. When we round one of the big spirals—which we seem to be doing right now—the universe moves everything in its path to power the shift.

As our focus changes, we will come to understand that all men, women, and children carry the Light within them. Gaia has that Light. Life in all its manifestations carries that Light.

We must hold steady the Light and our vision of peace during this critical time of purification. All of our planetary injustices and imbalances are being magnified now. As the political, racial, and economic divisions become more extreme, it takes incredible self-discipline not to despair or to get caught in polarization. It takes courage, love, and commitment to choose to light candles and give up cursing the darkness. On the other side of this divisiveness lies peace, and in that peace we will reap the harvest of each religion's wisdom. We can be emissaries of that vision of peace to the degree that we have first committed ourselves to resolving our own inner wars.

I was told in Spirit that our current initiatory experience could be summed up as "being in the world but not of it." As more and more people live the Christ consciousness, we will raise the vibratory level of the entire planet. We're on our way to learning how to spiritualize matter and heal the old schism between the physical and the spiritual. As this process takes hold it will bring tremendous change. And conscious change is the working mechanism of initiation.

PART II

The 7 Steps of Conscious Change

*T*hroughout the next section of the book I will be examining various aspects of change as it moves through a cycle of 7 Steps. This is intended to be a model and is certainly not to be construed as a rigid set of rules. At best any model for increasing our understanding of the way we grow is no more than a scaffolding upon which to hang insights. In spite of our love affair in the West with calculations, measurements, and statistics, the human spirit defies summary.

But we can share models that work, and they help to make the journey of transformation easier. Once we understand the nature of a process, we can work with, not against, the dynamics involved.

I suggest that you keep several points in mind as you read this book:

• All experience, no matter how mundane it appears, is about your spiritual life. Your relationships with family and friends; your profession; your use of money, sex, and social position— all are reflections of inner spiritual states.

• However impotent or uninvolved you might feel as you observe world affairs, your life is actually inseparable from the events on the planet simply because you are breathing, thinking, and acting on Earth. The macrocosm of society evolves through the stages of change just as you do personally, and you are a participant in, not a victim of, the collective changes.

• Any change in one part of your life affects all other parts.

• While there may be occasional clear-cut definitions between various cycles, you will find that they overlap, particularly at the beginning and end of any part of the process.

• Any change avoided or left incomplete pulls you back again and again to complete it. This is because a completed cycle alters your energy field and thus alters what you pull into your life. Authenticity can't be faked, because whatever is held in consciousness is the magnet for all that is drawn to you or repelled by you.

• You are probably experiencing a variety of changes simultaneously. As a result, you may find yourself at different stages of this model for each change. However once you become accustomed to the stages of conscious evolution, you may begin to discover that they are essentially variations on the same theme.

I recommend that you first read the material on the 7 Steps for its general content and for a clear understanding of the cycles. Then I'd like to suggest that you take a change that you have already completed and view it through the perspective of this model.

STEP ONE

The Form

The forest will answer you in the way you call to it.
—FINNISH PROVERB

*W*hatever you believe is true—for you. We do not act outside of our perception of reality. Whatever shape and structure our belief system takes on any subject is our "form." Our forms allow us to express ourselves within the parameters of whatever we perceive ourselves to be. *Good, bad, possible, impossible*—these concepts are meaningful to us to the degree that we believe in them.

Earth is a planet of forms. We need forms in order to express ourselves here. Our bodies are forms; so are our thoughts and emotions. We collect energy from the universal pool to fill out the forms we have designed. What eventually solidifies into physical reality is the self-fulfilling form we have fashioned with our thinking patterns and desires. Believe a thing is true and eventually it manifests. Nothing changes until the form we hold is challenged.

✗ "IF ONLY I BELIEVED
ALL I BELIEVE"

Several years ago I was finishing a counseling session with a delightful older woman. We were both quiet as I opened my eyes and settled back into alert consciousness. Then I heard her sigh. "Oh, I know you're right. If only I believed all I believe."

What a profoundly simple way of summing up much of our dilemma! How many times have you found yourself indulging in negative thoughts or behaving in a way that you knew, even as you were doing it, was not what you really believed? I suspect we all do this.

There's enough lip service and ritual given to the great truths of Spirit today to have us all walking on water. What sensitive person doesn't "believe" in love, justice, equality? Anyone who is even moderately awake on planet Earth today surely "believes" in the imperative of protecting the environment. We don't tell our children, our graduates, our congregations to "believe" in indifference, war, and greed any more than we tell them to prioritize their lives for a CD player or a diversified portfolio. What we tell them is about generosity, about improving the human condition, about actualizing their talents.

There is no arena of human experience in which we are more vocal, more emotional, or more adamant about our beliefs than spirituality. "Our God is a God of peace," we declare, as we design increasingly efficient ways of killing. "God is everywhere," we tell each other and then proceed to cross individuals, even whole nations, races, religions, and species, off the list.

So what's the problem? Are we all hypocrites? Do we simply pour the soft words of a noble belief system as tincture on our frustrations? Are we overwhelmed? Despairing? Or is it possible that we have a lot of ambivalence at work in the unconscious? Do we secretly suspect that our ideals are lightweight stuff compared with the realities of the material world?

How do we become what we believe? Perhaps it starts with

accepting that we're already living what we believe—it just may not be what we wish we believed.

I may wish to believe in love, but that means giving up my belief in fear. I may wish to believe in abundance, but that calls for releasing my hold on limitation. The fact is I am living exactly what I believe. If I want to know what I really believe about myself, God, reality, all I have to do is look at my world. It will report back precisely what my belief agenda is—hidden or otherwise. As Jesus was reported to have said, "It will be done to you as you believe."

An ideal, even if we intuitively sense it to be true, is not our belief until we live it from a molecular level. Then we become that belief. It is no longer an ideal "out there" that we can use or pack up like seasonal clothing. Who we are can no more be separated out than the color of our eyes. I may theorize that the universe is a loving place yet buy into the passing drama that is not so loving. But when I truly know the universe is loving, I become love. Love infuses everything I do, from praying, to making a salad, to disciplining a child. Love is in my thumbprint.

A belief that has become part of our being has the power to affect, even alter, everything it touches. Take words, for example. When words are repeated by rote, they often sound like clichés, boring and lifeless. But those same words taking flight from the fusion of will, desire, and conviction assume the alchemical power to transform.

When we become a belief, the frequency of energy it emits enters our permanent aura, our radiation into the world. The aura is made up of the totality of all our subtle energies—physical, emotional, mental, and spiritual. Moods, attitudes, even our physical highs and lows are like the changing colors and patterns of a lake as it responds to changing weather conditions.

All frequencies have a sound and a color. They can be felt in our auras by most people and seen by others. Even our slang shows that we perceive these emanations. We say someone is "green with envy." It's true. The color of envy does reflect in the aura as a bilious green. We speak of feeling blue; a person feeling down has a particular shade of blue in his or her energy. A truly depressed person's aura is filled with a lifeless gray.

When a person is angry, flashes of red can be seen in his aura. When the angry moment passes, the energy disperses and so does the red flashing in the aura. However, if that same person walks in the world consistently angry, the red energy becomes part of his permanent aura. He sends that anger into the world steadily, like a repeated news broadcast. While we may be irritated by the changing "weather" we all experience from one other, those permanent broadcasts affect the whole world.

We only get the color for our coat, permanent aura, when we are living a particular truth. For example, there is a deep, intense shade of blue seen in auras that is the color of devotion. You'd think it would be seen largely in the auras of pious monks. Yet I've seen that particular shade of blue in the auras of scientists more than any other single group, spiritual scientists as well as physical scientists, although the latter might bristle if I suggested they were seeking God in a test tube or at the end of a telescope or microscope. But if God is truth, that's exactly what they're seeking—the material truths of God. And they wear that particular color of devotion in their auras.

I'm referring here to true scientists, not technicians. While technicians may be very skilled manipulators of material reality, they are not true scientists. The true scientist, however brilliantly she/he has uncovered material realities thus far, stands like a child before the unknown. Real seekers after truth may master existing knowledge, but they won't try to enclose it in a cage. One side is always open to the universe for expansion. Einstein once said he knew everything he ever learned first through intuition, then spent hours in the laboratory proving it. We honor and reward those who protect our understanding of reality, but perhaps our biggest debt is to those who venture outside of it.

THE COLLECTIVE VIEW

One of the challenges of being conscious creators and not just reactors is to accept that we are influenced by the collective view of reality, even if we're not wholly convinced by it. Just as we share a similar physical form that we evolved together for thousands of years, so we share the thought forms that have organized the world for us.

When you and I set out to create a new thing, we have to examine the parameters of our society's belief systems and accept that we have breathed in to these forms just like everyone else. Not only are we conditioned by the voices of our family and intimates, we are also affected by racial and planetary messages about reality.

In our identification with material creation, we have appointed keepers of the myths to empower existing reality by reporting it back to us again and again. As Walt Kelly's "Pogo" once said, "We has met the enemy, and they is us!" The myth keepers of television, film, popular songs, advertising and political propaganda are often highly skilled in the art of manipulating symbols, and if they truly believe the tales, their retellings are very powerful.

We cannot really be their critics, for no myth has the power to affect us if we don't secretly believe in it. If one wants really to understand a people, it is good to study their myths. Often people feel relieved and reassured to have an old myth acted out for them, especially if it is entertaining. So our movies, TV shows, advertising, and magazines become powerful reflections of what we believe collectively.

However, television is also a major agent for the changing of consciousness. People suffering the ravages of war, starvation, or political greed were once safely removed from us. But through the immediacy of television and films, time and space are exploded, and we see that they are not the "other"; they are us. The simple reporting of facts is creating a slow, subtle awareness of unity in the human consciousness.

THE GRACE OF BEING

All great thinkers, mystics, spiritual teachers, avatars, scientists, and artists mastered the ability to move beyond cultural thought forms. We can materialize any new belief if we take seriously the words of the Incarnated Christ: "With God all things are possible."

The Sufis are masters at demonstrating a principle with a story. Here's one that makes the point about the difference between believing and being:

It seems there was a great Sufi teacher who was very erudite and highly schooled in Sufi theology and ritual. One day he was walking beside a lake, deep in thought, when he heard chanting drifting across the lake from an island. It offended his ears, for he knew exactly what the chant should sound like, and this noise was not it.

Being a responsible teacher, he decided to correct this distortion. So he rowed over to the island, where he found a euphoric little man happily chanting away. The Sufi teacher introduced himself, making it clear, of course, that he was an expert in these matters, and offered to teach him the correct way to chant. The little man was grateful and accepted the offer.

When the Sufi teacher was satisfied that he had done his duty, he got back in his boat and started rowing. He was halfway across the lake when he heard a strange sound—"splish, splash; splish, splash." Turning around, he saw the little man running after him across the surface of the water.

"Wait a minute, O great teacher," called the little man. "How did you say that last line went?"

There's another story, from the Hebrew tradition, that teaches us to look beyond tradition:

There was once a very great and holy rabbi. Whenever misfortune was threatening the Jewish people, he would go to a certain part of the forest to meditate. There he would light a fire and say a special prayer, and, miracle of miracles, the misfortune would be averted.

After he died, tragedy once again threatened the Jews, and one of his disciples, himself a rabbi, sought help from heaven. He went to the same place in the forest and said, "O Lord our God, ruler of the world, I do not know how to light the fire, but I am still able to say the prayer." And the miracle was again accomplished.

Many years later another rabbi feared for the lives of his people. But he had only heard vague tales about this tradition. Yet, desperate for a miracle, he went into the forest and prayed, "O Lord, I do not know how to light the fire. I do not know the prayer. But I do know the place, and I hope this is enough." It was, and the miracle occurred.

Generations later yet another rabbi wanted to help his people overcome misfortune. He sat at home and spoke to God, saying, "I have no idea how to find the place in the forest. I am unable to light the fire. I do not know the prayer. All I can do is tell you the story. I hope it is sufficient." Yet again the miracle occurred.

We don't have to figure out which belief system is the right one and then work feverishly to be in good standing with that system. The work is not about figuring out how to be good. We're already good because we're made in the image of God— how could it be otherwise? The big illusion is that we are not good. That's the illusion we bought and then set out to prove.

The work is not about figuring out what to do, how to get it right, how to win the gold star. It is about being, about the longing to be reconnected. Oh, we will still do plenty. For the more we awaken and the more aware we are of who we are and who everyone else is, the more empowered we are, and the more creative and loving we become. The loving automatically leads to service.

Reconnecting requires waking up to our birthright and remembering that we are already connected. It's not something we earn; we just have to accept it. Grace has never been withheld from us. We have withheld it from ourselves by our limiting beliefs about ourselves.

Once I took the subject of Grace into meditation and was shown the following image:

I saw a fountain of liquid Light. It towered in the air, brilliant and shimmering with color. I saw thirsty people approach this fountain, each bringing a container. Some brought only a thimble, which they filled, drank quickly, and then ran away. Others brought a cup, filled it, and disappeared. I knew they would return, driven by the dry winds of the desert. Then I saw a laughing child. He ran to the fountain, (or grew) stripped off his clothes, and jumped in. He disappeared into the water, and all I could see and hear of him was the occasional glimmer of a sparkling eye and the song of his laughter. And I understood that this was what Grace was all about.

How wonderful it would be if we could, like that child, simply jump into the perennial waters of the Grace fountain and accept our right to bathe and play there. Or, like some hero in a grade-Z movie, if we could only lay down our addictions and masks, and proclaim, "I have seen the error of my illusions about myself. Now I remember I am made in the image of God and I shall manifest that immediately." Know anyone who's done that without a struggle? Neither do I.

For most of us as we awaken to the Light, we find ourselves entangled in an elaborate construction of dogmas, defenses, fears, and tribal prejudices. Our human ego protests change; it much prefers to rearrange reality according to the information on hand.

PERCEPTION CHANGES REALITY

Perhaps we fear losing complete control if we don't have a fix on reality. And like the ancient tyrant who killed everyone in the town so that the one person who insulted him couldn't get away, we kill off much of our creativity in our fear-filled need to protect the known kingdom. I think much religious fanaticism stems from this need for control. I once read that a fanatic is someone who has lost sight of his goal and redoubled his effort.

Our history as a species is tied up with the making, defending, and destroying of successive waves of reality boxes. The box that says "The world is flat" becomes a new box that says, "The world is round." The reality box that proclaims "Slavery is an economic necessity" becomes the box that says "It's not right to own slaves."

A few brave individuals punch holes in the old reality box, first a few and then many, and finally everyone escapes. The great creators leapfrog beyond the known, but they often pay a heavy price at the personality level. My observation is that the persecution they encounter is their soul work, and they seem to endure it with a Spirit that is incredible to those afraid to venture beyond the tribal myths.

Sooner or later a few others build on the belief of a pioneering "heretic." Then a few more. Finally everyone sees in the new way. And the dance of creation continues. If I have a belief and fill it with a lot of energy—thoughts, words, passion, time—it becomes a living thing. It is impressed on a very subtle universal ether that will accept whatever I put on it, good, bad, or indifferent. It then becomes a magnet in that ether. Like cells adhere to each other. If you agree with the thought that I have created, it begins to gather power, considerably more than just one-plus-one. The principle of exponential progression multiplies the energy very rapidly. If thousands and then millions agree with us, it will become accepted reality, a new boundary.

Whether it's in the microcosm of one life or the macrocosm of our species, we form reality based on our perceptions; we build our systems to support these perceptions; and then evolution steps in and challenges them. We begin questioning the old, struggle between the old and the new, expand to embrace the new reality contract, and build another box. The perceptions we agree on establish the way the entire world is run, from governments to religions to personal lives.

Little wonder the Devil responded as he did when he and a friend were walking and they saw a man walking in front of them stoop to pick something up.

"What did he just pick up?" asked the friend.

"Oh, just a bit of the truth," replied the Devil.

"Doesn't that bother you?"

"Naw," said the Devil, "I'll just let him make a belief out of it."

If I believe I am "only human," then I will not be able to create beyond that.

So often we pride ourselves on being realists. "I'll believe it when I see it," we say. Maybe it's the better part of wisdom to say, "I'll see it when I believe it."

There is a story that is told about the Portuguese navigator Ferdinand Magellan, although I've heard it credited to Charles Darwin as well. During Magellan's voyage around the world he anchored off the southernmost tip of South America at a place now called Tierra del Fuego. He was met on shore by friendly natives who were astounded that he was there. How did he suddenly appear on their shores? He pointed to the sailing ships. But large boats with sails were outside their reality and they were utterly unable to see them. Finally, one of their shamans, who was able to consider the possibility of the unknown, saw the ships and taught his people to see them as well.

I know a woman whose mother died when she was three. The child's mind would not accept the death. When relatives held her up to the casket for one last goodbye to her mother, she saw an empty casket. Yes, of course her mind disassociated from the reality of the death. But it only underlines the capacity our brains have to deny any reality not understood or challenging to our concept of reality and safety.

I wonder how many sailing ships we miss because we believe so intensely that they're not there. One of our most famous fictional sleuths, Sherlock Holmes, loved to remind us that circumstantial evidence is a very tricky thing. It may seem to point straight to one thing, but if you shift your perception slightly, you may find that the evidence points in an equally uncompromising manner to something quite different. "There is nothing more deceptive than an obvious fact."

If I believe I am only what I have created—my talents, my body, my IQ, my emotional reactions—then I will be heavily invested in protecting this. But when I wake up to the truth that I am the being behind the creation, I free myself to look with new perception at my world. Most of us are deeply conditioned to believe we are what we do and experience. I am experiencing wealth or poverty; therefore I am wealth or poverty. I have a doctor's degree; therefore I am that doctor's degree. I resent my sister; therefore I am resentment. These beliefs are so imprinted on our self-identity that we build powerful tribal supports to reassure each other that what we do is what we are. However perceiving our experiences as who we are can create a very tenuous reality. One wrong business move or economic shift and there goes the job and our mortgage payments. One leaky blood vessel and so much for our IQ.

There was once an old man who studied the Bible for fifty years and was considered an authority. During an interview he was asked, "After all these years of contemplating the Scriptures, what is your very favorite verse?"

He smiled and said, "And it came to pass."

FLOWING WITH SPIRIT

At one point I was pondering our many religious beliefs and the sad irony that these forms—which you'd think would reconnect us to the Divine and to each other—so often serve to separate us. It led me to thinking about the challenge of being both Spirit and matter, so I took the question to Spirit for greater understanding.

I was shown an image of water flowing everywhere, boundless, full of Light. Then I saw various containers scoop up some of the water. One of the containers was tall and skinny; another was short and squat. Some were ornate; others plain. One was octagonal, another square. None of the containers had all of the water, but each had some. The water conformed to the shape of the container. When the water kept flowing into the containers and overflowing, it remained alive and pure. But when the water wasn't allowed to flow freely, it became stagnant and lifeless in the container.

I understood the water to be the moving Spirit of God, or whatever you choose to call the Source. It is without limit, flows everywhere, and is given freely to all. The containers are our human ideas crystallized into forms and structures. If a human container does not inhibit the flow of the water, if it is not stingy, the water will be replenished endlessly. But if it inhibits the nature of the water itself, it is no longer a good vessel, and the water stagnates. Even though I respect the containers, I'm personally drawn to the water. Though I may be temperamentally more at home with one container than another, I understand that's just what it is, a container for catching a bit of the truth, useful on this dimension unless it hardens into rigidity.

Once we have tasted the water, the containers are useful but not limiting. Because we can now identify with what is unlimited, we can accomplish the "impossible." Once the impossible has been done by one person, it stretches the container itself and redefines the limits. Harriet Tubman, for instance, was a hand-icapped slave when she listened to her guidance and helped hundreds of Southern slaves escape by means of the Underground Railroad. She didn't know that what she was doing was "impossible." Pablo Casals was clearly "too old" to be enchanting audiences with his cello at ninety-six, yet he continued to perform. No human being had run a mile in five minutes before Jim Ryun, but now runners regularly break that barrier as a matter of course. As Henry Ford once said, "Whether you believe you can do a thing or not, you are right."

The challenges we face today seem impossible if we continue to look at them through the eyes of the past. The loving and impersonal energies of evolution are pulling us toward expansion. We all intuit this shift now in process. If we are heavily invested in the existing forms, we may well fear the end of the world. Those of us who are not so invested in the old forms speak of an approaching "new age." Many see in our transition signs of the return of the Christ.

Imagine that the universe is giving a great big outbreath and pushing us toward our highest good. We may not understand how this evolutionary energy works; we may only see that it is powerful beyond description, yet loving of everyone and everything. We can use these powerful energies to expand and grow, to build new concepts and constructs. This is what a lot of people are doing. They are becoming agents of evolution, breathing in this new breath and aligning their will, thoughts, and choices in the direction it calls. Spirit is revealing itself in each of us in the here and now. The possibility of revelation is open to us, but we can only hear it if we believe this is possible. At some point we must decide whether to pursue our own relationship with God or simply to accept someone else's experience.

As conscious creators we're always walking a line between essence and form. Breathing in undefined essence, we breathe out a creation that is the sum total of our beliefs. The trick is to know that it is just a creation, a form, and not the essence itself. When we unhook ourselves from identifying with what we create, when we can recognize that we are creators, we are free to explore further, go deeper.

DOGMA

When he began, he was a true warrior, longing for the truth.

"I must go on a quest," he said.

The elders, satisfied that his youthful passion was controlled, his human ambition tempered, gave him the secret map. He traveled many seasons before he reached the High Land. Day after day he sat in the meadow atop the mountain, his life and breath suspended. There was only the silence. He saw nothing; he heard nothing.

Then, on the dawning of the seventh day, when the moon and sun were poised in balance, his quest was answered. Out of the Earth came a great white bird, its wings bathed in peach and gold light from the rising sun. It glided to a nearby tree and sang a song of such sweetness, the warrior wept when he heard it, lifting his hands in gratitude and supplication.

Without hesitation the bird flew to his upturned palms. For a long time they sat together in harmonious oneness. As the winged messenger told the eager young warrior many wondrous things, the warrior's Spirit broke free of its bonds.

Then he recalled his earthly home and the tribe he had left behind. "I must go and tell the others," he thought, and prepared to release the bird. But a thought nagged at him. Perhaps they won't believe me? I'll capture the bird and then they'll have to believe me.

The great white bird offered no resistance as the warrior's opened palm closed tight. Flushed with triumph and grasping the source of his revelation, the warrior raced down the hill toward home, never noticing how still the bird had become.

He gathered the people around him and told them the marvelous things he'd learned from the bird. Then, proudly, he presented the winged testament to his quest. But the eyes of the bird were fixed and empty. The soft white wings, once arched in flight, now lay flat and lifeless.

The people were puzzled. But they had never sought the quest themselves. Surely the warrior must know. At his direction they built a temple for the bird and told the story of his quest over and over again. Many young ones were inspired to seek for themselves.

But that was long ago. The warrior is no longer young and yearning. He sits alone in an airless, dusty room. It is said that he fashioned himself a cape of white feathers and that on certain days he sits before the stuffed white bird and waits for it to speak.

"I Didn't Believe
in Reincarnation the
Last Time Either"

Reincarnation exists until you know you don't need it.
—RESHAD FIELD

*H*ow do you think you got here in the first place? Dive head-first into this question without the safety net of someone else's explanations and prejudices. It might be scary, but it's necessary if you desire to plumb your own depths, for what you believe about your origins establishes the primary parameters of your reality. All of the changes you experience will be defined by those parameters.

The need to know how we got here seems to be built into the psyche. How do I arrive in a particular womb with a specific set of genetics, inheriting psychic, physiological, and sociological family patterns that reach so far back that they eventually disappear into everyone's history?

Is the universe so disorganized that an egg and a sperm can meet, fuse, and catapult us into ninety years on planet Earth without our having any voice in the matter? If so, what kind of God would decide that we should arrive just in time for a na-palm searing, or multiple sclerosis, or sexual abuse? Or even health, wealth, and happiness, for that matter? Do we indeed make our own reality? Is there divine Grace, and if so, what does that have to do with destiny or choices?

These are tough questions. But the questions themselves,

even the fact that we question, imply that we somehow know we existed before. Before what? Before we arrived here? How did I get here? Where do I go when I leave? Who is this "I" that poses the question in the first place?

One of the most dominant themes in human thought is that we return to life again and again until we learn to master all the lessons this planet has to teach us. Reincarnation as the means through which we spiritually evolve has been accepted down through the ages by saints, sages, and ordinary folk. In the West we have viewed this as a purely Eastern doctrine, but in fact that wisdom has been expressed in many cultures around the world, from the Essenes and ancient Greeks to Native Americans. Many Christians, from the early Gnostics to present-day believers find the concept of reincarnation not only in harmony with Christ's teachings but supportive of them.

HOW REINCARNATION WORKS

Allowing for variations in cultural packaging, basically the idea goes like this. We once existed in perfect rest and balance in the One. But then we were breathed forth from the heart of God bearing the image and the inner spark of our creator, with the gift of using our will to choose and create as we desired.

As we used that divine will, we became increasingly fascinated with the physical world, moving ever deeper into its density. As we came to identify ourselves more and more with our material creations—our illusions—we began to forget who we really were, perceiving ourselves as separate from God and from each other.

Our separation is our pain, and our cure is nothing less than reunion. The traditional spiritual teachings tell us that the manner in which this reunion comes to pass is through successive lifetimes, in which we gradually tire of the consequences of us-

ing our birthright of free will to create passing dramas that perpetuate more suffering and separation. At this point we begin to
use our will to seek conscious reconnection with the One Will.
This is when we discover that we've never really been separated;
we just thought we were. There was never a time when God's
Grace and love were not with us. Much of what we call evil is
simply ignorance and a denial of the Light.

Reincarnation is the means through which our individual will
is made conscious of its true oneness with the will of God. In
the process the consequences of choices, actions, thoughts, and
desires we make in one lifetime are experienced in other lifetimes. This is the cause-and-effect process called karma.

Karma is not a reward-and-punishment morality system. It's
a principle of nature. Whatever we say, do, think, or feel—
whether positive or negative—produces a reaction that will return to us, but not necessarily in the same lifetime. When the
conditions are precisely right, we receive back that which we
sent out. What we curse we bind to ourselves; what we bless
we free.

God's Grace offers us the unqualified opportunity to learn
and the ever-present potential for transcending karma. We do
this by awakening and surrendering to the Universal Christ—
by whatever name we call this energy—for total surrender is the
only way to bring about the reunion and eliminate the endless
round of incarnations.

MANY VIEWS OF THE
ETERNAL RETURN

Reincarnation has been explored throughout history under many
names—rebirth, reembodiment, metempsychosis, metemsoma-
tosis, even transmigration. Because we don't yet know the physics that would explain how we experience multiple realities, we

have created many theories about the way it works. However the fact that there have been a number of words and concepts built around reincarnation, many of which argue against each other, does not negate the possibility that it exists.

When observed truth has no provable context in which to place it, it becomes laden with superstition. Take transmigration, for example. This concept usually carries with it the implication that one would reembody in a lower life-form. That is not consistent with the theory of evolution; we don't go backward. Yet even today I'll occasionally meet someone who dismisses reincarnation by arguing, "Reincarnation? Isn't that when you think you'll come back as a dog?" Although this may be said with disdain, I sometimes hear a bit of fear in the voice, a fear that maybe God runs the universe like a top commander thundering, "Break the law and I'll bust you to private."

Perhaps transmigration as a concept came about less out of ignorance about evolution than from the observation that some people, such as magicians and witches, could project their conscious wills into lower forms. Shamans from many cultures have been credited with using animal forms to do their bidding or with successfully creating an illusion of an animal. Perhaps the child inside us still wonders if the bad witch really can turn us into a toad.

One concept about the way in which reincarnation works is that of the oversoul. This theory holds that the "I" in this life is but one of many expressions existing simultaneously in physical bodies, that we are all part of an oversoul, like individual cells in a single body, and that we each have within us the capacity to know all the other expressions of "I" experiencing other lives. This view sees each of us as both the whole—the oversoul—and the parts at the same time.

Lecturer and writer Dick Sutphen advises us to think of simultaneous lives as a multilevel chessboard. If we look straight down from overhead, we see many players on many levels. Move one player, and it affects all the other players.

Are these other lives also us? Yes, if we realize that space-time is not really linear. There is no beginning, middle, nor end, rather all these lives are happening in the eternal now. In which case the sooner we catch on to our divine right to create and to change anything, the sooner what we do in this life will offset all our other lives.

A variation on the concept of the oversoul says that we are who we are and have never been anyone else and that our knowledge and energy will remain with us throughout eternity. In essence, we have made ourselves up, and this "I" is free to make up other "I's."

Then there's the school of thought that says that earth life is simply an illusionary game created as an evolutionary process for the soul, that we make it up—all of it—even though the illusion certainly seems real enough while we're here!

Perhaps today a master such as Jesus might talk to us as a physicist, speaking of many alternate realities, many dimensions of time and space in which to live in consciousness.

Reincarnation is not a religion per se, although it is accepted or rejected by religious doctrines. Just as one can be a social scientist or psychologist of any faith, so can one belong to any religion and accept reincarnation as a working principle of soul evolution in the universe.

Seeking the ways in which God works with us through natural laws and systems is no more an exclusively religious issue than is how the human body or how the solar system functions. It wasn't so long ago that performing an autopsy was considered a sin. So was suggesting that the Earth wasn't the center of the universe. To blindly accept the pronouncements of any pre-science theology as final truth can set up a painful and completely unnecessary choice between our natural yearning for spiritual peace and our natural yearning for knowledge.

There is no split between Spirit and science unless we make one; science discovers the way Spirit manifests. And some of our sciences today are beginning to explore areas we previously considered strictly the territory of theology. The lines between objective and subjective reality are getting quite fuzzy. We know that we influence what we observe. Our consciousness and what we used to think was objective reality are proving to be inseparable. As Nobel Prize–winning physicist David Bohm said, "I find the study of mysticism no stranger than the study of the material world."

Correctly understood, reincarnation is part of a theoretical model of spiritual science, a discipline that studies how consciousness works. *Reincarnation* is a term that refers to one of the working principles of consciousness. When we separated the study of consciousness from the study of nature, we put science and religion into separate camps. No doubt we reaped some benefit from that, since we disempowered religious institutions from interfering with the pursuit of scientific knowledge. But in that separation of material and spiritual science we also intensified the split between our physical and spiritual natures.

BOTTOMING OUT

Another example of reincarnation as spiritual science was the experience of a young man who was referred to me by a psychiatrist. At age twenty-eight, for no apparent reason and with no history of similar behavior, he performed a violent act. Astrologers note that at ages twenty-eight to thirty, fifty-six to sixty, and so on we each experience a "Saturn return," meaning that Saturn, the planet of form, limitation, and restriction returns to where it was at the moment of our birth. Most people's lives undergo a major shift at these times—it might be a marriage, a death, a birth, or a job change. Whatever it is, it indicates that another chapter in our life story is beginning.

The psychiatrist told me that the man had an assortment of neuroses but nothing that would explain his sudden violent behavior. The first thing I saw psychically when I attuned to him were lifetimes spent in the military dating back to ancient history. The most recent lifetime was as a Nazi storm trooper in World War II.

The interesting thing that I was told in Spirit was that this soul had originally come to this planet out of love and a desire to help advance evolution. Unfortunately one of the ways we have spread culture, knowledge, and law has been through warfare. So he was drawn into military action over and over again, and with each life his original motive of accelerating evolution was increasingly lost. All this continual military experience left the yin side of his nature undeveloped. He was way off-balance with his inner feminine, and the psychiatrist confirmed that he had many problems understanding women.

When he had reached the age of twenty-eight in his lifetime as a storm trooper, the horrors of the Holocaust had shocked his consciousness into seeing the futility of war. He recognized that war was not the way to change things and in one irrational moment he shot himself.

Even in this lifetime the young man had chosen a pseudo-military profession, and when he reached the age when he had once killed himself as a storm trooper, he began to have violent, unexplained headaches. One day he simply lost control and exploded.

When I met with his family and told them what I'd discovered, his mother turned white. It seems he had compulsively drawn swastikas from the time he could control a pencil. No one in the family could understand it, since no one had been directly affected by World War II or harbored any political leanings in that direction.

From our human perspective the end of this story is not so happy. The insight that war was not the way to change things was devastating. He was like a car that had been racing at a hundred miles an hour, towards its destination, only to discover he was headed to the wrong place. He hit the brakes too fast.

He moved from prescriptions to street drugs in order to deal with his headaches and anxieties, and finally shot himself—again. I suspect he was suffering from soul despair and could not forgive himself.

When I saw him psychically at his funeral, he was quite happy to be free of the body and amazed that so many people had cared about him enough to come.

THE BODY REMEMBERS

Another example of how intensely the body prints out the beliefs held in the mind across time and space is presented in the story of an articulate, well-dressed, and gentle-mannered woman with many serious physical problems who came to me for counseling. It took her several minutes to catalog her twenty-year medical history. She had been in therapy more than once and was also satisfied she had had good medical treatment. But she had never satisfactorily answered the underlying question—the one she'd brought to me—"Why?" And the answer which had eluded her most diligent efforts was contained in her experiences in other lifetimes.

As I attuned to her, I immediately saw a computer printout of dozens of lifetimes with her present husband. They had shared every conceivable kind of relationship: mother-son, boss-employee, brother-sister, husband-mistress, and on and on. The one common denominator was that each relationship had been charged with competitiveness, jealousy, and enmity. As I looked at this list of negative relationships, it disappeared, and I saw a pulsing black ball with the word *hate* written all over it.

My observing self wondered how in the world I was going to tell this perfectly lovely lady that she was suffering from long-term hate that had concretized in her body. But I can't pray to be shown insights and then tell Spirit, "Thanks, but I'd rather have another one, please." So I took a deep breath and told her as gently as I could what I had seen, assuring her she could decide for herself if this held any meaning for her. Her composure dissolved. She burst into tears and said, "It's true, it's true. I hate him. I always have, and I never understood why I married him."

She had married him because she was compelled to—hate seeks its object as surely as does love. She was both attracted to him and repelled by him. Living in a tense state of ambivalence literally poisoned her body with hate. To be healed, the soul seeks balance and the reinstatement of its love nature. The body holds the memory of unreleased resentment from lifetime to lifetime.

REINCARNATION TODAY

Until recently the legacy of the scientists who pursued the knowledge of consciousness in earlier times has not been readily available to us. Most of them were driven underground. But all this is changing, and these treasures are now pouring into public awareness. Furthermore, physical scientists all over the world are turning their minds and laboratories to the study of consciousness—including the study of reincarnation.

Dr. Ian Stevenson of the University of Virginia, author of *Twenty Cases Suggestive of Reincarnation*, has been one of the early pioneers in subjecting this ancient spiritual teaching to modern scientific investigation. In addition our understanding of how consciousness creates experience or even creates matter grows as quantum physics explores space, time, and multiple and alternate realities.

In the United States reincarnation is often treated as an elective, take it or leave it, an amusing and titillating diversion. It even seems to be darkly threatening to some people. Why?

Maybe it's as simple as the "Frank and Ernest" cartoon that said, "I know I've never lived before, or I wouldn't be so confused this time around."

Could it be that to acknowledge reincarnation is to accept that no rescue team is coming to make all the world's problems go away? The rescue team, the masters and the teachers, have already arrived over and over again—and continue to arrive to show us the way to transform our personal and joint worlds. Is part of the fear that we might have to face and transform our personal, self-created demons and then work with others to transform our collective madness? Is it possible we will have to take Jesus, Buddha, Krishna, and all the other enlightened ones seriously and find our own paths through the "straight gate," and not simply expect to ride in on their coattails with our prejudices intact?

Our journey through the transformation process is made clearer by the enlightened ones in all cultures who have blessed this planet. Overcoming all of the world's traps, they have believed and then become the belief. They became masters by overcoming every obstacle you and I encounter. And by their lives, they teach us that we can and will do the same. Their struggles and triumphs have impregnated the collective mind with such clear, powerful radiations, which enable us to find our way home more easily. Co-creating with the universe, they amplify the evolutionary plan and serve us.

"I WILL—OR I WILL NOT"

The evolutionary plan which accompanied Paul in this lifetime presents us with much food for thought. Paul lives in Europe. He was six years old when I first saw him. He had originally been diagnosed as autistic, but his symptoms didn't continue to fit that profile, although he rarely spoke and was withdrawn. He was considered very handicapped in terms of his learning abilities and occasionally acted out serious behavior problems. Frankly no one knew what was wrong with him.

His parents and therapist brought him to me late one afternoon following a workshop I had been teaching. At first I could not get Paul to look me in the eyes, but then I discovered he would hang out with me on the mats on the floor and play. The first thing he did was to very methodically remove his socks, shoes, pants, and underpants, but not his sweater or his shirt. His therapist quietly commented that he had never done that before. We agreed to just wait and see what would happen.

After we made friends, I took him over to an easel, where I had been working with colored pens, and I took his hands and drew various shapes with the different colors. As he became interested, I backed off in order to get the perspective I needed to see his auric field. In English I asked him to draw a circle in green, and he did. Then a square in purple, and he did. I did this enough times to assure myself and those watching that what he was doing was no accident. For remarkably this child, who was considered barely teachable in his own language and chose rarely to speak it, was responding to my directions in English.

As I looked at his aura, I saw that he was in his body just enough to keep it running. Most of his energy was concentrated in the mental aspect of himself. From the waist down, his energy was so low that I wondered how he was even walking around. From the waist up, it grew stronger and stronger. Above his head I could see the concentration of his beingness, attached but doing its best to be as uninvolved with the life of Paul as possible. No wonder he'd removed his clothes from the waist down. He was having a checkup, and he knew where the problem was.

Paul had no will to be in his male body; in fact he used his extremely powerful will to avoid being in the body any more than he had to. He had nonspecific memories of having been in positions of power in which he misused his will, and he was afraid of his own will and power.

Finally he allowed me to make eye contact with him. One can make contact will-to-will through the eyes, and if that look is charged with love, it is very supportive and can cut through the barrier of words. It says, "I see you in there. I honor your will to choose. I send you a reminder of the love and Light that you are." Sometimes it is the only thing you can do for a person, though a very powerful one. Before he left, I gave Paul a small crystal as a concrete reminder of the prayer energy I was holding for him and also because children like crystals—"Earth candy," a friend calls them.

Later his mother wrote me that he had carefully placed the crystal on top of a picture of himself—over his heart—and would not allow anyone to touch it.

Six months or so after our visit I received a drawing from Paul. His mother attached a note saying that Paul had indicated that the picture was for me, adding that he very rarely drew pictures. She said that he told her to "tell Gloria that nobody lives in this house." The drawing was a house, but very clearly it was also a penis. Midway up, where the solar plexus would be, there were jagged red lines, and at the top there was a tiny yellow window, the only view out of the "house." Since yellow is the color often associated with the mental body, his picture confirmed my feeling that his will resided in his mental self—a self that was extraordinarily bright—but that he refused to infuse his will into his total self.

I knew that Paul had put the ball back in my court. So I listened to my instincts, checking them out with a couple of psychologists who work with children, and decided on the following: I cut out all kinds of pictures and pasted them on eight-by-ten-inch sheets of paper—there were dogs, cats, toys, teddy bears, even an angel. I sent them to him with a letter saying that lots of things could live in his house if he wanted, but that he had to choose what he wanted.

I know that his will is his divine birthright, and no one under universal law can interfere with that. All we can do is love him and offer him opportunities, support, skills, and time. It would be presumptuous for me to say I know what's best for Paul. He is considering other options to what he has been doing, and he continues to attract people into his life who will offer him options.

Perhaps this incarnation is a turning point in his evolution. Maybe he needs an incarnation to stay neutral and observe. He clearly doesn't want to be a boy. But I never had the impression that he wanted to be a girl. Whatever the extended purposes of this incarnation, he is certainly learning the power of will.

UNEQUAL OPPORTUNITIES

When I first heard the idea of reincarnation as a child, I instantly "knew" it to be true—for me. Certainly reincarnation makes sense out of the otherwise senseless. When we become aware of seemingly unfair situations, such as productive lives cut short by accident, violence, war, and disease, we rage at the lack of justice in human terms. I recently read a sad and funny anonymous quip that said that expecting justice on planet Earth just because you're a nice person is like expecting a bull not to attack you because you're a vegetarian.

Clearly people do not start life with equal opportunities. From a human point of view the only thing that a child born with AIDS in an African village has in common with a healthy child in the American suburbs is that they are both infants and dependent. Both give all of us a chance to improve ourselves collectively. But that is the second issue. The first is why?

Reincarnation clarifies the appearance of genius and all exceptional situations. And it is harmonious with what we understand thus far about physical evolution. Further it untangles many knots in sacred scripture that otherwise leave you wondering. For example: "Be ye perfect" seems unlikely when viewed from the perspective of any one life. But it is a clear directive that indicates perfection is the ultimate goal.

Perhaps the time has come to consider the possibility that divine justice and divine love aren't remotely like what we humans think they are. For all the contradictions, there is an order and a purpose to all our lives and while we may not understand how it all works, there is growing evidence that it does work.

Understanding reincarnation gives clarity to the knowingness that goes beyond reason. Moreover it offers insight into the unpredictable "fates" that bring just the right experience to us at just the right time—that synchronistic "magic"—the deja vu that brings the right people, that opens or slams doors, and that changes our lives.

LOVE HEALS ACROSS TIME

This story of the past lifetime of a very practical as well as intuitive woman in her late sixties shows that there are no simple karmic equations. From the time this woman was born, she experienced abandonment, first by her mother, who died when she was very young, and then followed immediately by her father, who gave her away. Her marriage to the only man she had ever loved was painful, for he spent the last twenty years of his life in an alcoholic haze that closed her out. While she coped with her disappointments, she paid for it with her low self-esteem and had little or no sense of being lovable as a woman.

Concluding that personal love was not for her, she began to work on herself, seeking to understand herself and her relationship to God. She learned to let go of the resentments and forgive the past. She regularly prayed to finish the lessons of this life.

One evening when she was in the lobby of an auditorium, she casually glanced up to meet the eyes of a man she had never seen before, a man some fifteen years her junior. That one look went straight to her soul. She felt she knew this man intimately, and the feelings it produced in her were unnerving.

She fled the meeting in tears, but they met again on the steps. She decided to tell him what had happened to her. He, too, had had the same reaction. That began a series of conversations that went on for days and deep into the nights.

She told him things she had never told anyone else. He was more familiar to her than all the people in her life. She had never before had a past-life memory, but suddenly she recalled exactly how and when she had known him—as his beloved wife and best friend. It was a life in which she had been loved and treasured. Independently of each other, both he and she picked up the exact same lifetime, including country, time, and circumstances. That is how powerfully the memory had been held by both of them.

In time they went their separate ways. It was never their karma in this lifetime to marry again or even to be sexually involved. What did happen is that her painful sense of not being lovable was healed. Because she had sincerely sought to complete the cycle, she attracted this reminder of a time in which she was highly loved and valued and so was able to release the anger, pain, and abandonments of this life.

When reincarnation is not understood, creating one's own reality and accepting destiny seem to be opposing concepts. They are not. They are like two horses that pull a carriage in tandem. They have to work together. The circumstances of our birth and many of the events that come to us are the raw material we have already created. How we perceive those materials and what we choose to do with them builds our future realities.

We are consciousness—and while consciousness can change form, it can never die. We are not dead when the body dies, we simply shift to another form—Spirit, not matter. Now you experience consciousness on Earth, now you experience consciousness in other realities. (Don't read that as living on other planets necessarily; physical matter is only one reality among many.)

It's certainly not as simple as the idea that if you killed Charlie last time, it's now his turn to kill you. It's closer to your holding in consciousness the memory of killing and being killed, the fear and the desire for revenge—all focused on a particular soul once called Charlie. If the Charlie you killed has released you through forgiveness, but you haven't released it from your own consciousness, then you'll meet a situation where someone just like the original Charlie will give you an opportunity to work through the unreleased energy you are holding.

TWO FOR ONE

I once knew two women who lived several states apart until it was time for their karmas to collide. The first was a young woman I had counseled many years earlier. She had come to me puzzled about feeling stagnant in her spiritual life. It was as if she had gotten to a certain point and wouldn't allow herself to grow any further. I was shown a life in which she had been an Aztec priest; one of her tasks had been to remove the living hearts of those being sacrificed on religious holidays. She resonated with this and told me that she had been haunted by dreams of herself splattered with blood since childhood.

Years went by, and I ran into her during a conference several states away from her home. I was with a close friend and introduced them as the three of us waited for the curtain to rise on an experimental drama. I never saw the piece, but I doubt it could have equaled the drama that unfolded.

To fully understand this story, you must know that my friend is a very self-contained and balanced woman, one who is accustomed to confronting her shadows without hysterics. While she didn't view herself as a finished product by any means, she was accustomed to using various techniques to aid her in her growth. She was aware that she felt blocked in her spiritual life by a fear that had no name, and she had been praying and meditating to work through this block.

As we waited, some very weird music began to play over the loudspeakers. It sounded like the score for *The Creature from the Black Lagoon*—ugly and dissonant. All of a sudden I felt a frantic pulling on my arm and leaned over to hear my friend begging through clenched teeth to get her out of there. Before I could say a word, she was running down the aisle, out of the theater, and across a meadow—with me running behind her and the other woman behind me.

She fell to her knees and began moaning, then throwing up, then moaning again. As her friend, I wanted only to hold her and assure her that whatever it was could be helped. But I had sharp, clear, and immediate direction from Spirit that I should help her go through it, not avoid it. I began to run my hand up her back, from the lower spine up, and soon her broken and terrified words began meshing with the pictures flashing in my head.

She was recalling with emotional horror a past life in which she had been a young girl drugged into paralysis, but not into unconsciousness. She was being taken up some steps in order to have her heart cut out as a sacrifice to the Aztec gods.

She was understandably very shaken after her recall was over, and I suggested that the three of us go somewhere quiet and get ourselves together. In the meantime the other woman had not said a word, but she was ashen. An hour or so later she turned to my friend and said in a trembling voice, "I think I know who it was who cut out your heart. It was me." My friend stared at her for a while and then reached out and told her, "I forgive you." They embraced each other for a long time, and the pain, fear, guilt, and blocks carried by both of them for so long was dissolved.

READING THE AKASHIC RECORD

In the life of the soul, whenever we develop a talent, use our circumstances and resources to the best of our abilities, and serve the good of all, we store this in heaven—"Heaven" being a state of mind. It's like having a vault filled with treasures, only in this case they're the talents we've developed over many incarnations.

There is also a record book in that vault, and it carries a detailed account of every asset and every debit. Now, imagine that you enter this vault to prepare for an incarnation. You look at the account books from the wise perception of the Higher will, not through the greedy eyes of the ego, and you pick a few things that need to be worked on. You might not choose to use all your treasures in any one life experience so that you can keep the focus on a particular lesson.

In the East this record of all we have done is referred to as Akashia or the Akashic record. The Bible refers to it as the Book of Memory. The Akashic record, the Book of Memory, is within. Ether moves through all things, and upon it is recorded everything exactly as it happens. It is highly magnetic. It is our record both individually and as a species, and it moves with us wherever we go. Here like attracts like. If you have imprinted fear, then, like Job, you will find that what you have feared has come upon you.

People with highly developed psychic sensitivity can read these records. However, before you believe the report of one of your past lives given to you by someone else, it is well to keep in mind that psychic impressions are filtered and interpreted through the mind and belief system of the one receiving the impression. Obviously the more work the sensitive has done to transform his or her own patterns, the more he or she can read yours clearly.

I had an experience with a highly skilled psychic in a foreign country that makes this point well. It was my first trip to this country. I had been told about a woman there who was considered to be one of the best psychics in that area. As I was waiting for people to register for a workshop I was teaching, she walked in, took one look at me, and, truly startled, began chattering away in a language I didn't understand. My interpreter told me that the psychic had announced that I was the reincarnation of one of the most well-known mythic figures in that country. I knew very well I was nothing of the sort. I doubt very seriously if such a figure ever actually lived, any more than that the gods and goddesses of ancient Greece were ever real people.

Later, when I became acquainted with this psychic, I tried to suggest that she was tapping into the archetypal realm. Archetypes are imaginary figures that have taken on a certain collective "real" life in our consciousness because their stories have been told and retold hundreds of times. They become symbols for certain types of energy. Even real people who were major villains or heroes of their time take on archetypal proportions as their exploits are repeated. Some quality of energy in a person can remind us of characters in legends. This psychic wouldn't buy it; she would not even consider that some quality of energy in me triggered a subconscious reference in her to the qualities she saw in the mythic figure. In her belief system that mythic figure had lived, and I was her, come back again.

I am not criticizing this woman. I found her sensitivity to be quite accurate and insightful about many things. I know very well that all of us have to interpret what we psychically sense, and it is shaped—or reshaped—in our minds by what we personally believe as well as by the symbols we hold in our subconscious. I tell everyone with whom I counsel that they must carefully weigh everything told to them and decide for themselves what is literal and what is symbolic.

Past-life memory may be symbolic, racial, or archetypal. The exactness of the memory is not so important as the type of energy it arouses in us. After all the melodramas of a particular life are over, what is left is the distilled essence of the experience. Being a tribal chieftain offers us the same dynamics for learning about the responsibilities of leadership as being a king or president of the United States. If we see ourselves or someone else as Napoleon, it doesn't necessarily mean that's who we were. It may simply be our subconscious giving us a symbolic reference for the type of energy we encountered.

Suppose you are terrified of losing a child to the point of being neurotic about it. You may have experienced such a loss in other life experiences, maybe by death, kidnapping, or slavery. Something today triggers that fear in you, and a "memory" surfaces of a life you may or may not have had literally. As the brain stretches to give a name to the fearful feelings of loss you are experiencing, it pulls on whatever you have in your subconscious. You might have seen a movie about someone losing a child, *Sophie's Choice*, for example, and found such a deep resonating response inside, that it felt almost as if that exact experience had happened to you. The "past life memory" appears like the movie. Memories gather around archetypal experiences such as birth, death, love, hate, war, religious and political power. Something in you recognized the dynamic and creates its own version of the movie.

While all souls are equal, not all are equally experienced in Earth existence. There really are old souls who are worn out, bored, and through with all the gymnastics of their own will. They may create very, very difficult lifetimes for themselves in order to run off the last of worldly illusions being held in consciousness. We puzzle over people who are self-centered and yet seem to be abundant in every way. Sometimes they are simply beginning to experience what their wills can accomplish. Their selfishness has less to do with being evil than it does with simply being young in their understanding.

One of the characteristics of a mature soul is its concern for the good of all. That doesn't have anything to do with choosing what appears to be a selfless profession. It has more to do with a total lifewalk of harmlessness and a consciousness of its own contribution. It makes no difference if such people are successful or not in terms of the world; they will use whatever resources and influences are available to them to put the best they have to offer into the world.

OLDER SOULS: TOUGHER LESSONS

One such mature soul I chanced to encounter was one of the most sensitive, loving people you would ever hope to meet, the kind of person you would expect would have only the best the world could offer. Not so. From the beginning of her life she was surrounded by selfish, self-centered people. When she married, she lived with an egocentric man who gave her little or no support. Her children were a constant trial to her. Even in their thirties most of them rarely visited her and were indifferent to her needs. Life was extremely painful and lonely for her, but she opted for love and forgiveness, not martyrdom.

Once when I was doing some healing work for her, I heard in Spirit, "She has walked a dark corridor with Grace." Spirit went on to tell me that she had incarnated to work on unconditional loving. She had done just that, no matter what came back to her. Painful as it was, she worked daily on releasing the children, blessing them, forgiving them.

She continued to love her children in spite of their behavior, and as the years went by, they began to respond to her ever-present acceptance and love. She has been more than their mother; she has been their teacher. At last she is beginning to reap what she sowed, even in this lifetime, but it has been a long and demanding lesson in maintaining unconditional love.

I have been shown over and over again that we come into a given incarnation both to learn and to teach. No other human being can fully know what purpose another is serving. For example a highly evolved soul may be ready for the lessons of personal ego sacrifice. One soul might choose to incarnate with limited mental ability in order to provide others with the opportunity to learn about love and caring. Another might come into this life as a male who's hit the jackpot—handsome, wealthy, and with every talent imaginable—yet must constantly struggle with overchoice. What to choose? How to use it? That soul is learning about focusing intention.

Whatever life we see now is only a page in an epic novel. If this is the point in the ongoing story in which the hero or heroine is challenged by the villain, the lifetime might appear tragic to us. But that is our human interpretation. It might well be the turning point in the whole evolution of the soul. It is not for us to judge.

Once Spirit said to me, "Do you object to the design of a bird's wing? Do you object to the color of a rock, or the orbit of a planet? Then why would you object to the design of another's soul? Do you think you know more about what is needed for another than his or her soul does? When you feel the need to judge another, you can be sure that you are out of balance yourself."

We can only accept that things are not what they seem to be and most probably are exactly where they need to be. That includes our quick appraisal of so-called Yuppies as well as the lingering superstition that the poor are somehow being punished by God. For all we know, Yuppies are souls running off the last of their materialism, acquiring "things" and status in some sort of last-ditch ego identification. We cannot know. In certain spiritual training practices in the East if a teacher observes that you have an unrequited addiction, you won't be taught to repress it. Rather the teacher might encourage you to indulge your addiction to the limit until you're sick of it. Then you'll be through with it once and for all.

When we can allow ourselves and others to just be—with no judgment—we begin to understand the wisdom and perspective that reincarnation teaches us.

But will that result in indifference to others' suffering, as some people suggest it might? My observation has been that just the contrary happens. The more we understand about our connectedness, the more we grasp that we are an incarnating piece of the whole, the more responsible we become as we relate to the whole.

If you are in a hole, and you are in my path, that is no accident. I'm given the opportunity to learn as much as you. I can have compassion and love you, or I can blame you for falling in and say you deserve it. I can offer you help out of the hole. I can put up a sign warning others. Or I can ignore the whole thing, saying it has nothing to do with me which is the biggest ignorance of all for it fails to see that you and I are in life together. We are in the hole, not just you. This becomes very important when we apply this insight to our major social issues, such as homelessness.

There comes a time in our growth when we give up any real preoccupation with reincarnation. Sufi teacher and mystic Reshad Field suggests that "if the sacred cow of reincarnation is still giving you influenza, then you had better give it up." After we have accepted that our life is continuous, weaving in and out of many experiences, then we can let go of who we might or might not have been. Sooner or later we all get to play every part. Meantime there's only now and the immediate demands and concerns of this life.

We may not know why a child incarnates and experiences a cruel battering. We only know that that child's life is not separate from our own. That child's experience may be a loving sacrifice for the good of all. And once it is brought to our attention, it offers us the opportunity to change the political, social, and psychological conditions that have allowed battering to occur. It is not only our own personal drama that is grist for the evolutionary mill; it is our response to the whole of life.

GETTING HELP—THERAPY
AND COUNSELING

Once we decide to make peace with our lives and move fully into self-acceptance, we have to get beyond blaming—even God, or whatever we perceive that energy to be. Even if we have been victimized in the worst of ways, we are still responsible for what we do with that experience. This usually requires that we first explore and own all of the feelings involved, including our rage, fear, and powerlessness.

It may not always be important to identify who did what to whom, when, and why, but it is very important to recognize and own the feelings that keep us stuck in a victim's impotence and repressed rage. At some point we have to decide what we are going to do with those feelings once we have named them. I have known people who have been through years of therapy and could articulate thirty reasons why they hate, yet they still held on to that hate.

However, good therapies help us first to identify, then to own, understand, and take responsibility for our reactions. We are led gradually into the actual transformation of the energy around personal issues. We know that the feelings are on the way out when there is no emotional charge either way—the feeling is neutral.

Until quite recently most psychologists have been careful to avoid anything that smacks of Spirit—or they've tried to do so. They are cautious about considering past-life influences in their patients. I understand that, having dealt with people who are clearly blocked in their emotional selves and who try to avoid confronting the pain with a smoke screen of spiritual double-talk. Perhaps cautious therapists, like myself, have met one too many Mary Magdalenes or Egyptian priests. I often wonder who were the cobblers and cooks in all those ancient civilizations.

WHAT GOES AROUND
COMES AROUND

It is very unusual in a counseling session to have one's past life discussed at great length. One particularly revealing counseling session I conducted however did reveal such an in-depth presentation. I did not know any of the facts of this man's current life experience before we started. But in this case I was shown a past life in great detail. And it turned out that the plot, characters, and dynamic were eerily similar to my client's current life.

In the earlier life this man had been a modest craftsman in a small town in Israel. Above all else he loved the Torah, and anytime he wasn't tending to his craft, he was at the temple discussing the ways of God. When his first girl was born, he was quite disappointed that the child wasn't a boy, but not nearly as much as when the second and then the third, fourth, and finally the fifth girl was born. With each birth he withdrew from the family more and more, spending increasing amounts of time at the synagogue. Over the years his wife became very, very bitter. On the rare occasions when he was home, he was hostile and indifferent to the girls, especially the younger ones. He only had time for the Torah. The youngest child became emotionally disturbed to the point of spending a lot of her time out of her body, unreachable by anyone. She was clearly mentally ill.

Then one day, while repairing the roof, the man fell and broke his back and had to lie in bed for over a year. Unable to go to the temple, he was forced to see what had happened to his once-sweet wife. She was beyond caring for him and did only what duty required. She focused much of her rage on the synagogue, viewing his spiritual obsessions as one might a mistress.

The oldest child had at least experienced some parental love and grounding in her earliest years, and while she felt rejected, she still reached for his approval and love. She became his nurse. Frustrated at being unable to discuss his beloved Torah with anyone, he began discussing spiritual ideas with his eldest daughter—creating friction between her and the mother. As he lay there, he also began to realize how ill the youngest girl was and felt the pangs of guilt.

When this man came to see me in his current lifetime, he was the father of several girls and the husband of an angry wife. He spent all of his spare time at his church. He was considered by most people to be a very spiritual man, since he was so devoted to studying the teachings. He had met a woman at the church with whom he could talk about such things, and he had convinced himself that she understood him spiritually. He did not see that his relationship with his wife and girls had anything to do with his spiritual life, and he was ready to leave his wife and girls, the youngest of whom was not emotionally stable.

I didn't recognize all the characters in this rerun, but it was clear that his new love was his eldest daughter from the life in Israel—even then he had thought she was the only one who understood him. His wife of today was the wife of yesterday, and neither of them had forgiven and released the mutual hostility of the past life. He was still substituting spiritual concepts for spiritual transformation—Protestant theology had simply replaced the Torah. It was the ideas and not their guidance that fascinated him. But the soul knows the difference. We don't progress because we can talk the rap, we have to become what we believe.

It was not my place to tell him what to do, but I did lay out the dynamics for him to see. He had very strong reactions to the description of the life in Israel, even to the point of tears. Strong emotional response is often a clue that the information— or symbolic value—is accurate.

Nowadays, however, more and more therapists are realizing that it is virtually impossible to do their work without dealing with both their own and their clients' spiritual beliefs. I know many who use the concept of "past lives" as a means of going deep into the recesses of people's psyches, where the waters of mind, Spirit, emotion, and imagination blend. Clearly if there is an emergency in the emotional self, the healing needs to take place there. But for therapy that aims ultimately for wholeness and self-actualization, one can no more separate people's Spirit from their emotions or body than one can separate blood from a living organ.

There is no way of separating psychological influences from the soul's choice of lessons. For example, suppose a soul has fears about being in a female body. Perhaps that person has spent many lifetimes experiencing limitations or persecutions as a woman. Not only might that person choose to find balance through a lifetime filled with the challenges of being female, but the soul is likely to begin the whole thing in the womb. She might come to a mother who has serious doubts about how much she likes being female herself. While in utero, sharing her mother's blood, the girl is imprinted with the psychic vibrations of her mother. All the things she fears are modeled for her from the first day she is born. No doubt she will have plenty of psychological issues that must be addressed, but her karmic choices provided her with the perfect classroom for her soul's lessons.

Although past-life therapy is not a substitute for untangling the emotional knots of this life, it can be a useful adjunct. Over the years, I've worked in collaboration with many therapists. The therapist takes the cassette tape of one of my counseling sessions, which might include past lives, and then works with the patient in a steady, week-by-week processing of the information from the reading. Through this process I've seen people unlock powers frozen in the past, lay down fears that no amount of previous therapy could dissolve, let go of ancient hatreds, release phobias, grasp complexities in a sudden Gestalt of knowing, and cry away long-held pain.

My experience has been that a past life is recalled because it has a direct bearing on the experience at hand. It is not remembered for amusement. Past-life recall is not a parlor game.

I have been with many people in the throes of remembering

a painful experience from the past they have not released. They are not detached observers, but rather can find themselves reliving the key emotions of the experience. When an energy is locked in consciousness, it is beyond time and space. It lives in the NOW. So if a hatred was developed, say in fifteenth-century Spain, and it has not been released through forgiveness and understanding, it might as well have happened this morning. It has the power to influence us as a living energy. There's a good chance that the hate has set up a magnet that is active in the current life. We don't have to remember the Spanish experience to know what energy is still active; we simply need to be honest with our reactions, prejudices, likes, and dislikes of today.

I find that a good percentage of our life-to-life holding patterns constellate around lack of love for the self. We tend to hold on to feelings of guilt, shame, loss, powerlessness, and self-punishment. However, these emotions can be identified, accepted, and released through processing techniques that we know work. The most important thing is forgiveness of self and others. God is not holding out on us for our past actions. It is we who refuse to forgive ourselves.

REMEMBERING WHO WE WERE IN CHILDHOOD

The bleed-through from the experiences of other lifetimes shows up in predispositions; attractions; passions, both positive and negative; compatibilities; and spontaneous resistances. Some children have memories that come spontaneously, especially before the age of four or five. After that the imprinting of this life and its demands take over.

Children can be very matter-of-fact about it all. I knew a three-year-old boy who casually said to his mother, "I shot

Daddy, and I'm glad I did." Busy with dinner, his mother brushed this off with "Don't be silly. You love your daddy." But she began paying attention when he said, "Not now, Mommy. Before. You remember, when we lived in California and Daddy was this bad man from Mexico and he was trying to hurt you. I shot him, and I'm glad I did." Not too hard to figure out why the three of them are back together again.

Another little friend of mine, also three, expressed some of the challenge of relationships when she screamed at her mother angrily, "I liked it better when I was the mother and you were the child!"

I think children shut down conscious memories for a couple of reasons, although the integrated knowledge is always there. First of all, children need to focus on the lessons and opportunities of this lifetime. One of the controls we have built into healthy psychic equipment is an overload valve that shuts down when our multidimensional selves have difficulty staying in touch with present reality. The more we can integrate all aspects of body, mind and Spirit, the more we can open up the valves.

But I also think there's another reason why children forget. Many adults don't take children's remarks about other lives seriously. Sometimes they accuse a child of making up stories, not only about past lives but about psychic experiences in general. This is the beginning of very serious problems for many people.

For example if Johnny's mother says that it's only his imagination that he saw Grandpa in the corner—"Grandpa is dead and gone. That's impossible."—or worse, accuses him of lying, then Johnnie can become doubtful and mistrustful of his perception of reality. This becomes the seed for self-doubt of other perceptions. I have sat with many reasonably balanced and sophisticated adults who had dissolved in tears of grief for the psychic children they had buried within them.

AMAZING GRACE

I have a friend who says she intends to finish everything this time because she refuses to learn multiplication tables one more time! Surely the lessons of reincarnation can seem endless. Do we ever cease running our own mazes? We are continually seeking answers from books, theologies, teachers, and counselors and are in many ways just like fish constantly swimming to and fro in the ocean, when all the while the ocean itself is the answer, and its name is Grace. Its bounty has never been withheld.

It is through Grace that we are able to lay down the burdens of our lives. We have only to forgive ourselves and each other.

It is through Grace that we are given the opportunities to purify all our misconceptions.

Grace holds us in wholeness even as we see ourselves as separate.

Grace contains our darkest secrets and our greatest triumphs, judging neither.

Grace is love so profound, so unconditional, that we cannot name or limit it.

Grace transcends karma; it exists in God's time. The birth of Grace within us signals the completion of the endless rounds of birth and rebirth.

The Universal Christ—by whatever name you remember it—is the embodiment of Grace.

Even as we begin to awaken to the Light within, it is important that we be patient and gentle with ourselves as we seek to disentangle ourselves from limitations.

Our human ego protests when we start to challenge old concepts of self. It much prefers to arrange reality according to the information on hand. But regardless of what the ego likes or doesn't like, the old ideas of self will be challenged when we seek self-knowledge. Whether it arrives quietly or knocks us down, any challenge to our old forms, our old beliefs, signals us that conscious change is in progress.

EXERCISE: THOUGHT FORM CHECKUP

This exercise is designed to point out those negatives you may be energizing with your thoughts and words in your everyday life. Commitment means paying attention to all the ways you are building a reality for yourself. The suggestion is that you consider the word or thought or both and then think about whether you are affirming it occasionally [+] or regularly [*].

Have you said or thought to yourself . . .

IDEA	THOUGHT IT	SAID IT
I am too fat.	[ ]	[ ]
I am too skinny.	[ ]	[ ]
I am too old.	[ ]	[ ]
I am middle-aged and therefore [fill in blank].	[ ]	[ ]
I am too hippy [flappy, short, busty, flat-chested, etc.]	[ ]	[ ]
I am not coordinated [not graceful, etc.].	[ ]	[ ]
I have bad eyesight.	[ ]	[ ]
My allergies are acting up [my back is out, etc.].	[ ]	[ ]
My family has heart problems baldness, diabetes, etc.].	[ ]	[ ]

[Other negative body affirmations].	[ ]	[ ]
I can't draw [sing, dance, etc.].	[ ]	[ ]
I am afraid of [fill in blank].	[ ]	[ ]
I am shy.	[ ]	[ ]
I am too talkative.	[ ]	[ ]
I am not as smart as [fill in blank].	[ ]	[ ]
I can't quit smoking [eating, nagging, etc.].	[ ]	[ ]
I can't visualize.	[ ]	[ ]
I can't meditate.	[ ]	[ ]
I don't "see" psychically.	[ ]	[ ]
I am [list other negative self-images].	[ ]	[ ]
I'll never earn more because . . .	[ ]	[ ]
I am a woman.	[ ]	[ ]
it's not spiritual.	[ ]	[ ]
the world is unfair.	[ ]	[ ]
I am too old.	[ ]	[ ]
there are no opportunities.	[ ]	[ ]
"they" won't allow it.	[ ]	[ ]
Men are all [fill in the generalization].	[ ]	[ ]
Women are all [fill in the generalization].	[ ]	[ ]
Kids today are spoiled [etc.].	[ ]	[ ]
All politicians are corrupt.	[ ]	[ ]

We're headed for a
   depression.   [ ]   [ ]
You can't fight big
   business [city hall, etc.].   [ ]   [ ]
Israel and the Arabs will
   never live in peace.   [ ]   [ ]
The great catastrophes are
   inevitable.   [ ]   [ ]
[Other assumptions and
   generalizations]   [ ]   [ ]

*How many times in the past month have you thought or
   said . . .*
I am a child of the Divine.
I am okay just as I am.
I am grateful.

Try taking one of the negative affirmations that
you've been giving yourself regularly in both word and
thought and write an affirmation that is positive. Use the
power of the *I Am* to decree what you desire. For example if you checked "I am too fat," then consider giving your subconscious the affirmation "I am grateful that
my body is becoming perfectly balanced."

Whenever you feel tempted to empower the negative, simply take a deep breath and choose instead to
reinforce the positive. As this works for you—and it
will—tackle the other negative reinforcements one by
one. Pay close attention to those thoughts and statements
you preface with *I Am*. You're decreeing a reality when
you use them.

It might be awkward at first to reword all *I Am* statements in a positive fashion, but you'll get used to it. If you are consistent, you'll discover that this is one of the secrets that underlie your power to shape reality.

EXERCISE: GETTING HONEST ABOUT YOUR GOALS

There is a big difference between wishing you could create something and really desiring to do it. Consciously changing the old starts with being brutally honest about what you really want. This exercise will be most effective if you do it one step at a time and don't read ahead.

1. Take five minutes and list on the left side of a sheet of paper all the goals you have for this lifetime. Don't eliminate anything—playing a good game of tennis, being a world-class baker, speaking French fluently—these belong on the list right along with career goals.

2. After you've done this, take three minutes to select the five things that are the most important to you. Put a star beside them.

3. Now, suppose I were to tell you that you have exactly one year left to live. Which of the five is the most important to you? Circle it.

4. Next, on the right side of the paper, list everything you're doing in your life right now to forward that goal.

5. After you have completed the list for your first choice, take the other four you've starred and list everything you're doing now with your time, money, talents, energy, and commitment to bring these goals to pass.

What are you doing with your resources right now? Who is responsible for your choices? If you discover that you're not putting into motion the very things you say you want to create, then take that realization into your personal work on self-awareness. How are you spending your time and energy? Who established your agenda? Is your week being eaten up by other people's notions of what you should be doing? Are internalized parental voices—or those of peers, a spouse, the media—calling the shots for you?

STEP TWO

The Challenge

"The real voyage of discovery consists not in seeking new landscapes but in having new eyes."

—MARCEL PROUST

Conscious change is set in motion when the original belief form is challenged. Something happens to detonate the security of the status quo—crisis, trauma, or disillusionment. Or the challenge can creep in as a restlessness that signals you have outgrown an old attitude. The challenger to the known accepted view of reality can come through education, travel, exposure to other points of view, or interaction with someone of broader perspective. But whether it arrives dramatically or subtlely, the challenge to the old form sets change in motion. You cannot return to the old form—it no longer works. The shift is in process.

CHALLENGE: STRESSES AND STRETCHES

Discomfort—the major agent of conscious change—has received a lot of bad press. We don't change unless we're willing to experience the uneasiness that any challenge brings to our old beliefs, our old forms. We know from medical and behavioral research that any kind of change, good or bad, causes stress. A marriage, a new baby, a new job, or a move will cause stress as easily as illness, divorce, a death in the family, death, or business failure.

Dr. Hans Selye, who gained international recognition for his work on stress, defined it as "the non specific response by the body to any demand made upon it."

On the Holmes-Ray Social Readjustment Rating Scale, various human changes are assigned stress points. I know a young couple who were sure their marriage was doomed to failure and sought counseling from a psychologist. The first thing the psychologist did was to have them take the stress test. Between leaving home, getting married, having a baby, and moving to another state away from family and friends, all within a year, they had stacked up enough heavy stress points to run their scores off the charts. Once they realized this, they were able to put their marital difficulties into proper perspective against the panorama of the enormous stress-filled changes they'd been experiencing. They quit overreacting to the stress as an indicator that something was wrong with the marriage, and began a healthy appraisal of how to handle the stress each was experiencing.

New jobs, new people, new environments—new anything—all present potential challenges to who we think we are, but they also offer us shiny new possibilities in life. Sometimes the challenge arrives violently, with no warning. Suppose part of your identity is "I am a wife." All it might take is one telephone call on an ordinary Monday morning, and suddenly you're a widow. Or perhaps part of your identity is "I am financially secure." Along comes Black Monday and you're back to square one. Or maybe part of your identity is that you're in charge of your own world regardless of what others are doing, but then Chernobyl explodes into the atmosphere, and suddenly the whole world is potentially in your backyard.

H. G. Wells once said that the future is a race between catastrophe and education. Without the catastrophe you're not motivated to change; but with too much catastrophe you're paralyzed and incapable of change.

The suddenness of challenge can also present itself pleasurably, however—you win a trip, meet a special person, inherit money. But whether the news shocks or elates you, it is going to do more than change your physical life. It is going to give you the opportunity to see yourself and reality with new eyes. Challenge represents what Marilyn Ferguson defined in her book *The Aquarian Conspiracy* as the "entry point" of change.

According to systems theory, people and social institutions evolve only when they can't produce the needed results any longer. As long as they're working, they stay intact. The same is true of our personal lives. We may have a personal system, a set of beliefs, that work for a few years, a lifetime, or several lifetimes. As long as a given belief structure is bringing the people and events we need into our classroom, the form is still working. The issues and possibilities for learning are hot, alive, vital. But when the form is no longer offering us opportunities for growth, when we're starting to sleepwalk through it all, things start to fall apart.

When stress has been accumulating over years or lifetimes, it eventually reaches the boiling point. The challenge is that moment of eruption when the controls of the form can't hold the fort any longer. And it seems as though all order goes with it.

The family of a young teenage girl requested healing for her because she was constantly in trouble and resisted help. As I attuned to her, the first image I saw was of water spilling everywhere with no boundaries (the emotions were out of control). The next image I saw was the girl's head and body separated, telling me that no rational management was present. Then I saw a car careening downhill without brakes, and I knew it was going to crash. My own daughter at that time was about this girl's age. As I watched these destructive scenes, I lost my objectivity, slipped into my maternal self and uttered, "Oh, no!"

Immediately all images of the girl disappeared, and I was looking at a panorama of the universe. In one tiny corner was a microscopic white box, and I was told in Spirit, "Don't you ever forget that that is all you are ever seeing in one moment."

BIRTHQUAKES

Sometimes the challenge seems to erupt with terrible and sudden destruction. But like an earthquake that builds up pressure in the slow shifting of earth plates, the outer "sudden" event has grown out of existing circumstances filled with a pressure that has to be released. They become what a friend calls birthquakes.

For example Paula grew up and later married in an extremely Fundamentalist church. By the time she had had three children, she was an abused wife. Fearing for her own safety and for that of her children, she sought sanctuary in the church. She was told in no uncertain terms to return to the husband, who was "by God's authority head of the household." Furthermore she was told that if she sought counseling or considered divorce, she would be considered dead to her family and the church. She fled with her children. All of the forms she had lived within— God, family, marriage—were challenged. A long and difficult period followed as she sorted through the fragments of her life, but gradually she began to see herself in new and healthier ways. As painful as it had been to experience the brutality, the disillusionment, and the losses, she says that it was those very things that forced her out of fear-based life.

OUT OF THE BLUE

The event that challenges your world originates in the blueprint of your soul and in those with whom you share your life. Often it takes the perspective of time to understand what you were being challenged to learn. But when the soul is ready to release its time capsule, "impossible things" will happen.

One of these out-of-the-blue things happened to me in 1968, and it changed my life. I was a young woman raising two small children on my own and working as a design editor for a national design publication. Two good friends of mine were going to Peru on a design research trip and wanted me to go with them. I thought they were crazy; every penny I made was needed for my family responsibilities.

They suggested that I get my publisher to send me, or even less likely, that one of their companies might finance me. I could only laugh at the idea. But my friends proposed this to my publisher, and, for reasons I don't understand to this day, he agreed.

So off I went on this "impossible" trip having a wonderful time, blithely oblivious to what the trip was really about—until I arrived at Machu Picchu. Today we've all heard about the mystical pull of Peru. Not so in 1968. This was years before Peru became a travel staple in the New Age movement. I didn't even know that Machu Picchu existed. I had never talked with anyone who had been to Peru, nor had I read anything about it. And I knew nothing about the effect of powerful Earth sites on our energies.

No sooner had we arrived at the Lost City of the Incas than I began to feel strange, but I chalked it up to a disagreement with the food from the night before. As we started walking single-file up a narrow path to a sundial, somebody behind me wondered aloud what we would find when we got there. Suddenly my mouth opened, and I began to describe what we would see and what its significance and purpose had been. In my mind

I was seeing scenes dropping into place before my eyes like slides.

Nobody was more surprised than I. How did I know that information? It was more than strange. It was terribly unsettling. My sense of reality was being seriously challenged. Later I wandered away from the group, trying to regain the sense of reality I'd brought to that mountain. But a powerful change had taken place.

Since my childhood I'd been seeing random pictures in my head. I never questioned them, nor did I attach any importance to them. Children don't ask if you see the way they do; they just assume that you do, if they think about it at all. But ever since that moment on Machu Picchu, the mental pictures I'd been seeing since childhood have no longer been random. Now they come on request.

I had no idea then that I would use this capacity, which is called clairvoyance, as a tool, for my life's work didn't unfold for another seven years. Although this sudden and unlikely trip had blasted me open psychically, once I returned, I tried to dismiss the experience as strange but unrelated to my life in any serious way. But from the perspective of today I can track the changes that brought me to this moment back to that experience on Machu Picchu.

FROM ADDICTION TO CHOICE

We always have the right to choose what we will do with any challenge. We can always refuse the lesson. The challenge will merely arrive again in new packaging. Spirit is lovingly patient and impersonal; it is interested in our evolution in consciousness, not in our comfort at any particular time.

Take the example of a woman who believes she is only valuable when she is in relationship with a man. If at any point she chooses to use the challenge of yet another disappointing love affair to examine her beliefs about herself, she can break the pattern. Otherwise she is stuck in the second stage of change—the challenge. She will maintain her belief, get challenged, endure all the disturbances of challenge, and then start the whole process over again.

I've known women in their fifties who hold the same image of themselves that they held as teenagers, their talents undeveloped, living in terror of aging and totally unaware of the richness of their beingness regardless of who is or isn't in their lives. Many of these women have been caught in the challenge to women's roles that is prevalent in our culture right now. Their individual soul lessons are part of the collective challenge expressing itself.

Being addicted to a form is not the same thing as preferring it. The shift from addiction to preference is a concept fully explored by Ken Keyes, Jr., founder of the Cornucopia Center in *A Handbook to Higher Consciousness*. He finds that when we're stuck in an addiction, we think we can't do without what we're addicted to. It's the same with our sense of self, that which we think we have to have in order to be happy. Once we move from addiction to preference, we realize that we don't *have* to have anything to be happy, but we prefer to; we choose it voluntarily.

The woman addicted to men can meet the challenge by coming to understand that she is worthy regardless of who is or is not in her life. She may then decide that she prefers to be in a relationship. The difference is choice; she's no longer being dragged around the same track over and over again.

Sometimes challenge says to us, "Listen, this old idea of who you are has you trapped. Now is a good time to break it." The minute we really hear this, we discover there are many systems around to help us move beyond old forms. Alcoholics Anonymous and Adult Children of Alcoholics have high success rates at helping people deal not only with alcohol-related problems but with the problems that stem from any dysfunctional family. Their Twelve-Step guidelines for recovering from addiction start with admitting that you have a problem in the first place.

EXPANDING OUR PERSONAL MYTHS

We've all constructed personal myths, usually over the span of many lifetimes. And to the extent that we believe them they guide our lives. But when it is time to grow beyond these myths, challenges will come.

In an article in *ReVision* magazine, David Feinstein and Stanley Krippner suggest that our personal myths are the product of four interacting sources. The first is biology. They say that our beliefs, both personal and cultural, end up as symbols and narrative rooted in the structure of the brain. Information and attitudes are neurochemically coded. In addition temperament and hormones also influence what we believe. Secondly, our personal myths are to some extent a microcosm of the mythology of our whole culture. The third source, they say, are the details of our personal history. And finally, our personal myth takes its final shape as a result of transcendent experiences that embrace the episodes, insights, dreams, and visions that inspire and expand our perspective.

They suggest, and I agree, that when a personal myth is being transformed—whether it is individually, as a nation, or as a whole species—those changes become milestones in the evolution of human consciousness and form in their words, "the heat of human history." We are at such a point on our planet.

Psychologist and philosopher Rollo May says that when a myth about our reality is no longer working for our highest good, when it is not bringing us the experiences and growth our souls have scheduled, it will create "mythclasm," and the myth, the form, gets challenged.

I remember a sincere young man who could hardly wait to become a minister. But his first year at college was traumatic, for he was exposed to facts and logic he had never met in the safe mythology of his family and local culture. He told me that was nothing compared with the shock of graduate school. One by one his favorite childhood stories had to be sacrificed on the altar of truth. It was his very dedication that ensured that he would attract the education that would force him to find a richer truth. Had he not had such a deep desire, he could have found himself a much less challenging school.

We draw to ourselves what we really want, not what we think we want. It's not a bad idea to ask ourselves now and then, Whose truth are we living? Whose dream are we dreaming? Kay Boyle once said, "There is only one history of importance, and it is the history of what you once believed in and the history of what you came to believe in."

CHALLENGING PERCEPTIONS

The first couple of years after my work in healing began to unfold, I lived in a state of challenge. All my preconceived ideas about what was real were brought up for examination. Like most people educated in the West, I was heavily invested in left-brain logic. I intuitively knew there had to be more than I had been taught in Newtonian science, but at that time I knew nothing of unifying fields of energy, space-time, relativity, or alternate realities.

On occasion the explanations for someone's illness fit into my understanding of the power that thought and emotions have on the body. I wasn't too surprised to see retained resentment end up as a gall bladder problem, or a refusal to release the past express its rigidity in a disturbed colon. I have been carefully taught not to say that anger will *always* express itself as this or that, or that resentment *will definitely* cause such and such. I find it simplistic to say "always." People are far more complicated than that. It is probably more accurate to suggest that a disharmony will "possibly" express in a certain place.

But many times in the work I would be presented with a situation that totally defied any known explanation I had of reality. There was simply no way to explain how I could concentrate on someone hundreds of miles away and accurately diagnose a problem. I could see a person in my mind, feel energies moving through me and toward that person, and often the person would recover.

Many times what I experienced defied all logical understanding. A friend of mine, an advertising executive, called one day to ask if I'd work with the daughter of one of his co-workers. Holly was four years old at the time and she was literally impossible to handle. Her parents were frantic. She was so much out of control that she would throw things through windows. The parents had taken her to several kinds of doctors, including allergists and behavior therapists. No one had any idea what was wrong with her.

My logical mind, with its ideas about reality, supposed that we would find a severe chemical imbalance. Imagine my surprise when I attuned to Holly and found two children living in her space. I was told in Spirit that another soul had attached itself to Holly at birth and had been with her ever since.

The only treatment I perceived for this was angelic intervention. I saw beautiful Light beings lovingly but firmly removing the soul that didn't belong there. I was told that Holly would be disoriented for a while but that she'd be fine in time. Further I was advised to tell the parents only that the work had been done. They had nothing in their own belief systems that could understand what had happened. They might jump to the conclusion that their child had been possessed, which was not the case.

About a year later my friend asked Holly's father how she was doing. "Oh, she's great. She acted very strange for a while, but now it's as if we have a new child."

Holly's will was fused with normal biological development. The will of the entity that didn't belong there was very strong and very attached to Holly. It was not replacing the will of the child as much as it was dominating the behavior and confusing the child. The entity was guided by the angelic presences to the dimension where it karmically belonged.

SHELVING THE PUZZLES

My concepts of reality were so regularly challenged in those early years that I had to create several techniques for integrating the shocks, since I had no intention of becoming a "space cadet." I was committed to doing the work, but I was equally committed to remaining balanced and grounded with it.

One thing that worked for me and that continues to help when I find myself in the throes of challenge is to build a shelf in my mind labeled "Awaiting Further Enlightenment." When I don't understand how something can be possible, and I don't want to limit myself by forcing it into my existing knowledge or prejudice, I just put it on the shelf and let it go. I make the assumption that sooner or later I will attract the information I need to help me understand it.

Sometimes that shelf is overflowing with more questions than answers. And then again, answers come when I least expect them. When we panic in the face of challenge because we don't know all the answers, we can temporarily close down the opportunity the challenge is offering us. I use the word *temporarily* because if it's our time to learn something, it'll come around again in another form.

When one of our dearly held beliefs, whether it is societal or personal, is battered by challenge, we can feel as though we are flying apart. "I don't know who I am anymore." "Things are happening too fast." There seems to be no order or direction. Like a star experiencing entropy, all that we thought was real seems to collapse. Then we are blown into expansion. But the process will once again lead us to contract, and the re-formation—a new form—begins. Sometimes all we can do when the challenge comes and we feel our parts flying to their edges is hold on and wait.

PAYING ATTENTION

Often during this part of the cycle of change, challenge will bring ambivalences, self-deceptions, and inconsistencies to the surface. If we say we believe a certain thing and yet live a different way, then all the ways we're not living the truths we espouse will be brought to our attention, and not always gently.

For example we have said, from the moment the United States declared its independence, that we believe that all people are created equal. Yet, one Civil War and 125 years of social struggle later and we're still being challenged to live what we say we believe. We are still manifesting a reality based on a deep-seated belief in inequality. Until all people do indeed live in equality, we will continue to be challenged. There is no way of manipulating the universe with platitudes and "good intentions."

Over my desk there is a poster that says, "Today Do Nothing to Offend the Harmony of the Universe." I have declared that I believe in that. But there was a time when the universe said, in effect, "Let's see if you're really paying attention to what that looks like in your life."

At that time I was living in an isolated area in the North Carolina mountains. One day a visiting friend and I drove out on the Blue Ridge Parkway to spend the day. We decided to stop and pick a bouquet of wildflowers. After a few minutes my friend said, "I don't think we should be doing this. I don't feel right about it."

"Why not?" I asked. She shrugged, and we continued to pick a large bunch. The next night I was reading a travel book on Tibet. It was not a book about consciousness at all—or so I thought. On the second page the following words jumped out at me. "And in their belief the two worst things you can do are harm a child and pick a wildflower."

Two weeks later I was teaching a week-long course at a conference. One of the rituals that I like to use for this particular class involved giving a flower to each participant. I didn't think the conference committee would like it if I submitted a bill for fifty cut flowers. So I collected a huge bouquet of wildflowers outside the city, brought them back to the room, and stored them in a coffee carafe in an obscure, shady little corner. When I returned two hours later they were mysteriously gone. One would think I'd have paid attention at this point. But it took one more incident.

A week after the conference my daughter and two-year-old grandson were visiting me in the mountains. He and I had been walking happily for over an hour in the meadow, collecting all sorts of rocks. As we started back, I asked him, "Wouldn't you like to take a flower to Mommy?" As he reached over to pick a wildflower, he was stung by four bees. It was a scary moment, for we had no idea if he was allergic to beesting, and we were at least thirty minutes from the nearest medical help. Fortunately he was okay, but it sure upset me.

The experience was less about wildflowers per se than it was a lesson in fine tuning, consistency, and paying attention. I had said that I believed in not disturbing the harmony of the universe, but I had been totally oblivious to the part wildflowers play in a larger ecosystem.

At last I finally got it.

THE HOUND OF HEAVEN

Change doesn't always shout; sometimes it whispers. Challenge at its most subtle can be a nameless yearning for something that has no name. In the midst of the most ordinary life perking along with everything in place, this yearning can seep in like fog and settle around everything. A friend wrote me, "I recognize in me a feeling, a longing so ancient, so prevocal and prerational, a voice almost like the howl of a lone wolf as it pours out its longing to the moon. I have no words to communicate it, but the longing has something to do with wanting to go so much farther. I think it is a longing for change—and for God."

The poet Francis Thompson called this longing the "Hound of Heaven." Others have spoken of the "divine discontent." I cannot recall a time in my life that I didn't hunger to know why and for what purpose we are here. The questions would go underground when I was busy with daily business, only to surface again later more strongly than ever—it's as if the longing itself provided the fuel to search. A dear friend who is eighty-two offered me a philosophical way of living with that longing: "I would rather be a seeker," she said, "than congratulate myself on what little I have learned."

Sometimes challenge might come as a creeping boredom. All that was satisfying at one time loses its attraction. One day a person looks around at the rat race and finds the money and job status just aren't enough anymore. "Is that all there is?" A young woman goes to the trendy club as usual and finds that the very things that excited her last week have lost their edge. The priest, so dedicated when he started, finds the passion has leaked out of his life and he discovers he is performing empty ritual.

The challenge stage of change catapults us to the edge of the unknown. And that brings up fears, all kinds of fears. Theoretically we may know that joy, fulfillment, and all the answers lie in the unknown. Pragmatically, we may become suspicious.

Sometimes the ego thinks that the challenge is an accident, something not really meant to happen. There's an old military expression that says you won't die unless the bullet has your name on it. Maybe what we're afraid of is the bullet that says, "For whom it may concern." Accidents are often manifestations of beliefs that have been denied or not recognized. If we really feel that our life is out of control, we might create an "accident" that externalizes the inner frenzy. If we have a secret belief that we "can't win for losing," we might create all kinds of equipment breakdowns that cost us money and time. At some level we give ourselves permission to "catch" a bug, if only by our refusal to pay attention to the body's needs. There's a reason why we find ourselves where an accident occurs.

I recall hearing a lecture by Dr. J. Allen Hynek, the UFO researcher who formerly headed the Air Force Blue Book program. After his speech, which was a plea for open, nonprejudiced inquiry, he opened the floor to questions. A man said that he had heard it suggested that UFOs might actually be space brothers here to help us with our evolution.

Before Dr. Hynek could answer, the audience burst out laughing. After the laughter died down, he asked his listeners if they really knew why they were laughing so hard. He reminded them that they probably did the same thing when they were in the fourth grade and heard people talk about sex. Sex was the mysterious unknown, and the best defense against its mystery was ridicule. The audience instantly became quiet.

When form is faced with challenge, the ego sometimes does laugh. It's a nervous laugh—ego doesn't want to be found ridiculous, and it fears criticism. It's also quick to say, "This is not true because it doesn't compute with what I know."

So how do we deal with the challenge phase of change? The most important thing we can do for ourselves is to accept it and be fully present with it. We also need to pay attention. Our world, both inner and outer, always tells us what's going on.

If we can let go of asking—just for the moment, and as soon as we realize we're doing it—"Why is this happening to me?" we can save ourselves a great deal of anxiety. It's when we get stuck in thinking that somebody has to be responsible for this that we're tempted to start blaming ourselves or others. That only delays the whole process. At this point we need to tell ourselves, "No one is right or wrong; no one is to blame, including myself. This is just what's happening. There is purpose in it, and I choose to make it okay not to understand at this moment what that purpose is. In time I know I'll understand."

GRATITUDE

The next best thing we can do with challenge is to be grateful for it. I used to wonder why the master teachers always guided us to be grateful, to say thank you. Certainly God doesn't have an ego that needs praising. But through my healing work I've come to understand why. Gratitude is an energy that works miracles in all of our dimensions.

I first learned this by being asked to work on a young man who had been in a small-airplane crash. When I first worked with him in Spirit, his energy field was fragmented and traumatized, as you would expect. I was told to bring him back into the work in three days.

When I worked with him again, I could hardly believe what I saw. There were thousands upon thousands of tiny little explosions of light taking place all over his body. I was told that I was seeing the "energy of gratitude at work." Gratitude releases a tremendous healing power within the structure of our cells; it is like a miniature atomic explosion. That is why we are told to be grateful: We are empowered by gratitude. Gratitude is a choice, in time it becomes a habit.

Our challenges are perfect classrooms. If we listen quietly, we might find that underneath our ego's frantic responses to the challenge, a wiser part of us is already grateful.

The temptation is great at the point of a challenge to want somebody, anybody, to make it all go away. I call this "looking for the fairy dust." Sometimes we pray for Spirit to take it away.

I was once faced with a challenge that had me so bewildered that I went to Spirit begging to be told what to do. At that moment I didn't want any of the usual wisdom lectures; I just wanted to be told what to do. After I calmed down, Spirit said to me, "Do you think you are loved so little that you'll be robbed of the only way you have to grow—the decisions you make every day?"

Then I was shown the image of a baby learning to walk. The baby would occasionally fall down and hurt itself. Loving hands appeared to help it back to its feet, pat its behind, and back off. "True love," I was told in Spirit, "honors the inherent ability of the baby to walk. It does not say, 'Because you have hurt yourself, I will carry you through life.'" Our challenges come because it is time for us to learn to crawl, then walk, then run. Without them we'd be continually stuck in infancy.

Another technique that helps during challenge—and other stages as well—is to develop what is often called the witness or the observer. This means that you assign some part of your awareness to stand outside whatever you are experiencing and simply observe. It doesn't interfere with your reactions. If you cry or laugh, protest or surrender, it simply watches and takes note. The challenge is what you are experiencing, it is not who you are. The witness helps you to see the difference.

It is important at this stage, as well as others, to start where you are.

The story is told of a woman who lost her car keys. She was standing under a lamplight feeling around for them. A man came along and offered to help. After a while he said, "Are you sure you lost them here?" "Oh, no," she said, "I lost them over there in the dark. It's just that there's more light here."

During a challenge, it feels as though we're fumbling around in the dark, and it might be more comfortable to go back to the light of the old, reliable forms. But the answers aren't there. They're in the dark unknown.

But don't forget that in time the dark cycles to light.

EXERCISE: TEACHERS, CLASSROOMS, LESSONS

Among the major questions brought to a counselor are "What are my lessons?" "Who are my teachers?" "Where are they?" But in truth we don't need anyone else to tell us this. The answers lie in our everyday lives. This simple exercise will help remind you.

1. Take a sheet of paper and make three columns.

2. In the left-hand column list every person of importance in your life. This will, of course, include parents, siblings, lovers, spouses, children. But it should also include your next-door neighbor, your boss or business partner, a fellow volunteer, your close friends, and anyone with whom you interact frequently.

3. In the second column, beside each name, write down the context in which you know the person— school, work, home, church.

4. In the third column write, beside every name you have listed, the quality or emotion that comes up first for you when you think of that person. This is for your eyes only, so be honest with yourself.

5. Now, in *big block letters*, write over the first column, "MY TEACHERS"; over the second column, "MY CLASSROOMS"; and over the third column, "MY LESSONS."

6. Think about it. Honor your teachers, your classrooms, and your lessons. You created that perfect space to learn and the perfect people to learn through.

STEP THREE

The Resistance

You'll never get me into one of those things!
—Caterpillar looking at butterfly

*T*he inevitable third step of conscious change is the battle between the old and the new. The old form does not give up the territory easily. As we begin to consider a new way of viewing reality, all of our deeply conditioned patterns of thinking and feeling rise from the basements of our mind and shout "Oh, no, you don't." New ideas stir fears of the unknown, fears of breaking with acceptable modes of thinking held since childhood, patterns dictated by culture and family, perhaps even from other lifetimes.

This is the time of transition, when the *what ifs* and the *yes, buts* predominate. "What if this new way of thinking is wrong?" "What if I fail?" "Yes, I like this new idea, but on the other hand, this is the way I've always thought." That which is new appeals, but the old has the pull of history. Vacillation and indecision spill over and manifest as outer symbols of conflict. Yet resistance is a natural part of conscious change—and a period of the cycle that cannot be rushed, unless you want to redo it later.

HOOPS OF FIRE

I've often heard people say that as soon as they got serious about wanting to grow, their lives became chaotic. For example the first thing that generally happens when you decide to beat an addiction is that it gets worse. Decide to give up cigarettes, alcohol, chocolate, or the lover who isn't good for you and all you can think of is cigarettes, alcohol, chocolate, or the lover who isn't good for you. The minute we announce we want to be more patient, life suddenly becomes one steady frustration.

The standard cry at this point is "What am I doing wrong?" Not a thing. You are right on schedule. The chaos is a sign that change is at work. The challenge to your old form has exploded like a bomb in the status quo, and the defense system goes on red alert.

When I first began to get consciously serious about my spiritual life, my personal world immediately turned upside down. At that point I'd spent a number of years studying various psychologies and was under the illusion that I knew myself pretty well. But the more I studied, meditated, and affirmed what I aspired to, the more confusion I experienced. Finally I was able to quit resisting the process and began asking how to understand it.

In Spirit I was shown a moving image. In the background there was a gold crown and in the foreground a hoop of fire. Telescoping from that hoop toward the crown there was a continuous series of hoops of fire. The first two hoops were some inches apart, the next two only an inch or so. As the hoops moved closer to the crown, the distance between them got smaller and smaller until they became a wall of fire. I understood that the gold crown was not a reward for accomplishment; rather it represented a piece of personal self-mastery. When we seek the crown of self-mastery, everything within us that is not under this personal mastery fights back.

When we set out upon this path, we first pass through a

single hoop of fire and experience some relief. But the more serious we are about this quest, the more the resistances come up, until, as we near the goal, they become a continuous wall of fire.

When we are experiencing the fires of resistance, the fears of a lifetime begin to flare up. They burn, and for a while everything seems scorched. It does not necessarily mean that we're doing it wrong. It could well be that we are doing it exactly right. Each crown of self-mastery that we claim, however small, is worth it. But during the resistance stage of change it doesn't seem that way.

If we've never examined the beliefs we internalized from parents, teachers, ministers, and artistic or business mentors, their voices might speak loudly during resistance. Some people feel as though the blaming, shaming, screeching furies of self-doubt and fear have been let loose. Others will find their egos fighting back with the smooth, cool voice of logic: "Well, now, I know that this new idea appeals to you, but let's look at the facts calmly, shall we." Of course that voice is usually referring to the old, familiar facts. It's a master of rationalization.

THE JOYS OF AMBIVALENCE

Any number of things can happen as we work our way through resistance. Often we find ourselves a study in ambivalence. "Yes, I will" on Monday morning becomes "No, I won't" by Monday night. One part of us keeps trying on the new idea like an exotic costume; another part of us would just as soon slip into an old comfortable robe. Sometimes we feel we've actually lost the ability to make a clear decision.

For example most of us find we're ambivalent about what we want in a personal relationship. If we came of age in the last twenty years, we've been part of the changing concepts of men and women in relationship. I've found that this cultural shift is by no means finished with its resistance stage. And that resistance often brings up ambivalent ideas about husbands, wives, or lovers.

One of the workshops I teach is on relationships, and in that course I ask people to take a test examining their attitudes. Almost everyone turns out to be ambivalent about what they think they should want and what actually makes them feel good. For instance they may want to want equality in relationships. A woman might say—and really believe she means it—that she doesn't care what kind of money a man makes. She's happy if he drives an old car and goes camping on the weekend. She just wants their relationship to be one of equals. And yet, pushed to be honest, she will often admit that the man who is driving a new car on his way to a promotion really turns her on. A man, coached well by liberated women, might admire a woman who is his professional equal, but secretly admit he is more at ease when he feels he is in charge.

Both are telling the truth about what they think they want; they're just ambivalent. The old forms of the ideal man and the ideal woman are deeply embedded in our psyches. They don't give up without a struggle. Clearly my example is stereotyped to make a point, but we can't creatively use a struggle unless we're honest about its existence.

Yes, but and *what if* become a way of life when we're living through resistance:

"Yes, I know I don't want him to treat me that way, but what if I speak up and he leaves?"

"Yes, I would like to go back to school, but he (she, they) won't let me."

"Yes, I disapprove of the chemical dump, but what if I protest and get fired."

"Yes, I'm for equality, but, hey, I've got a business to run."

"What if I'm wrong?"

"What if I fail?"

And most troubling of all, the unspoken questions: "What am I going to have to give up?"

The old form has the sweet assurance of tradition. We know what to expect even if we don't like it. The new idea has no history; we have no idea what to expect, and fears breed quickly in the unknown.

I know a doctor who struggled for months with *yes, but*. His form had been his traditional training that taught him to perceive illness as though it were a breakdown in a machine. Medication was the way to fix it. However as he became increasingly exposed to holistic attitudes, he became very interested in how the mind and emotions affected the body. That wasn't too challenging. He could find a place within his old form for that. But when he witnessed spiritual healing, which was clearly "impossible" according to his old form, he was severely challenged.

Being a real physician—not just a technician—he honestly wanted to grow in his understanding. Because of that he seriously began to challenge his original beliefs. At this point his logical mind waged a furious battle; existing science was the big cannon. He also had to deal with his fears of how the AMA, his colleagues, and his patients might react. He finally resolved the conflict and became a true holistic doctor, but not before he'd had to wrestle with his resistances as Jacob had had to wrestle with the Angel of the Lord. Interestingly it was science, the "new physics" that explores consciousness, that helped him build a bridge across the gap that had separated spiritual and scientific truths in his past.

LOSING OUR SENSE OF PLACE

One of the reasons this stage of change is so uncomfortable is that we are losing our sense of place. Years ago I read a perfect description of this feeling. The writer (whose name I've forgotten) said that it's as if we've left the security of our curbstone. We're heading across the street, which is where we want to go, but we're right in the middle of the street, equidistant from the curbstone we left and the one we're going to. When we're on the old curbstone, even if we don't like it, it's familiar. When we're ready to step onto the new curbstone, the excitement of almost being there helps carry us through the fear of the unknown. It's when we're in the middle that we lose our sense of place. That is the most frightening part of the journey. When the traffic gets heavy, part of us wants to back up, part wants to run ahead.

When I think of losing this sense of place, I am reminded of the terrible psychic disorientation of many of our Vietnam veterans. Many of them truly believed they were fighting for their country and that their country had a righteous cause. This was the form they started with. They were challenged by the senselessness of the war, but played it out, even though they were caught in agonizing personal battles. But when they returned home, instead of gratitude, help, and support, they were treated like lepers, shameful symbols of our collective madness. It took us twenty years to quit torturing the messengers of our changing myth, twenty years of the veteran having no place. Although we haven't yet retired the myth of the warrior, once we began admitting our own ambivalence, we could embrace our sons again, and healing could begin.

Dr. Ira Progoff reminds us of the enormous potential that exists when we are midway into a change. "Insofar as the past is over and the future has not yet transpired, the midpoint is an open movement of possibility. Properly used, it becomes like the eye of a hurricane, a quiet center at the center of life, a free unconditional moment of opportunity."

THE BACKLASH EFFECT

The resistance stage of change shows itself in the energy of backlash. While the new is gathering force, the old is regrouping for a counterattack. We took major steps forward in the sixties for civil rights and social programs, only to experience the backlash of a conservative "return to traditional values" in the eighties.

The women's movement is an example of the backlash effect. Challenging one of the oldest forms we have as humans, the myth of the patriarchy, it calls for nothing less than a revolution in our most basic assumptions. From the sixties on, visible and viable leaps were made as more and more men as well as women supported the redefinition of equality between the genders. Laws were changed, schools were made coed, business opportunities for women increased. Movies, television, magazines, and advertising began to show us women who were interested in something more than detergents and "catching a man." Hundreds of books and television talk shows opened a forum for dissecting injustices and offering new options.

But all the while the age-old form that defined women lay coiled like a serpent in our collective consciousness, striking out wherever it found a vulnerable place. We might change a few laws, but we were not going to pass "the law"—ERA—that would settle the issues of inequality once and for all. We could see the beginnings of a new myth when at last some of our daughters could enter the hallowed halls of previously all male institutions. Meanwhile, increasing numbers of our daughters were being attacked on the street. Even as we placed a woman on the Supreme Court in Washington and considered another for vice president, the "feminization of poverty" became a growing reality across the land. On the one hand we wanted our girls to aspire and achieve; on the other we just wanted them to be beautiful and forever young. We were and are ambivalent.

During this same passage we didn't know what men should

be anymore. On the one hand the film *Tootsie* gave us a new perspective on male and female, and *Kramer versus Kramer* showed us a sensitive father. On the other hand we paid millions of dollars to watch *Rambo*, and thousands of ten-year-olds, complete with fatigues, grenades, and boots, cloned the old myth.

There are a lot of old forms that are going to die in the next few decades. High on the evolutionary hit list is the repression, denial, and misuse of feminine energy—the female aspect of God. Now She is working through our evolution, and She is telling us firmly that if we want to survive, we cannot trash the waters, land, and skies anymore; we cannot willfully commit genocide on whole species, economically enslave members of our own family, or reserve knowledge and resources for the benefit of the few. Some of us have always listened to the eternal feminine. But in the past few decades even more have begun to listen.

THE MORPHOGENETIC FROG POND

Every time one more person opts for cooperation instead of conquest, the seedbed of our entire society becomes more fertile. When a species is ready to make an evolutionary shift, it will develop new organs, phase out others, add or subtract color, refine its wing or leg power to flee from predators—in essence, whatever it needs to meet the new demands from the environment.

The way this is done is suggested by botanist Rupert Sheldrake in his theory of morphogenetic fields, which posits that everything that is alive, from the tiniest atom to the largest planet, is surrounded by a field of energy that establishes its unique pattern of being. Dr. Sheldrake believes that "accumulated experiences of a species constitute a kind of formative memory."

When universal energy is poured into the energetic force field of a living creature, say a frog, genetic patterning (memory) maintains the frog's form. Any noticeable change in a species takes a long time. Even when evolution says it's time to change the pattern of frogness, not all frogs change at one time. But at some point a new pattern enters the frog world. First, a few frogs demonstrate the new possibilities, then a few more. When enough frogs have caught on to the new pattern, a critical mass builds until—in one quantum leap—all frogdom makes the shift to the new model. A new memory pattern is established. Probably quite a number of frogs prefer the good old days, but they won't last too long in the pond.

So it is with us as individuals. When we're making a change in the collective consciousness, it is not likely that all of us will cooperate immediately, no matter how much we know it's the right change. Ideas about ourselves have their own morphogenetic fields of energy. We have a model of what reality is and we expect life energy to pour into that familiar mold. When we become aware of a new idea, we must be patient while it is being resisted—after all, a new mold is being made. We don't have to become a whole and perfect person for the energy of the new concept to shift the pattern. But we need to use our will to persistently affirm the possibility of the change.

From the social scientists we know that a new idea considered radical, heretical, even dangerous in its inception will nevertheless be well seeded in a society when as little as 5 percent of the population accept it, and that it is well on its way when 20 percent accept it. However, between 5 and 20 percent lie 15 rocky percentage points. That's where we find resistance, with it ambivalence and backlash factors, raging at fever intensity. Threatened with death, the old form fights back.

THE BUTTERFLY EFFECT

The critical shift in growth comes when the desire to change is greater than the fear of the process. Once we're 51 percent in love with God, we're over the hump. Even the most agonizing battles have a different quality when we understand that the outcome was already decided the minute we said, "I want the truth."

We don't always experience a lot of support in our environment when the struggle begins. The people and circumstances around us are not necessarily changing just because we are. Our personal environment has been built on the magnets of the past. Our job, church, friends, hobbies, attitudes, personal relationships, all our preferences, addictions, and attitudes have been steadily mirroring our creations to date. Start to change and the mirror cracks.

In science the theory of the butterfly effect says that the air over the United States shifts when a butterfly moves its wings in Japan. Just imagine the impact on a relationship when you introduce even a subtle change. Relationships are harmonious to a large degree because of agreed-upon realities and roles. They function fine until one of the partners starts to change and the other is threatened.

It is very common after a conference, a workshop, or a therapeutic session, wherever we have made a major breakthrough in perception, to rush home full of enthusiasm—and immediately crash. We're ready to change, but our world is exactly where we left it, and all the old defenses come up. Family and friends have no idea what we're talking about; often they can be so deeply threatened that they become accusatory: "You're not the girl I married." "You've changed." "You weren't brought up that way." "You're going off the deep end."

The deep end is probably anything on the other side of their perception of us and reality. But that's small comfort when we're trying to reconcile a young, fragile, not-yet-integrated insight with an old, established relationship.

I caution people who have had awakening experiences to ground themselves well before they leave the setting in which they have turned on to new ideas. There are a lot of techniques for doing that. One is simply to slow down, take a deep breath, and put the new feelings in a healthy context. It's important to remember that family, friends, and co-workers have not shared the experiences that made this breakthrough possible. They may be bewildered by the new ideas or not interested. And certainly no person changes on demand.

Many times all the other person needs is an assurance from us that we're not going to leave them behind as we grow. As we live with the new insight, that quality gradually becomes part of who we are. The other people in our lives will learn far more from our living demonstration than from demands or proselytizing.

Some of the best advice I know for accepting that situation was given by the poet Rainer Maria Rilke to a young writer in *Letters to a Young Poet*:

"But everything that may some day be possible to many, the solitary man can now prepare and build with his hands that err less. Therefore, dear sir, love your solitude and bear with sweet-sounding lamentation the suffering it causes you. For when those who are near you are far, then your distance is already among the stars and very large; rejoice in your growth, in which you naturally can take no one with you, and be kind to those who remain behind, and be sure and calm before them and do not torment them with your doubts and do not frighten them with your confidence or joy, which they could not understand.

"Seek yourself some sort of simple and loyal community with them, which need not necessarily change as you yourself become different and again different; love in them life in an unfamiliar form and be considerate of aging people, who fear that being-alone in which you trust. Avoid contributing material to the drama that is always stretched taut between parents and children; it uses up much of the children's energy and consumes the love of their elders, which is effective and warming even if it does not comprehend. Ask no advice from them and count upon no understanding, but believe in a love that is being stored up for you like an inheritance and trust that in this love there is a strength and a blessing out beyond which you do not have to step in order to go very far."

TRUE FEELINGS OR JUST REACTIONS

During the cycle of resistance to change, it is helpful to distinguish between feelings and emotional reactions. "Get in touch with your feelings" is the rallying cry for most growth modalities, and of course that is essential. Otherwise you live in repression and self-deception. No matter what ideal you aspire to, you have to start with where you are. And that means being as honest as possible about your reactions.

A lot of what appear to be feelings are really just programmed emotional reactions. I might deeply feel that forgiveness is what I want to give, but when an old injury is stimulated, I might have a spontaneous reaction of anger and self-justification. Reactions tell us what we're still responding to from the old model of ourselves. However our deepest feelings guide us to where the reactions still are and inspire us with the new direction. Emotional reactions are very sharp and make us pay attention; feelings are heard in quieter moments.

The more we listen to our deepest self and commit ourselves to where we're guided, the better we can see the difference between who we are as opposed to what we're experiencing. Reactions show us what needs clearing out. At times it may be a bit like visiting the dentist because we want healthy teeth. But the day will come when we can watch a reaction with a certain amount of detachment: "Oh, there I go again, getting angry. I wonder what I'm afraid of?"

Cycling through resistance serves our need for balance. We reach and then we pull back in order to steady ourselves. It acts as a check on excessiveness by giving us regular reality checks. It helps us acquire discrimination and learn the power of the will.

In *The Journals of Abraham Maslow* the pioneering psychologist observed, "The voice of the Divine within is counterposed not by the voice of the devil within but by the voice of the timid."

The more we fight resistance, the tighter the knots get. But we can also choose to see it as a necessary and meaningful part of the process of change. It will pass. Be patient. How long we stay in this stage depends to a large degree on how willing we are to be honest with ourselves, nonjudgmental about our ambivalences, and fully present with the issues they bring up.

There are a number of things we can do for ourselves in order to ease this passage. Therapies can help during this stage. So will talking and writing about it, and releasing tension through physical outlets. Prayer helps, too. Not the prayers of a supplicant seeing self as apart from God and begging for release from the pain. Rather the prayers of a voyager offered in gratitude, affirming that God is in us and that our highest good is in progress. The moment of understanding and awakening is soon to come.

EXERCISE: VISUALIZATION FOR STRESS CONTROL

Sit quietly where you will not be disturbed. Take fifteen or twenty slow, even breaths—breaths that reach deep into your abdomen. Focus your mind on your breathing. Once you are able to watch your breath going in and out several times in a row, then go on to the next step.

In your mind's eye picture yourself sitting down inside your own forehead, right between your eyebrows. You might imagine yourself on a prayer rug, in the lotus position of hatha yoga, or whatever is comfortable.

In this position you become the observer. Notice any tense spots in your body. When you find them, send the next few breaths into those spots. Contract, then release, all your muscles. Do it two more times—a muscle is most relaxed after being contracted. Now, as the observer, notice what your emotions are doing. If you discover tight energies—fear, anger, envy, whatever—then use your breath to release them. As you exhale, see those negative energies breathed out. If it helps to give them a color, you might want to use gray for fear, red for anger, bilious green for envy, and so forth. On the inhale, breathe Light into your emotions, and release.

From the position of observer, notice the thoughts darting around in your head. Don't try to resist them. Simply make the decision not to follow their lead. Very gently watch the thoughts come and go. If one persistently demands your attention, gently breathe it away and bring your attention back to watching yourself breathe. When the next thought comes, do the same thing. Part of the success of this exercise is not to fight the thoughts, but rather to be gentle, observant and clear in your intention.

Next imagine that there are tiny holes in your fingers and toes and that these are drains for everything that is tight and tense. Just let it all flow out. Use your out-breath to empty yourself. When that is complete, plug up the holes and begin using the in-breath to fill yourself with pure Light.

When the process is complete, simply rest for a time in your physical, emotional, and mental bodies, aware that you are none of these vehicles but rather the relaxed being in charge of them.

EXERCISE: BALANCING YIN-YANG POLARITIES

This mental exercise helps to create a state of inner balance between your masculine and feminine polarities. For any effective imaging exercise, you first want to get very comfortable and then deeply relaxed. Exhale your breath to release all tensions and preoccupations.

Image the familiar yin-yang symbol—the circle with the black and white sections separated by a curving line, with a black dot in the white section, and a white dot in the black.

In your mind's eye trace the circumference of the circle several times and then trace the curved dividing line several times. Now image yourself totally in the white section. Breathe white; feel it on your skin; smell it. Only white exists. Stay with this experience of the whiteness for a minute or so.

Now, in the midst of the whiteness, observe that there is a small circle of black that is pulling you toward it. Feel its magnetism until you disappear into the blackness. It is a nonthreatening dark. Experience it, breathe it. Let it become a total part of your sensory experience without any judgments, just be aware of how different it feels from white.

After a couple of minutes observe that there is a circle of white that you are moving toward. Then dive back into the white, and once again there is only whiteness. Stay with this for about a minute, and again feel the magnetism of the blackness pulling you toward itself.

Make the shift back and forth several times until you feel easy and poised with both whiteness and blackness. This is a good exercise to do when you feel yourself going to one extreme or the other.

STEP FOUR

The Awakening

Running around the boat does nothing to ensure progress through the water.

—ANONYMOUS

When the form has been challenged and the resistance endured, the awakening follows. The awakening is the breakthrough—the insight that brings the critical shift from the old to the new.

The clear "Aha! I've got it" of the awakening often seems to come suddenly. But it only seems sudden. It was actually conceived in the struggle and of the previous stages and birthed with that "Eureka!"

This part of the transition is very joyful. *Why not?* replaces *Yes, but.* The natural magic of synchronicity brings new ideas, new experiences, new people, new books, even new dreams into our lives. The mood is exploratory as our desires change. The right brain, the portal to the intuitive self, begins to send out new information, new kinds of answers to old questions. Before long we begin to realize that our world has grown larger forever.

HERE COMES THE SUN

In the resistance cycle we make the pearl. In the awakening cycle we bring it to the surface.

Just when we think we can't stand the tension of resistance another minute . . . we've had it . . . we're convinced there are no answers . . . we're weary with ambivalence . . . we're ready to give up . . . or do give up . . . Eureka! Suddenly there it is— the answer, the direction, the insight, the sweet resolution to the conflict that has been consuming us.

We've entered the awakening cycle of change. What relief. What magic. What a high!

The awakening can come gradually, as gentle as the dawn rolling back the night. Or the awakening can burst upon us unexpectedly, like the summer sun piercing storm clouds.

Awakening can come when we give in to the power of "I don't know," and we begin to see new options. It can arrive in a chance meeting, at a lecture, or in the mail. However if the resistance stage has been long, we can be suspicious. As a friend once said, "I see a light at the end of a tunnel. I just hope it isn't a train coming."

For astronaut Dr. Edgar D. Mitchell, awakening happened aboard a spaceship. He wrote that his perception of life and reality changed in the moment he first looked at planet Earth from space. Seeing our world as "a blue and green jewel set against a midnight sky," with sudden insight he realized there was a God, that there was order and a plan for this Earth. But his moment of ecstasy was immediately followed by black depression when he realized how we were endangering the Earth. He came back from that flight committed to spending his time and resources to raising human consciousness. To bring his vision to pass, he founded the Institute of Noetic Sciences which provides through publication, research and public programs a stimulating forum for dialogues between spiritual and physical sciences.

Awakening doesn't arrive because we demand it but because

we desire it at some level of consciousness. It may arise from the sincere desire to resolve the conflict at hand, or from the deeper, unconscious desire of our soul intention—or both. But whether it comes suddenly or gradually, it carries us to our next point of growth.

The awakening is no accident. In our lifewalk every major step along the way is scheduled by our souls. Awakening reminds us to look at our inner clock and to acknowledge that we're right on time.

During resistance, however, we can hit a point when we feel we're not driving the car, that we can't change the routing. Everything seems stuck or out of our control. This can be so frustrating, so agonizing, that there's a great temptation to "do something even if it's wrong."

At such times the best thing we can do is nothing—or what seems like nothing. Not resisting a situation we can't change is a very powerful "doing" of its own. It withdraws the energy that feeds the difficult situation. When we match energies with something, we empower it. But when we withdraw the anger, the fear, the negativity that is bonding both sides of the resistance, there is no energy to keep it going. Very often this is when the awakening comes.

Nonresistance isn't passive. Passivity suggests powerlessness. But nonresistance is extremely powerful. It means we're consciously choosing what we wish to empower. Nonresistance is the action of wisdom that assessess a situation and realizes there is nothing to be gained from fighting it. Once we allow ourselves to relax and accept a situation or an ambivalence that we can't change at the moment, it becomes much easier to draw on our own resources to cope with it. At this point our sense of humor, our perspective, and our objectivity all come flowing back.

Taoism teaches us Wu-Wei, the art of accomplishing by not-doing. Nothing is forced; nothing is undone. As Leo Tolstoy said, "There is infinite movement within one moment of rest."

"But if we can't force an awakening," we ask, "if we can't make the trip go any faster, then what are we supposed to do? Why bother?"

Well, for starters, if we're not paying attention, we might not even recognize the awakening when it comes. We arrive at the awakening point precisely because we've arrived there. It's one of those cosmic conundrums. We can prepare the soil, plant the seeds, fertilize, and weed—but we have to wait for nature to do the rest. The turmoil in the psyche during resistance is a necessary part of the growth cycle. When we turn over the soil for the spring planting, we not only bring up the rich, loamy dirt, we also bring up the rocks. Acceptance of both shows us the possibilities, as well as what has to be cleared out.

Part of our readiness for awakening is to trust in whatever we perceive God to be, to trust in our own life's plan, to trust that we are totally connected to everything else in the universe. Trust is the universal law of attraction. It's at this point that we begin to understand that we don't have to beg, shove, or manipulate the universe—we only have to relax into our place in it.

A doctor wrote me recently and said, "I think I have finally figured out that spiritual progress is not something I am going to figure out. But if I just do my spiritual practices, I change, things change, and I don't have to figure it out or manipulate it. What a blessing."

SYNCHRONICITY: GOD'S COINCIDENCE

There's a story about a rainmaker who was brought into a village that had been enduring a drought for a long time. When he arrived, he found the villagers upset and anxious. The atmosphere in the village made him feel that way as well, so he retired to a hut, where he did nothing but get quiet. His quietness spread, and the villagers became calm. Soon the rains came. He had done nothing but bring his own energy into harmony with the universe. And then the natural forces brought rain.

The mysterious "coincidences" that arrive like needed rain in our lives often contribute to the awakening cycle of change. On the surface they seem to be illogical and improbable events: How could I have met that person at precisely that one moment? Receive that financial help just in the nick of time? Happened to pick up that particular book? The whole thing smacks of magic. It's little wonder that some of us credit the magic to some force on the outside that decided to take us out of our misery. Others of us amazingly insist that microsecond timing is pure coincidence. Either way we have a hard time making "coincidence" rational.

In our prescientific days we perceived the whole universe as being involved in the affairs of humans. The heavens prophesied the birth and death of great ones; a comet announced the birth of a new ruler. Wars, floods, and other devastating natural phenomena paralled dire turns of events in human experience.

In the West we have been educated to perceive reality in a safe linear fashion. Something happens because something else set it in motion yesterday. Add to that our perception that people, trees, birds, animals—all things that live—are separate little units of life acting independently of each other.

Well, it turns out that life is more like a circle than it is a straight line. Time warps, space bends, and we're all connected in the morphogenetic field. We're going to have to give up even our favorite myth of "objective reality" and see that we are participants in forming any reality, not just observers. Cause and effect, it seems is a multidimensional dance we're doing through the past, present, and future with everything that lives.

Consciousness is the bridge being built between the worlds of mind and matter. Each of us is a point of consciousness focusing his or her attention in space and time. We direct energy into the patterns we believe are possible. If we can't conceive a thing, we can't create it. If we perceive a thing as good or bad, we instantly telegraph instructions to our neurochemical systems on how to react. Consciousness perceives, desires, repels, and attracts whatever it thinks it needs and desires or not—from a sea of infinite possibilities—and then assigns values.

You and I exist in wholeness, but we forget that we are plugged into many other realities. While we may be aware that we are building in a three-dimensional world, we may not be so aware that we're reaching through space and time for the building materials.

Now and then the judge that sits at the controls of the left-brain computer dozes off, and information begins drifting up from the subconscious and the superconscious through the right brain. Just as dreams and psychic experiences transcend the limits of space-time to help us resolve the push-pull of resistance, so does coincidence. It lifts us out of the ordinary focus and into a fuller relationship with ourselves and all of life. *Coincidence* is really a counterfeit word; it's a stand-in for the important dynamic of energy called synchronicity.

We cannot begin to grasp synchronicity until we acknowledge that we all share a common ground. Turn-of-the-century biologist Paul Kammerer called this "the umbilical cord that connects thought, feelings, science and art with the womb of the universe which gave birth to them."

Dr. Carl Jung brought to the West recognition of this dynamic interplay between the psyche and the material world through the concept of synchronicity. This idea was already interwoven into the view of reality in the East. The ancient Chinese, for example, didn't perceive events in a linear matter, but rather they saw events, as the I Ching says, "clustering in time."

Jungian analysts see nature taking an inevitable course in a personality type they call "The Gambler." These are people who have painted themselves in the proverbial corner. They have exhausted every option and resource. There's nothing left to do but wait for the universe to do something. And it does. All of the person's focus turns to that critical moment, energies concentrate, and unpredictable synchronistic events then occur.

Tom Chetwynd in the *Dictionary of Symbols*, defines *synchronicity* as "meaningful coincidence, significantly related patterns of change." Synchronicity is not considered random—it is the purposeful movement of energy.

In his book *Synchronicity*, F. David Peat says, "Synchronicities are the jokers in nature's pack of cards for they refuse to play by the rules and offer a hint that in our quest for certainty about the Universe, we may have ignored some vital clues."

Synchronicities seem to show up more during the awakening cycle of change than any other. Or perhaps we're simply more aware of them. I suspect the more dramatic ones are encoded in our life plan, since they show up so often at key turning points: birth, deaths, first meetings with significant people and ideas, "instant" solutions to long-standing puzzles. When the desire is real and the timing is right for the good of the soul, the need is signaled everywhere at once, and the appropriate help is magnetized to the need.

A friend of mine was traveling to California on business. Quite unexpectedly he decided to stop in Texas on his way home to North Carolina. At the Dallas airport he jumped into the first taxi he saw and was soon deep in conversation with the driver, who spoke of his brother, who had an advanced case of glaucoma. Although the brother had been struggling with the disease for a long time, he was now at the point of giving up, but the driver was still praying for a miracle. My friend told him of the healing work that I did, and the driver requested it for his brother. The two of them exchanged addresses. My friend brought this request to North Carolina, and the healing work began.

Three weeks later my friend received a three-line note: "My

brother is healed. The doctors are mystified. Praise God." What force had attracted someone who knew a healer into that man's taxi at precisely the right time? Synchronicity!

I know a minister who was stuck in the resistance stage because of the unexpected death of his beloved nineteen-year-old daughter. He simply couldn't reconcile his religious teachings with the loss. For her funeral, butterflies had been printed on a memorial card because the young woman had been very fond of them.

When the father's grief lasted for months, his secretary wrote to a very famous minister asking for his help. The minister was out of town when the letter arrived, but his secretary responded on her own initiative because she had been so moved by the plea. She commented in her letter that a strange thing had happened when she sat down to write: "A butterfly landed on my finger."

A few weeks later the minister and his wife went to the ocean, still searching for peace. They parked their car close to the beach and walked for an hour or so. When they returned to the car, it was surrounded by hundreds of butterflies. The minister told me that he couldn't articulate logically why that resolved his conflict, but it did. It told him more about the continuity of life than all his theologies and provided the awakening from his deep resistance to his daughter's death.

Sometimes our dreams work with physical events to bring awakening. I have a friend in Iceland who is a dedicated physician and spiritual devotee. He had been raised in a liberal home that taught universal spiritual principles. In that model, Jesus was acknowledged to be master, but one of many. When my friend was exposed to the strong opinions of Christians who disallowed any possibility of divinity other than Jesus, he was thrown into conflict. He couldn't seem to resolve it, and then he had the following dream:

He was standing in the middle of a large Mormon cathedral

while a service was in progress. Suddenly Jesus appeared wearing a white robe and sandals, just as he was pictured in classical Christian art. My friend said he felt a moment of acute anxiety. "What if they've been right all along?" he asked himself. "What if there really is only one master, and it's Jesus?"

However as he watched, the Jesus of his dream floated down the aisle, and just as he passed the dreamer, he turned and winked. The loving feeling that was communicated by Jesus was: "I'll show up however you or anyone else needs to see me. If you need to see me as Jesus in white robes, that's the way I'll reveal myself." My friend woke up feeling a deeper understanding of the Universal Christ, and his conflict was resolved to his satisfaction.

Synchronicity stepped in to resolve a conflict for me when my healing work was first unfolding. It illustrates how we magnetize to us experiences that dovetail perfectly with our inner life.

I had started my career as a journalist and shared the belief system of most of my contemporaries: You work hard, and you progress professionally in recognizable ways, including monetarily. I had stopped working as a journalist when the healing work first opened up, and it took some time for me to find my new direction. I never dreamed that healing and counseling would unfold for me as a full-time profession. It all started with the misery of resistance. How would I earn a living? People would think I was crazy. What did God want from me anyway? The hotter the resistance got, the more I threatened to go back to work as a journalist. Meantime I was praying for guidance. And the awakening came, although not the way I expected.

I was offered just what I'd been praying for—the perfect job. As I sat in the interview, trying to feel pleasure in the enthusiasm the interviewer was showing, I felt more and more ill. Here it was, exactly what I'd said I wanted. And yet I was miserable. Every issue around my resistance was spelled out in capital letters. It was as if Spirit said to me, "Well, here's a clear-cut choice. What are you going to do?"

I could hardly get out of the office before I was in tears. I jumped in my car, put my head on the steering wheel, and said, "Okay, God, you win." So much for my preconceived notion that my big moments with God would be bathed in light filtered through stained glass with angels singing in the background. All I heard was honking cars. Spirit uses the moving energy of synchronicity anywhere we are.

PSI Q: THE PSYCHIC QUOTIENT

Sometimes the awakening part of the cycle arrives in a totally inexplicable fashion, as a "psychic experience." A mother bolts out of a deep sleep at 3:00 A.M., only to learn later that her son was killed in an accident at exactly that moment. An executive follows a "hunch" with no data to support it and makes millions for the company. A doctor, on nothing but instinct, orders a test that saves a patient's life. A neighbor has "a feeling" where you misplaced the important documents, and she's right.

As William James comments in *The Varieties of Religious Experience*, "Our normal waking consciousness, rational consciousness as we call it, is but one special type of consciousness, while all about it, parted from it by the filmiest of screens, there lie potential forms of consciousness.

"We may go through life without suspecting their existence, but apply the requisite stimulus and, at a touch, they are there in all their completeness. No account of the universe in its totality can be final which leaves these other forms of consciousness quite disregarded."

Once we've had one of these unsettling experiences, we can never again define reality in quite the same comfortable way. For just at the edge of our peripheral vision we've caught a glimpse of a whole other world. And it momentarily sets aside our orderly notions of what's real and what's unreal.

This was well put by Dr. Charles Richet, who won the Nobel Peace Prize in 1913 for his discovery of anaphylatic shock. Facing criticism from his colleagues for his study of clairvoyance, he responded, "I didn't say it was possible; I only said it was true."

In a society that all but worships the rational, we are sometimes threatened by an encounter with the unknown. It's no longer "out there," like the mysteries of space that we trust science will explain one day. No, the mystery is intimate, inside us.

"Why is it," asked Lily Tomlin, "that when we talk to God, we call it prayer, but when God talks to us, they call it schizophrenia?"

When we know that something extraordinary really did occur, we often look to our religious leaders to tell us if it's good or evil. Religion invariably gets the first shot at the unknown. When we didn't understand storms, we attributed them to the rage of the gods. When the world of microbes was unknown, infections were seen as the punishment of the gods. Nevertheless the phenomena we lump broadly under the term *psychic* are inherently neither good nor bad, spiritually speaking.

Just as each of us has an IQ, so each of us also has a Psi Q, our psychic quotient. Psi Q is the potential within all humans for perceiving and interacting with nonphysical realities. There is nothing supernatural about psychic skills. Naturally super, and supra, perhaps—but not supernatural.

It's unlikely that we could find any culture on planet Earth that has not had people with high Psi Q's, those who are able to consistently, on demand, use abilities that tend to occur randomly in most people. The manner in which societies have dealt with psychically gifted people varies from honor and near deification to ridicule, persecution, and death. They are seen as either God's messengers or God's enemies. But no matter whether those with heightened psychic awareness are integrated into a culture or hiding in its shadows, they have always been among us—shamans, prophets, seers, healers, visionaries, clairvoyants, and even entertainers.

The eleventh-century British monarch King Canute was so attuned to subtle energies that his court perceived him as a magician. He tried to tell them otherwise. They wouldn't listen. So he took a group of his courtiers down to the coast and set his chair at the edge of the waves when the tide was out. When the tide began to turn, he stretched out his hands and commanded the sea to stop, which, of course, it did not. But at least some of his people understood the lesson: The wise person does not resist nature but attunes and works with it.

RIDING THE WAVES

There are dozens of radio and television waves passing through us right now. The reason we don't hear music or the news is that we don't have our internal receiving equipment set to convert those waves of energy into recognizable patterns. However a psychically skilled person has receiving equipment that is tuned to information passing through the ether.

The ether is the connecting medium of all life. Thoughts, words, symbols, personal history, ideals, feelings—all that we are—moves out from us into the ether like waves. Beliefs, strong emotions, even memories form patterns in the waves. When these patterns meet the beliefs and emotions of other people, they do one of several things. They can, like wave patterns, entrain with each other and build a stronger emotion or belief, which is the way contracts and myths are formed; or they can cancel each other out or produce contrasting and opposing patterns.

Most of the time we are focused on our own personal physical realities, and we are unaware of—or deny—the existence of these waves that bombard us all the time. However we all sense and react to them, even if we don't know why.

Now and then, when our inner guard relaxes, we pick up one of these transmissions psychically. Accident, childbirth, surgery, a near-death experience, or a threat to a loved one can, in one second, explode one's usual sense of reality. People with extraordinary Psi Q can pick these transmissions up almost as soon as they ripple the ether. They can see, sense, or sometimes "read" the wave patterns. Some people can predict with uncanny accuracy—although no one seems to be able to do it all the time—the likely manifestion of the pattern.

I know a young man who had never had a psi experience until he was knocked out during a basketball game and found himself floating at the top of the gym looking down on his body; a woman who could quote verbatim conversations that took place during her operation; many people who found themselves "alive and well" even though medically declared dead for minutes; and more "nonpsychic" parents than I could count who were suddenly and accurately aware that their children were in danger.

As evolution pushes us to understand more about our potential, we seem to be standing at the edge of our prejudices and ingrained ideas of how the world works. We might learn a lot by employing T. H. Huxley's advice. "Sit down before fact like a little child and be prepared to give up every preconceived notion. Follow humbly wherever and to whatever abysses Nature leads or you shall learn nothing."

Psi research is right there on that edge. The yogi who can control his own heart rate; the child who can bend metal with his mind; the woman who can leave her body at will; the healer who can affect molecules encased in a supposedly impenetrable cloud chamber; the dowser who can locate water—these people and many more are leading us toward an understanding of the possibilities within ourselves that were barely imaginable just a generation or two ago. The next step is to figure out how these things happen and then harness and teach the skills.

The last portion of the twentieth century will probably be recognized in retrospect as much for its exploration of human potential as for putting whole libraries on a microchip or launching spacecraft. We're stretching, accelerating, and moving across disciplines—from brain-mind research to the physics of consciousness. The day is not far away when we will have the instrumentation to measure a human aura and to see energy blocks in the body before they develop into disease.

In the meantime seeing auras and all other expressions of Psi Q present quite a challenge in the scientific laboratory. Elusive, now-it-works, now-it-doesn't, psi phenomena are often resistant to predictability or repeatability under the usual scientific empirical methods. Perhaps we haven't been able to get the right answers because we haven't been asking the right questions yet.

Einstein once said, "The mere formulation of a problem is far more essential than its solution, which may be merely a mark of mathematical or experimental skill. To raise new questions, new possibilities, to regard old problems from a new angle, requires creative imagination and makes real advances in science."

One of the challenges in investigating Psi Q is that it works best when it is stimulated by motivation. I remember how quickly I became bored when participating in ESP experiments in college. After my ego was satisfied and my curiosity wore off, I didn't really care which card came up next. I've never gotten bored using it with people. I recall hearing a well-known psychic lecturer who could bend laser beams. She gave up doing scientific testing in spite of incredible results because, she said, "I wondered what anyone could do with a bent laser beam anyway."

I know a man who is world famous for his successful psychic work with police departments in many countries. He failed to display psi abilities completely in a laboratory setting. Without the human stimulus his Psi Q didn't operate.

Another reason Psi Q is challenging in the laboratory is that people tend to try too hard or they are too emotionally invested in the results. Psychic accuracy often decreases when emotional expectation increases.

Physicist Dr. Russell Targ has designed and run experiments in "remote viewing"—seeing at a distance—and national ESP tests as part of a government sponsored, multimillion-dollar research program.

In the *Brain/Mind Bulletin* he advised participants not to over-invest themselves as they would probably score better if they didn't, saying, "A playful state of mind has long been associated with psychic success."

Dr. Targ said, "In astronomy you can see the faintest star only by averted vision. If you try to look at it directly, you can't see it. ESP seems to work that way, too."

People who consistently use psi energies know how true this statement is. Psychic impressions can be much like dream images you try to recall. One might be imprinted vividly, and you can call it up on request. But with many images, when you grasp for them, they disappear like smoke.

Psi Q abilities have no more to do with spiritual evolvement than does IQ. The abilities are neither moral nor immoral. They just are. A person can have a highly trained voice and use it to bring beauty to the world—or choose to sing pornography. Nuclear energy can light up the planet or blow it up. It is always the consciousness that uses the resource that makes the application constructive or destructive.

I don't identify myself as a psychic anymore than I identify myself as an intelligence, a body or any other resource I might use. I simply use my psychic skills like any other ability I possess. No matter what resource we have—intelligence, money, position, talent—we choose what it will serve.

FINDING HELP IN OPENING PSI Q

There are many, many realities—bands of energy—the highest of which even the best psychic cannot tap unless the intention is very pure. To align ourselves with the higher frequencies—such as another's soul pattern—we have to have cleared out the desire for self-aggrandizement. That doesn't mean we must be without personal ego. Such a thing is probably not possible short of complete mastership. But it is possible to set our ego aside. This requires being able to live unconditionally and non-judgmentally, with a measure of humility—we can't be taught anything new if we think we already know it all.

One important requirement of being able to "read" any frequency is to establish a sympathetic resonance with it. Another is to be free enough of our own biases to receive a clear, unprejudiced impression. Even the clearest receivers have to interpret what they see or feel. Interpretation depends on several things: the data, symbols, and experience stored in the receivers' brains; their willingness to be taught new information; their ability to plug into the collective mind and draw upon the whole of human experience; and their ability to stand back and view information and the whole situation with as much compassionate detachment as possible.

Just as the opening of psychic capacities may be part of the awakening stage of our growth, so must these abilities go through an awakening of their own. The body—particularly the nervous system—the mind, and the emotions all have to be prepared to handle interaction with higher frequencies. That preparation does not necessarily occur at the feet of a teacher or in esoteric training. Life can be our teacher. The preparation comes with living responsibly, honestly, and consciously—in all ways, including physically—with the challenges and opportunities in front of us every day. Our greatest teachers may appear to be the people in our lives who give us the most grief. Learning to forgive everyone everything (particularly oneself) and to love everyone (especially oneself) regardless of appearances can be our most important lessons in life.

If you really want to understand how your body, mind, and emotions work together, the study of a spiritual science—such as Theosophy, Rosicrucianism, Yoga, and many others—can save you a lot of trial and error. Plus it can help you avoid the pitfall of superstition. I am not pushing a particular philosophy any more than I would suggest that you only study psychology. However, it is valuable to find good sources of information about how energy works in the physical body in collaboration with consciousness: how and where energy enters your body; where the major energy-collecting points (chakras) are; and how they are connected to your neurochemistry. If you do not have any background in a spiritual science and are interested, I would recommend that you start by going to a good metaphysical bookstore and asking for basic information on subtle bodies and chakras (energy centers).

It is true that as one releases a limited view of reality and opens the mind to more possibilities, one's Psi Q tends to increase. There are safety gates inside the average healthy person that protect the organism from overloading itself with experiences it isn't yet ready to integrate. While those gates can be blasted open through severe trauma or with drugs, generally the reality one experiences under those conditions cannot be integrated or repeated on demand.

Good spiritual training promotes this integration and balance. In most systems stern warnings exist about becoming preoccupied with psychic phenomena. And with good reason. Getting preoccupied with the razzle-dazzle of psychic phenomena can detour you from your goal of self-knowledge.

Many people I know who are now serious spiritual students had a major breakthrough at that level, an "Oh, wow!" experience that fueled their passion to know more. The trick is not to get addicted to the "Oh, wow!" or mistake it for the real thing.

I recall a story Ram Dass tells of giving Guru Maharaj-ji an elephantine dose of LSD and being shocked when he had no reaction. Finally his teacher said that the LSD was okay, but he wondered why anyone would want just to visit the Christ when it was possible to go there and stay.

It's not a good idea to explore "other worlds" until you have a handle on the one you're conscious of living in. Developing Psi Q is not the way to avoid personal problems and life challenges. Over the years I have observed people alienate their families, ignore responsibilities, and avoid what are clearly psychological problems by creating a smoke screen of psychic double-talk. From the beginning, Spirit advised me, "Take a baby step and integrate. Take another step and integrate."

That has been indispensible advice, and I highly recommend it. When we begin having more than random psychic experiences, we need to keep making reality checks. The wisdom that teaches "Before I was enlightened, I chopped wood and carried water; and after I was enlightened, I chopped wood and carried water" applies to new psychic insights as well. After we've experienced them, we still have taxes to pay, children to raise, jobs to be done.

I often tell people that if they want to develop their Psi Q, that's fine, but first, stop and ask yourself honestly, "Why? What do I want to do with those skills? Do I want to use them in service for my own growth and to benefit others? Am I willing to keep working on my own personal issues?" It's wise to check out any unresolved ego needs for attention and power over others before you deliberately set out to develop psychic skills. The point is always to be grounded and balanced, for psychic abilities make wonderful servants but terrible masters. The best advice I know was credited to Jesus the Christ and has been echoed in spiritual trainings from the ancient past until today: "Seek ye first the kingdom of Heaven"-Nirvana-Bliss-Paradise-Reconnection. Psychic insights can simply help us recognize some of the turnings on the way.

CHANNELING

We have only begun to understand the potential of the human mind. Our ability to perceive nonphysical realities and to communicate with intelligence that exists in other dimensions is just beginning. The understanding of this capacity is made even more puzzling to us as we also see the pathologies of certain mental illness. We fear people who are incapacitated and confused by the voices they hear and the things they see. Yet, ordinary, balanced people can have spontaneous communication with nonphysical beings through a near-death experience or an altered state of consciousness induced by sickness, trauma, drugs, an out-of-body experience, intense prayer, or a heightened spiritual awareness.

We exist in many frequencies of nonphysical energy that are emotional, mental, and spiritual. Just as one might take the cursor on a computer and move it around as desired, there are those who have the ability to move their consciousness at will to other levels of perception. These people can focus their awareness on command on any available frequency. People from all cultural, psychological, and religious backgrounds report communications with other beings in these frequencies. When they report the communications, they are often said to be channeling. The language of communication with other dimensions that is found in spiritual, esoteric, and parapsychological literature varies and there are few clear cut definitions. However, this experience of interdimensional communication is so universal—and yet still so mysterious—that definitions of the phenomenon must be created and put in context.

One "channeler" might set aside the sense of personal self altogether and give the appearance that another intelligence is speaking through them. Their voices and body language change. Such a person might be known as a trance medium. Another "channeler" doesn't leave a personal sense of self in order to contact other intelligence and maintains his or her own voice, mannerisms, and personal identity. These individuals are often referred to as mediums—meaning they serve as a bridge between worlds of perception—but they remain reporters of other intelligences—not creators.

People have been channeling—receiving guidance from Spirit—as long as there have been people. Sacred Scriptures from around the world are filled with wisdom, visions, and dreams credited to nonphysical beings. From the Christian Holy Bible to the Hindu Bhagavad Gita, from the prophecies of a tribal shaman to the modern *Course in Miracles*, God has taught humans the ways of the Divine through angels, guides, guardians, teachers, deceased relatives, spirit doctors, saints, ascended masters, space brothers and sisters, and beings from alternate realities.

Channeling has been with us since time immemorial, and it's just as mysterious now as it has always been. Although it seems anachronistic in a technological, materialistic society, the fact is that millions of sane, educated people continue to believe in communication from Spirit. The word *channeling* is itself a bit of a catchall. It covers everything from personal spiritual inspiration to messages from other dimensions. For one person it means that the words and ideas "heard," felt, or sensed are literally those of another intelligence. For another person it means that the words and ideas come straight from God. For still another it means that the words and ideas emerge from the highest potential within the Self.

In the purest sense channeling is about being attuned to the very highest guidance within ourselves and allowing that guidance to come into our conscious minds and physical lives. It puts us in rhythm with the energy of the universe and allows it to flow through us. The material plane is very, very dense and full of fear. Pure Light is pure love, and we act as channels every time we bring that love into fearful places.

Pure Light is stepped down enormously in this dimension. If it were not, it would short out our nervous systems. When we pray, channel, and hold healing thoughts, we act much like an electrical transformer that steps down energy from one frequency to another so that it doesn't overload the circuits.

Channeling can be an excellent tool to help in the awakening stage; however there is no bigger arena for an overactive imagination, personal self-deception, and the possible deception—even exploitation—of others than channeling. It is filled with potential dangers for the psychologically vulnerable.

Nevertheless it is as superstitious to dismiss a phenomenon out of hand as it is to believe everything one hears. It is impossible to build a case for it in logic, but whether we understand it or not, there it is. So all we can really do at this point is keep an open mind, listen to our highest guidance and our own common sense, and explore this tool for ourselves.

THE LAW OF ATTRACTION

When we become interested in working in these realities, we must examine our motives and intentions with great care. The law of attraction is always at work. We receive at the level of our desire. And we have to know ourselves pretty well to know what we are truly desiring. If the desire, no matter how repressed, is to avoid the challenges of our personal lives by escaping into another realm, then the magnet of desire is marked escape, not service. If the desire is to have an imagined power, then that's the magnet, not service.

We receive what we ask for. It's important to realize that information and communication pulled to us through muddy motives can take us into culs-de-sac that are dangerous for our mental health, and that, in turn, can interfere with our growth in all ways.

My experience has been that the higher beings in Spirit are contacted when the motive is high. But they are committed to the good of all. No highly developed being is interested in helping us justify our ego games. In fact they will lovingly but quickly straighten us out on that. They are all-inclusive in their love and work—not exclusive.

In fact this is one of the best clues we have about whether or not we're in touch with beings of very high energy. Be very, very cautious when there is talk of exclusivity. When I hear anyone claim that he or she is the only channel on earth—or one of only a handful—for a well-known saint or master, I am immediately suspicious. But if he says he is *a* person—not *the* person—then I listen to what he has to say.

First of all, Jesus, Buddha, Saint Germaine, Saint Michael, Maitreya, Kuan-yin, the Virgin Mary, and other Masters are not personalities in the way you and I think of an individualized personality. They have broken those limiting bonds and are no longer restricted to space-time as we perceive ourselves to be. Masters, by definition, have complete control over the cellular structure of all of the lower bodies (physical, emotional, mental). They can materialize however and wherever they desire. They are more like the sun. If you pray to the sun, you receive a ray of the sun, which is indeed sunlight, but it's hardly the only ray in existence.

Secondly, we can easily make contact with an archetype. If we pray to the Archangel Raphael, for example, we could make contact with a thought form that the collective unconscious has built around the image of Raphael. If the ultimate master for us is the Buddha, then we might feel we're receiving a message from him.

I learned early on that we can choose the level at which we wish to be taught. But there are some ground rules. If we want to learn from beings who radiate unconditional love, then we must be willing to work on learning to love unconditionally. If we want to co-create with a very high intelligence that is dedicated to earth's evolution, then we, too, must desire to serve evolution.

Spirit communication of a very low order also exists. There

are mischievous and even detrimental entities who can wheel and deal quite impressively on the lower levels of subtle energy that encompass desire and emotions. But that is where their ability stops, unless you give them power in the physical plane by providing a channel for them. As a species we have polluted our collective consciousness with fear. This has given these lower entities lots of raw material to work with in playing to the ego and creating dependencies. Higher energies do neither, and they would never suggest, encourage, or participate in the harming of another being in any way.

Discernment is an important part of the training of a student of truth. "By their fruits you shall know them" is a solid criterion to use. I would suggest that whenever you feel you have contacted an entity of any kind, you do as sacred Scriptures suggest: Test it. The higher the being, the more it will respect your clarity of purpose. Affirm that you seek truth and truth only. Hold a firm image of Light in your mind; ask if the Spirit serves the Universal Christ and wait for confirmation. If you are not assured that it does, or if there is no response, then demand in the name of the Universal Christ that it leave your presence. This should be done in love and with sureness—not in fear.

Just because someone is no longer in the physical body does not mean it automatically knows more than you do. As Dr. Charles Tart said, "Dying does not necessarily raise your IQ." Your sincere desire to grow and serve is what attracts high teaching. And there is no faking it. In the higher realms one's motives can be read as easily as you and I read a newspaper. Selfishness, greed, hate, grudges, arrogance, and judgments show up as black constrictions in the auric field. Please don't hear that as a statement that Spirit is judging you. Higher teachers know that this Earth plane is a schoolhouse. If we had it mastered, we wouldn't need to be here. The judgments we receive come from this plane, not from the realms of Spirit. The love there is unqualified and rejoices in every effort we make.

I find that it is rare for inner-plane teachers to tell us what to do about our personal problems. They are more inclined to offer insights and share wisdom. True guides and teachers on the Earth or in any other dimension won't attempt to turn you into a robot by resolving your challenges. This would rob you of the very means through which you grow. Working with Spirit is an act of co-creation. You retain responsibility for your self. No wise entity wishes to make you dependent.

One of the hallmarks of good spiritual guidance from other planes—and from this one as well, I might add—is that you feel empowered by the contact, not just impressed. Oh, you'll probably be impressed first. But you'll come away from such contacts encouraged, inspired, and optimistic about your life.

Spiritual growth and service by no means require that we be aware of Spirit guides and teachers. When we evoke the energies of love within ourselves, we automatically invoke the energies of love from the universe. And our love is redoubled and transmitted through our thoughts and intentions into the world.

An awakening that breaks the resistance cycle and launches us into the awakening may not involve synchronicity, Psi Q, or a conscious contact with Spirit. It may arrive through the most mundane of activities. But make no mistake: The change is about our spiritual life. Everything that happens to us serves ultimately to bring us toward greater understanding.

The moment of breakthrough passes. It has served the purpose of taking us from one point of understanding to another. Next comes the time of commitment to the new direction.

I want to share with you a prayer that I have used for years in healing and counseling work. Of course any prayer is only effective if it is fused with your real intention and heart's desire. I would encourage you to write your own, but in the meantime many of the principles of intention and protection are covered in this one.

A HEALING PRAYER

Dear Mother-Father-God

I ask to be cleared and cleansed with the white Christ Light, the green healing Light, and the violet transmuting Light.

For my highest good and within God's will I ask that all disharmonious vibrations be removed from me, sealed within their own Light, and returned to the Source for purification, never again to re-establish within me or anyone else.

I ask to be used as a channel for healing for [name, situation]. I seek this for [his, her, its] highest good, within [his, her, its] own will and within divine will.

I ask that this room be surrounded by Light, that this [person, situation] be surrounded by Light. I ask for the protection of the triple shield of the white Light of the Universal Christ.

At this time I accept those forces of healing that work through and with me, accepting only that which serves the Universal Christ.

I express gratitude for all my many blessings, above all, the privilege of serving others.

EXERCISE: MEETING
THE COMMITTEE

This visualization is designed to help discover which aspect of ourselves is in control of certain functions. If you're willing to trust the images your unconscious will kick out during these exercises, you can learn a great deal about yourself. If you are currently working with a therapist, I would suggest that the two of you consider doing this exercise together. It's even helpful to do it with a friend. You might want to talk your experience into a tape recorder, as it is easy to forget details.

Some things to remember:

• You should not do this or any other exercise if it makes you uneasy. Not every exercise is for everybody. Trust yourself. If you have a tendency to go into an altered state easily and don't know how to handle it, I would suggest that you only do this with a therapist, a minister, or a counselor.

• Whether you are male or female, you have both masculine and feminine energies at work. So go through both visualizations.

• Don't judge anything. It's all just information. There's no right or wrong, good or bad. If you resist an image because you don't like it, you could deny yourself a valuable insight.

• Pay attention to every detail. As with dream images, every little item is a clue.

A. MEETING YOUR FEMALE COMMITTEE.

1. Locate a place where there will be minimal distractions. Begin by getting in a comfortable position and allow yourself to relax. Take fifteen or twenty slow, deep breaths. With each breath consciously release tension. Then quickly scan your body mentally. And tighten and release any tense muscles.

2. Reassure your subconscious by saying a prayer affirming that this experience is for your highest good. See yourself surrounded and filled with pure Light. Affirm that you seek truth and truth only.

3. Now, in your mind's eye create an image of yourself walking beside a lake at twilight. Make this image so vivid that you can hear the water lapping against the shore and the sounds of life settling down for the evening. Feel the slight dampness of the falling dew under your feet, the softness of the evening breeze on your skin. Look up and notice that the stars are appearing. There is going to be a full moon tonight.

4. Soon you will come to a bridge that leads to an island in the middle of the lake. What does the bridge look like? Stepping on to it, you begin to feel anticipation but don't hurry yourself. As you cross the lake, notice how bright the moon is, how sparkling the water in the silver light. There are swans floating quietly near the bridge.

5. As you step off the bridge, you come to a path that leads through a forest. It is a well-worn path, and the forest is a safe place to be. What kind of trees are there? Is there any wildlife? The moon paints the path with light as you walk directly to a clearing in the woods.

6. In the middle of the clearing is a fire already lit. You are expected. Around the fire, in a circle, are places for people to sit, although you are the first to arrive. What kind of seating is there? Stones? Logs? The moon is directly overhead. Find the place in the circle where you are most comfortable and sit down. Become familiar with the circle. Is there anything there that draws your attention?

7. Now you are going to invite some of the women inside of you to join you in this circle. Each of them will bring you a gift. The first is your Power Woman. Call for her to come forth, and accept her regardless of how she shows up. Does she come down the path? Is she alone? Is there an animal or bird with her? What is she wearing? What is her age? Hair color and length? Jewelry? Notice every detail. How does she walk? Does she remind you of anyone you know or have read about? What is her attitude? Do you like her? Does she please you or scare you? Does she say anything to you? What is her gift to you? Invite her to sit down. Where does she sit in the circle?

8. Now you are going to invite your Wise Woman to join you. She, too, will bring a gift. Observe all the same kinds of details that you did with your Power Woman—dress, age, attitude, and so forth. Your Wise Woman and your Power Woman know each other. Do they like each other? What is her attitude? Accept her gift and any words she has to offer. Then invite her to sit down in the circle. Where does she sit? On your right? Your left? Across from you? Where is she in relationship to the Power Woman? How does it make you feel to have these two sitting with you?

9. Now you are going to meet your Fear Woman, the one you've been afraid to meet. Invite her into the circle and don't resist the way she presents herself. She will bring a gift also. Make the same kinds of observations you did for the other two, paying particular attention to what you like or don't like—her walk, attitude, clothes. Notice everything. What is her relationship to the Power Woman and the Wise Woman? Who reacts to her and in what way? How does she relate to them? What is her gift? Invite her to sit in the circle. What does she do and where does she sit? Does she have anything to say? How do you feel about her?

10. The next invitation is issued to the Unknown Woman, the woman you didn't even know was inside. She comes with a gift, as the others have. Make all the same kinds of observations you have with the others. Does she remind you of anyone? What thoughts come to mind as you see her? Pay attention to every detail, including whom she does or does not relate to. Does she actually know the others? Are you surprised at her? Afraid of her? What is her gift to you? Ask her to sit in your circle and notice where she feels comfortable.

11. There's one more that has to be added to this circle, and that is your Little Girl. Call for her to join your circle. Does she come willingly or do you have to help her? How old is she? How is she dressed? What is her attitude? Which one of the women in this circle makes her feel the safest? Is she frightened of any one of them? Is she thrilled to be included? Suspicious? Where does she go when you ask her to sit in the circle? Now ask the women to bless her, each in her own way. Do they do that willingly? How does the little girl feel?

12. Now look carefully around the circle. Express your gratitude that each of them is present. Tell them you plan to bring difficult decisions to the circle in the future to listen to what each has to say. Ask the group that if there are any other women you need to meet, would they please bring them to the next meeting.

13. After you have expressed your thanks to each of the women, prepare to leave the circle. As you start back through the woods, take one last look at the group around the campfire and express your gratitude. The more you are appreciative and accepting of all facets of yourself—the shadow and the light—the more aspects of your self will surface. This is your circle and your committee. You can return anytime you like. But for now you need to leave. Dawn is approaching.

14. Follow your route back across the bridge. The sun is starting to rise as you step onto the mainland. Take deep, full breaths and direct the energy into your feet and legs, into the trunk of your body, into your head. Become aware and at ease with your physical surroundings. Now open your eyes. Declare that you are balanced, harmonized, and attuned.

Note: You will probably be too tired to hold a council the first time you meet your committee, but in the future you can re-create this circle and bring problems to it. By listening to what each has to say, you can discover where your ambivalences lie, make "deals" with committee members, and use your imagination to facilitate cooperation with all parts of yourself.

B. MEETING YOUR MALE COMMITTEE

This part of your visualization is done in a similar fashion to the meeting with your female committee, but this time you begin at dawn, walking up a mountain to a clearing at the top. It is high noon when you sit in your circle and begin asking for the Power Man, the Wise Man, the Man You Fear, the Man You Don't Know, and the Male Child. Instead of gifts, imagine each man bringing a banner on which there is a significant symbol. He will plant the banner behind where he sits. Be very attentive to every detail of dress and attitude, and to the men's relationships with each other. If you don't have an immediate intuitive knowing, I don't recommend that you try to figure out what all the symbols mean. You'll have plenty of time to work with them later. For now just be the observer and receive from your own creative mind.

C. MEETING YOUR JOINT COMMITTEE

When you feel comfortable with both your masculine and your feminine committee members, you can create joint meetings. It's very revealing to discover who holds the power, who speaks up, who doesn't. You can learn a great deal about where the splits are in your dual nature and how to heal them.

STEP FIVE

The Commitment

Knowing is not enough. Risk knowledge with action and then you will know whether it is genuine, pretension or just information.

—SRI GURUDEV CHITRABHANU

*A*s we explore the delights of the awakening, our old form begins to lose its hold on us. But as the dust settles from the excitement of new inquiries, decisions must be made. And this brings us into the next stage of our odyssey—the commitment— the covenant to change.

At this point we begin to pay serious attention to habits and attitudes that were deeply ingrained in our original form. There is a conscious knowledge of seeking a path for ourselves rather than simply accepting the one we inherited from others. "Know thyself" becomes an important value. There may be changes in diet, routine, and where, how, and with whom we decide to spend our energy. During the commitment stage people often seek a system or discipline that will give structure to the new direction, sometimes taking classes or workshops and becoming more dedicated to various therapies that clean up the past. In terms of our spiritual evolution, the commitment period is when we expand inward to discover God.

WALKING THE TALK

The awakening says, "I see it; I get it!"

The commitment says, "Great. Now what are you going to do about it?" As Rene Daumal says in *Mount Analogue*, "You cannot stay on the summit forever; you have to come down again. So why bother in the first place? Just this: What is above knows what is below, but what is below does not know what is above. One climbs, ones sees, one descends. One sees no longer, but one has seen."

Once we have experienced an awakening, we're never quite the same. We can't live as we did before because we can't pretend we haven't seen a new and higher truth for ourselves. The trick is not to get addicted to the awakening cycle itself—it's not the end of the journey.

When people get hooked on the awakening part of the cycle, they can become growth junkies, rushing from one experience to another—the newest "hot" technique, a teacher with something "new" to say, the experience that will re-create that mountaintop high over and over again. It's also easy to begin following what someone called "the path of paraphernalia," acquiring bells, crystals, pyramids, beads, books, tapes, and a thousand quotes.

Each of these paths and techniques has an intrinsic worth, but we cannot keep substituting symbol for substance. Insight—awakening—is not the same as integration. Any newfound truth only becomes a potent force when we can see it working.

It's one thing to see divinity in the eyes of a fellow seeker during a meditation retreat. It's quite another to see it in your service station attendant, your child's coach, or the IRS agent.

Once we've come down from that heady experience on the mountain, we usually discover that our material world is pretty much the way we left it. If we want to become what we now believe, we have to make a serious commitment to retraining all parts of ourselves.

It takes a lot of commitment to rewrite our scripts because the old form is firmly encoded in the archives of the subconscious. On the other hand, we're also wired for change. There are 2 trillion connections among the nerve cells of the brain. Astrophysicist Carl Sagan says that that means that there are more potential mental states in a single human brain than there are atoms in the known universe. We're not stuck with our old-form patterns unless we choose to be.

As Marilyn Ferguson says in *The Aquarian Conspiracy*, "The difference between transformation by accident and transformation by a system is like the difference between lightning and a lamp. Both give illumination, but one is dangerous and unreliable, while the other is relatively safe, directed, available."

Becoming the truth we now perceive is done by making choices. We're always choosing, although we're not always conscious of it. Even doing nothing is a choice. To hate, to love, to criticize, to speak, to shut up—these are all choices. To say "I couldn't help myself" is the choice to give away choice.

A paralyzed man was telling an interviewer that he had trained to be a world-class athlete before his accident. The interviewer asked him if his handicap hadn't colored his life. "Yes," came the quick answer, "but I've chosen the colors."

During the commitment cycle of change, we're making the choice to bring the new idea about ourselves into reality. However this is when we need to remember that the material world we see when we first make the commitment is the result of choices we made long before. By the time we see the light from a star, it's thousands of light-years away from its home. Early on in the process of change—usually during the resistance—we tend to get caught up in appearance, the evidence of the old form. During commitment we make the choice steadily and patiently to bring the new vision into the material world in spite of appearances. One of these choices, as the old truism says, is to light candles instead of cursing the darkness. The light penetrates the darkness not by resisting it but by simply being itself.

By owning our power to choose consciously what we want to do with our energy we sharpen our spiritual crafts. While we can't determine what someone else will do, we do have full power over how we're going to respond. Shaping our responses is enhanced by learning the difference between observing and energizing.

We observe that the world is acting out its confusion of change. We can choose to energize an image of peace.

We observe that a person has a disease. We can choose to energize an image of health.

We observe that some of our old programs are still running on high. We can choose to energize our awakened vision.

At earlier points in the process, challenges to our old programming can make us feel threatened. But during the commitment stage we learn to observe our responses. "Oh, there I go again, reacting to this or that." The old automatic responses become the triggers for identifying old programs that still need our attention. It is not by denying but rather by identifying the old responses that we gradually reeducate them.

If you're angry, for example, just be angry. It's far better to own it than to make yourself sick by swallowing it or deluding yourself through a false piety that denies the anger. Try saying, "Okay, I'm still angry about that. So what's the anger telling me about my own self-image? What do I choose to do with this anger? Will it run me or will I run it?"

Anger is, after all, only energy. It's what we're experiencing; it is not who we are. Once faced and owned, anger can be used creatively. Take a person who is angry because she's been watching a TV news report about baby seals being abused. That person can choose to turn off the news and say, "I don't want to look at this; it hurts me too much." But if she does, there's a good chance that choice drops down into the subconscious and feeds a sense of powerlessness that might be tied up with all the other perceived brutality on the planet, including personal experience. Perhaps the anger symbolizes an unconscious ambivalence. I know that my own ability to act on my anger about animal abuse took a straighter mark when I put away a fur coat that I concluded symbolized a principle I could no longer accept.

Another person, faced with the same anger, might look at the facts, be straight with the anger, and ask, "What, if anything, do I choose to do about this? Where is the energy of my anger best spent? In fighting the seal hunters? In contributing to awareness of the rights of seals? In creating a consciousness that looks at all of life in a more inclusive way? In writing to a congressman? In saying a prayer of gratitude for the seals' sacrifice so that our collective indifference can be reflected to us?"

The choices are endless.

Consciously, or unconsciously, we make choices all the time about what to do with the energy of any given situation. We might not be able to change a co-worker's negative attitude, but we can choose whether or not to match it with equal negativity, which could keep the dance going ad infinitum. Pointing fingers polarize and resistance empowers a struggle. Or we could withdraw our reactive energy and choose how we desire to act.

I once saw a perfect demonstration of this by lecturer-teacher Patricia Sun. During a beautiful and powerful presentation she mentioned this very principle. A few minutes later, when she asked if there were any questions, a man in the audience stood and told a tasteless "dirty" joke. Sun did not react—not in words, not in body language, not in facial expression, not in anything. Because of her lack of response to this attempted taunt, the joke bombed and the whole audience ignored it. There was no indignant whispering, no turning of heads to see who had committed this outrage. It was as if it had never happened. Had she reacted with indignation, anger, insult, or hurt, the audience would also have reacted, and the bad joke would have taken the power of the moment. As it was, it died a natural death due to lack of energy.

When we choose what we will do with our energies, we

claim our real power. We begin to act and not merely react. We claim our birthright to create by choosing the words, images, desires, and actions that establish new blueprints at a causal level. We no longer waste energy shuffling around the effects of earlier creations.

Many of us are discovering, for example, that if we match energies with war consciousness, we make no progress. It only reinforces the very thing we want to overcome. Instead more and more of us are finding it is better not to put energies into being against anything; it's far more effective to be for something. This allows us to reroute energy into creating a new planetary consciousness big enough to embrace and celebrate all our differences as well as our commonalities as citizens of planet Earth.

It takes a great deal of discipline and tenacity to take the insights we've had and bring them into manifestation. There are always plenty of old assumptions around to discourage us. "Better look after number one." "There will always be wars." "Women are by nature [fill in the blank]." "Men are by nature [fill in the blank]." And then there's the bottom line: "That's human nature!"

Commitment to a new view offers us the opportunity to stop and review these assumptions. Are they really true? Is that really how I am? How we are? Or is that a tribal assumption passed down from generation to generation with such authority that it is accepted as truth?

When I hear stories of creative new solutions, I think of the word *Jehovah*, one of the names we have given God. It means "I am imagination and manifestation." Each of us carries the power of *I Am* within us. The universe isn't responsible for what we choose to do with the *I Am* power—we are. It's good discipline to pay attention to how we use this power. Whenever we say "I am . . ." our subconscious immediately sets up a program to bring that pronouncement about. Every time we say "I am afraid," we reinforce the fear. And every time we say "I am confident a solution is coming," we give the subconscious a boost toward attracting that solution.

I once worked with a woman who ran from doctor to doctor and healer to healer. She never received help. While there were probably many reasons for that, one of them was that she didn't take responsibility for her own pronouncements. She began her sentences with "I am afraid" twenty-two times in one conversation. By continually affirming her fear, she closed down the possibility of receiving the help she claimed she wanted. Ambivalence is an energy just like any other. Create an ambivalent energy and send it into the universe and that's just what you get back—double messages.

There is no limit to what we can do when we claim the *I Am*, when we let go of past limitations, dream anew, and then commit ourselves to bringing the new vision into the Earth. Poised between our Godness and our humanness, we become, as Talmudic scholar, Rabbi Adin Steinsaltz described himself, a "commuter between heaven and earth."

THE VOICE OF DOUBT

Our breakthroughs become reality to the degree that we commit to our new vision. Like a young plant reaching for the sun, we need fertile soil and nutrients to reach our full potential.

The first thing we need to nurture is our faith in our own highest inner guidance. Danish philosopher Sören Kierkegaard said, "Everyone comes to earth with sealed orders." Having faith in our path helps us to read those orders.

You might not feel ready for the commitment. Few of us do. Sacred Scriptures remind us of this dynamic of change in various allegories. It's told that Moses resisted his mission at first, telling God he wasn't the man for the job of leading the people out of Egypt. He even argued that because he stuttered, he wouldn't be a good enough speaker. In the Hindu epic *The Mahabharata*, that same dynamic is at work when the youthful warrior Arjuna argues with the god Krishna, insisting that he isn't ready for leadership yet.

We often find that as we build a new faith in our truth, our old version of reality rises to plague us with feelings of unworthiness. "Who am I to think I can live this way? How can I be an instrument of a new vision?"

We tend to assume that others don't experience these passages of self-doubt when they face a new level of commitment. I think almost everyone does. I passed through it in the early days of my healing work. No matter how much I was learning through my own journey or the healing and counseling work, I still needed to surround my own discoveries with statements from recognized authorities. It took a long time before I could simply say: "This has been my experience in Spirit. See what it means to you."

In the early months of my work I would often say "I really don't feel worthy to do this work," thinking I was being humble. I would refuse to lecture, insisting I wasn't ready. Then a good friend loved me enough to say, "That's just ego talking." She was right. I have since learned that true humility follows inner guidance even when the outer self is unsure. "My guidance is to stay home with these two children? Fine, I'll do that." "My inner guidance is to get on a stage and speak up? I'll do it." "Paint the picture . . . collect the clothing . . . give up negativity . . . whatever the guidance, I'll do it." That's humility.

A budding new teacher I know expressed to a more experienced colleague the fear of not being ready or worthy. The advice was: "None of us feels ready or worthy, but the truth is always ready and worthy to be told."

I was once told in Spirit, "Humble yourself to power." It took a while to really understand that. Most of us have a distorted notion of power, perceiving it in human terms as political, social, or economic clout. God's power is often seen as a force outside of us that can either clobber or bless us, rather than the force that moves and expresses itself through us. When the personal ego usurps that force to serve its own ends, it does so in ignorance. I may happily take a whack at the world with a passing show of power, but all that it creates—good, bad, or indifferent—returns to it. The principle of return—"Everything that goes around comes around"—is a very impersonal but loving law.

When we commit to another piece of our truth, we align ourselves with true power. No matter how small the movement seems to us, we are in training to align ourselves with the universal flow.

THE CREATIVE POWER OF FAITH

We are each a cell in the common body. When we choose to create, to activate the Godness within us, our movements affect and influence the whole. But until we really know this at a cellular level, our commitment to our own awakening remains an act of faith.

Faith is one of the most powerful forces at our command. Whatever we have faith in is also what we believe in—and belief is the basis of our reality. Whatever our sealed orders are, faith reveals them to us. Having faith means we're taking responsibility for our choices and that we're paying attention to our inner guidance.

One of the finest healers and teachers I know lives in the country on the outskirts of the suburbs of a small Mississippi town. This place is really remote. He was guided to go there from several states away, and now people from all over the country seek him out. Once when we had been talking for hours, I blurted out to him in a moment of enthusiasm, "You should be doing workshops and lectures everywhere." He smiled at me gently and said, "Oh, no, my dear, this is my assignment." Faith leads us step-by-step to our assignment. Your assignment in this world in uniquely yours. Others can encourage, inspire and mirror you, but no one—not the clearest psychic, not the best spiritual teacher—can tell you what is right for you.

I was reminded of this years ago when I heard stress expert Dr. Hans Selye speak. He said that if a tortoise is made to run like a racehorse, it is stressful; but if a racehorse is made to slow down to the pace of a tortoise, that is equally stressful. I wanted to run right up onto the stage and hug him. All my life I had been told by others to slow down, but my inner guidance knew that my cruise control was not set at a tortoise's pace. I think that was the first time I really accepted my own pacing.

Once we start paying attention to what's happening in our own environment, we begin to see that the universe is giving us all sorts of clues about our path. If we believe in love and are making a commitment to being love, there's a good chance the universe will send us thirty people in a row whom we don't love. Our assignment: Love those thirty people. Many times we ask God to teach us, but when the lesson arrives, we say we had something a little less demanding in mind. Or it goes right over our heads because we're not paying attention.

Following a two year spiritual intensive in the mountains, I returned to the city full of my insights and expecting more. But everytime I turned around my time and energy were being pulled into material concerns. I was so busy doing workshops and consultations, I often felt there was little time for my own spiritual practices. Finally I paid attention to a few of the clues, and they were found everywhere. My new bank account number, my new house number, my car license, and my new telephone number all came up number 4. Four is the number of physical manifestation. Clearly it was not a time of new inspiration—it was a period of anchoring insights into the physical world.

Consider the tale of the man trapped in a flood, who wasn't

worried because he thought he had faith. So when the waters first started rising and a motorcyclist came along and offered him a ride to safety, he turned him down, declaring that he had faith that God would save him. The waters rose, and soon a man arrived in a rowboat. He passed that up as well. God would save him; he had faith. He was finally forced to stand on the roof of his house. Soon a helicopter flew over, and the pilot yelled down that he was dropping a rope and would take the man to safety. Again he declined, declaring his faith in God's protection.

Well, he died. And he was furious. When he arrived in heaven, he demanded to see God and began protesting this offense to his faith.

God replied, "I really don't know what went wrong. I sent a motorcyclist, a rowboat, and a helicopter."

When we commit to faith, we shift our life flow from ego control to divine control, and "impossible" things begin to happen. All sorts of things occur that seem totally unlikely. Doors open as if by magic. The right people synchronistically appear in our lives. We even learn to worry less. A friend a mine responds to worries about how difficulties will work out by saying "that's God's problem. I just work here."

With faith, synchronicities become a way of life. As *A Course in Miracles* says, "There is no order of difficulty in miracles. One is not harder or bigger than another. They are all the same."

Faith cannot be counterfeited. It's not the same thing as calculated risk. It's not an idea we can simply try on for size and discard. It's a day-by-day process of reeducating every doubting cell in our bodies until our whole beingness is living in faith. The doubts do come. But instead of denying them, we learn to use them to discover what we're still holding on to. Often our faith is stretched thin because we're clinging to outmoded ideas about what is good and what is bad.

When someone commits to faith, it is not unusual to have that faith tried to the limit. Faith is optional when everything is rocking along as scheduled. But faith is often forged in the crucible of confusion and doubt. During such moments the psyche can be plunged into dark and fearful places where no faith exists.

Years ago I remember waking up in the middle of the night with a cold terror in my solar plexus and my mind suddenly questioning whether everything I believed was wrong. I tried to pray. Nothing. I tried to meditate. Nothing. No matter what I did, I couldn't feel insights or comfort or relief, and I received no answers from Spirit. I got mad at God, tried to negotiate— all the usual stuff. Nothing.

Finally I just surrendered to it and let the darkness be what it was. I quit fighting it. And out of that darkness emerged all kinds of things I was hiding, questions I thought I could bypass.

Once again the universe was reminding me that we can no more walk in a little bit of faith than we can be a little bit pregnant. The more I allowed myself to face and accept the darkness, the more the Light penetrated it. I learned to affirm that Spirit was moving in that darkness even though I couldn't see it at that time.

It is not always an easy labor to birth faith. But once we do, we wonder how we ever functioned before. Faith liberates our abilities and relationships from the tyranny of manipulation. The leap is to accept that one's life has a plan and that whatever or whoever we've brought into it at any given moment has a purpose in that plan, even if we cannot see any rhyme or reason for it at the moment.

Once I was led to give up a substantial part of my income in order to take the next step in my journey. My ego didn't particularly like that as it could not see how I would make a living. Of course, I first tried to manipulate events according to the way I thought I could stay safe and protected. My fear and not my inner guidance was calling the shots at that point.

During a meditation I saw an image of myself swinging on a trapeze while another trapeze was coming toward me. It became clear that I was to let go of one trapeze in order to catch the other one. Now, it was also clear that there would be a moment of free-fall in which I wouldn't be holding on to either trapeze. I could feel my solar plexus sink as I asked, "What if I fall?" The answer came, "If you trust in human law and fall, you'll get hurt; if you trust in God's law and fall, you'll always be caught by a golden net."

I have had to let go of many security trapezes since then, and I have discovered that this is consistently true. Solutions, support, money, people, opportunities—they always arrive somewhere during the free-fall. They haven't always arrived when my ego thought they should, and they've rarely taken the shape my preconceived ideas would invent. But I always see in retrospect that they arrived perfectly timed and packaged.

I want to share an experience that underlined this for me. At the end of 1987 I received a check that I had planned to use for income while I wrote this book. Instead I entered a long and physically painful process that rendered me all but helpless for five months. Out of work and with my body acting out mysterious symptoms no one could diagnose, I really had to let go of everything but my faith. Daily, even hourly, I affirmed that there was only God. I felt that if I ever acknowledged there was any other power, I would lose my faith.

The money I had received lasted through this period. But of equal—perhaps even greater—importance, people came into my life in the most astounding way. Not only was my mother available, but two friends were both between jobs (in itself a powerful "coincidence") and literally took over the endless tasks that everyday life demands and sickness accentuates. They cooked, cleaned, ran trips to the bank, the store, the doctor. They became my nurses, secretaries, message therapists, all-around supports. Another angel-friend I had known only casually up to that point appeared. Working on a degree at a local university, she gave over her spare time in order to take on numerous tasks that persisted for over a year as I slowly regained my strength.

Throughout this passage, whenever there was a need, it was met. My editor was concerned about me, not about deadlines.

My publisher never once pressured me. When the closing on the new house presented a financial surprise, a friend was there to help. Whenever the pain was severe, a healer was there. Throughout the course of my strange symptoms my doctor was careful, intuitive, and kind. When I was close to discouragement, a letter of support would arrive. Many times during the passage I would receive letters from people in different parts of the country and even foreign countries who had no idea anything was wrong but felt concern and the need to write. Several had dreamed about me.

My point is not to outline all that I learned from that passage. It was a potent and rich classroom, full of lessons in receiving and surrender, gratitude and compassion. But above all it showered me with affirmations of faith. The lessons I was scheduled to experience couldn't be avoided, but I received all I needed to support me in the process.

CLARITY OF INTENTION

Spiritual wisdom advises us to be very clear and uncompromised about our commitments, reminding us, "You can't have it both ways."

There are a lot of ordinary ways to check out our own double messages to the universe. We say we really want to work for world peace. So who in our world are we fighting? We say we're committed to cleaning up the world. But is our own nest a mess? We say we're committed to bringing beauty into the world. Have we filled our surroundings with objects that offend us?

The signature of everything we believe, and are therefore really committed to, is in everything we do. Our environment is a constant feedback program. And sometimes having a garage sale is the most conscious thing we can do!

Focused intent is a law of energy—not a sentimental notion. It can be used, and often is, to serve selfish and cruel purposes. Those who seem to succeed in seemingly negative ways often do so because they are one-pointed. No matter what someone else thinks about how they use it, these people have developed the power of the single eye. It doesn't even occur to them that they could fail. They attract the raw energy to feed their desires as easily as a magnet draws iron filings.

There was a story of the man who took his son out into a sunlit meadow and held a magnifying glass over one spot until a fire started, teaching him how the power of focused attention can gather energy.

Just the opposite often happens with well-intentioned people who really want to serve the good but are ambivalent. The more we want to understand, the more we bring ourselves face-to-face with the oldest of our shared conflicts. And power is near the top of the list. So is money.

MONEY AND POWER

We seem to have confused the warning against worshipping money with the ability to use money as a resource. Nearly every devotee I know who aspires to grow spiritually—including myself—has had to wrestle with questions around money. Our spiritual histories are full of directives to renounce money in favor of God.

One of the points of renunciation is to destroy addictions and illusions. There is no question that money can be very addictive and a potential identity trap.

Yet denouncing money can be as big a trap as the allure of money itself. It puts money aside and says "you are not of God." I am suspicious that any resource that we exclude from wholeness is less about God and more about the polarization that grows out of our fears. We have historically assigned money to one moral polarity or the other. We have either thought that having money was a sign of God's blessings or that it reigned supreme as the arch enemy of spirituality. Instead of being neutral, perceiving money as a human creation, the agreed-upon symbols of value, we have set money up as a battleground between Spirit and matter. If your commitment requires money, it will be magnetized to you if you are uncompromised in your belief about what you need. You can also block money if you subconsciously think you don't deserve it.

At this point you have to ask yourself some crucial questions:

Can I handle money with responsibility but indifference?
Do I truly see money as just another resource—like my talents, time, or energy?
Do I try to leave God out of my personal finances and go it alone?
Do I really believe that who I am is not a question of how much money I have?
Is my identity clear enough as a spiritual being that I can afford to have money?
Do I secretly suspect that somebody out there is either blessing or denying me money?
Are my attitudes toward money really mine, or have I merely internalized others' opinions?

When you are committing to your highest purposes, a great deal of power may begin moving through you. It's not your personal power, it's universal power—God's power, if you will. But it does come through you personally. I know a teacher who says that people are a lot more willing to be God's love on Earth than God's power. Ask yourself:

Is it okay for spiritual power to act through me?

Does some part of me find that not okay?

Am I afraid of it?

Do I fear I will misuse it?

Am I not worthy of it?

If my commitment takes me into a key position, that affects other people and makes changes, can my ego remain neutral about it?

As serious spiritual students, we have to resolve our personal ambivalence about money, power, and a number of other issues. And this can show up during a cycle of commitment. To fully anchor the commitment we are being led to make, we need to develop a clear focus—the single eye.

A good technique for reinforcing a commitment is to do what a friend calls "making yourself at home" with it.

My friend is a singer, and she'd gone to New York with fame on her mind. Very soon she met a man, and they became good friends. When she told him that she knew exactly the record company she wanted to be with, he advised her to "make herself at home" in that company. So every day she imagined herself singing under the label of that company. She began to think of herself as one of their artists. She lived it and breathed it. And within a year she was signed by that company.

However there's a corollary to this story that's worth hearing. The record company couldn't find a property that suited her voice. She was legally bound to them, but she wasn't singing. It took her another year to get out of the contract and redirect her career.

This tale is a good example of focusing the single eye. Just let me offer a word of caution: Be very clear and careful about what you pray for, because you're likely to get it. Whatever you commit to is your prayer.

PRAYER, PATIENCE, AND POISE

Spiritual craftspeople pray. Our prayers are not something repeated listlessly, by rote. We form our prayers with the images
in our heads, the desires in our hearts, the intentions in our wills,
and the words of our mouth. When we worry, we are actively
praying for what we don't want to happen.

I've shared with a lot of people a prayer image I was shown
in Spirit a long time ago. The image was a balloon. What we
choose to pray for is the design of the balloon itself, it's shape,
color, and dimensions. The air in the balloon that lifts it is our
passion. Without genuine feeling involved, the balloon won't fill
up. Attached to the balloon are tethers made up of worry, fear,
and anxiety. If you hold on to them, you keep the balloon on
the ground. You must let go of the tethers for the balloon-
prayer to fly.

Not long after I first received the balloon-prayer image, I
heard the story of a little girl who lived in Florida who really
wanted to attend the Olympics. She was walking on the beach
when a balloon floated down that said, "Welcome to the 23rd
Olympiad."

VISUALIZING WHAT WE WANT

Consistently holding a desired image—visualization—is one of
the most powerful techniques we can develop. Visualization is
not a philosophical concept. It's a principle of using energy. It
can be used for good or for not-so-good. Either way what we
create will return to us.

When we actively use prayer images to support healing, we
must learn to pick the images carefully. I recall a frantic telephone call I received in the middle of the night. A young man
was burning up with a fever of 104 degrees Fahrenheit, and all

of his vital signs were erratic. The first task was to align myself to Spirit and seek an image that would help stabilize him. I debated about the image to use in this case, because I know how powerful images can be. Certainly his body was running a fever for a reason. I decided to focus my image looking over the shoulder of a doctor toward the young man sleeping peacefully. The doctor was writing the words "All systems stabilizing."

As I attuned to him and used this image, I was aware that his parents were surrounding the young man with fear energy. I suggested that they remind themselves of the potency of their own energy, and the unlimited power within the boy and go back to the bedside sending pure love and reassurance. Within a half hour the boy's fever had dropped to 101, and within an hour his vital signs began to stabilize.

People who use visualization as a support for cancer treatment and other life-threatening illnesses have discovered the importance of careful image selection. For example, after Carl's cancer diagnosis he began visualizing the cancer cells being killed by soldiers. It was only after work with his therapist that he realized this could not be effective for him as he had been a committed pacifist for a long time. His subconscious would not easily welcome a warlike image. He settled on using an image of the cancer cells being rescued from their path of destruction by angels and taken to a place of reeducation where they could become "good" cells. It worked for him, and he is convinced that his belief in the principle and his consistency in practicing it positively supported his medical treatment and cure.

I know a man who wanted a new car. He pinned a picture of a blue Chevrolet to his bulletin board. He actually wanted a red Toyota, but he couldn't find a picture of one, so he assumed that the picture of any new car would do. And he began to affirm that the new car was coming. He had no doubt that it would, nor any hang-up about deserving it. His prayer was answered when he topped his company's sales charts and was rewarded with a new car—a blue Chevrolet.

I'm cautious about repeating stories such as these, for they oversimplify complex dynamics. Obviously we live in a consensual reality jointly created by all of us who live in it, and not everyone is holding the same image. We have to be deeply committed and unambivalent in order to consistently feed an image that is unlike our partner's, our family's, or our culture's.

Nevertheless if we can't see the image in our minds, we can't create it. A peaceful world, for example, has to be visualized by a number of us long enough to replace our ingrained belief that war is inevitable. That takes real commitment.

Visualization is not as easily mastered as it might seem. The brain stores memory in clusters. Put one item off the cluster, and the rest of the memories are triggered. To visualize well one has to stop that process and hold the mind to the one image you want. Left unattended, the mind, which is often compared to an energetic monkey, will run wild with its own agenda.

TAMING THE MONKEY

As an exercise in taming the monkey, select a simple object you'd like to visualize, something like the face of a clock. Before you begin, decide exactly, in as complete detail as you can manage, what the clock will look like. Once you decide, don't change it. Then relax, breathe slowly, and image your clock.

At the first glimmer that the "monkey" is about to take over and change the face of the clock, drop the image. Don't attack the "monkey" or grit your teeth and fiercely attempt to hold on to the image of the clock. Just gently withdraw any mental attention from the distraction—think of gray nothingness for a second—then, just as gently, reimage the clock.

It takes patience to seed a new idea in the subconscious, and patience is an acquired skill. It's built on faith. For a period of time after we make our commitment we're not likely to see as many results from our new choice as we do evidence of the old patterns. But don't be seduced by the past or by appearances. The laws of energy will work. We simply have to believe in them and patiently feed our new commitment with positive images, desires, and words.

Never underestimate the power of words. They are one of the main ways in which we build a new reality. Words instruct our subconscious. When we say we want one thing and reinforce its opposite with careless words, we totally confuse the subconscious. All sacred scriptures emphasize the importance of the word. "You shall decree a thing, and it shall be established unto you," (Job 22:28) seems to sum it up.

To *affirm* something means "to make firm." We can affirm our good or affirm our negatives. When we affirm what we do want and quit talking about what we don't, we're making firm in the ether the good that we desire.

Even inanimate objects respond to our blessing rather than our curse. I recall my freezer being fixed once by a repairman. When I asked him what he did, he said he talked to it: "Ain't nothing but a bunch of molecules, you know."

We are creating a new prototype for ourselves with our new commitment. And like all prototypes, it will seem strange, even awkward at first, and it will probably have a lot of glitches that must be worked out. At this point it's easier to say "This is just the way I am" than to say "This is the way I choose to be."

IMAGING PEACE ON EARTH

Many people across the world are acting as prototypes now for humanity. As agents of change, they are challenging even the most cherished myths about what humans are. Every time one of us makes a commitment to a new possibility, it is communicated instantly to all of us. However, it takes time for the new ideas even to be recognized.

We know from the findings of neuroscience that the brain functions like a computer that uses "neuron microchips." These individual cells function in a complex network of interdependence. It is the network of the neurons working together, not each individual cell, that is critical for optimum functioning.

The implications are staggering if we consider that each of us is a neuron in the planetary brain. The child in Bangladesh is a cell in our brain; so is the stock broker on Wall Street and the prisoner of conscience in Central America. And so are you. Your thoughts are equivalent to a neuron firing information about reality to the global brain. The direction of our evolution depends on how we act together to form new patterns, new myths of reality, new programs that can recognize life in new ways. Once again we encounter Dr. Rupert Sheldrake's fields of morphic resonance. As he says, "When one thing forms, a crystal, for example, or any animal learns a new behavior, it will influence the subsequent learning or formation of all other crystals or animals of the same kind."

The point at which oneness is recognized as the unifying ground for all life is expressed by physicist David Bohm as the field of "enfolded order." By contrast, all that we see and recognize as individual objects and identities are "unfolded order."

Anyone who desires to bring harmony, peace, and love into the Earth needs to learn to move personal awareness to that place of "enfolded order." To do this is to move beyond the appearance of separateness. Time and space are meaningless, because there is no here and there, no yesterday or tomorrow. There is only here and now. We blend with the beingness of someone living in Japan or Australia at that level as easily as we can our dearest friend or next-door neighbor.

211

MEDITATION: THE PLACE OF
INNER CONNECTEDNESS

For anyone seeking alignment with the spiritual self, meditation of some sort is essential. Meditation is often characterized as listening to God, while praying is talking to God. During meditation, awareness shifts from preoccupation with the choppy surface waves of our lives to the deeper rhythms and currents moving within us, gradually leading us to that place of connectedness with all life.

Meditation is not about seeing pictures and hearing voices; it is rarely a light-and-power show. Meditation attunes our outer self to our inner self so that we become aware of how God speaks to us in all things.

Paramahansa Yogananda once said, "The wise man understands that even though mortal life is a dream, it contains dream pains. He adopts scientific methods to awaken from the dream." Meditation is a scientific method.

There are dozens of techniques that have grown out of as many approaches to spiritual science. If you don't meditate now, I would suggest that you search around for the method that resonates with you. Remember, the law of attraction is always working. If you sincerely want to find the methods that are right for you, frame that desire in your heart, mind, and intention. If you are clear about your request, you'll hear about a group, or the right book will fall into your hands.

Once you find the techniques that work for you, stick with them. Your subconscious will begin to cooperate and support you if you are consistent. Remember, you're not seeking something outside yourself. As mystic Thomas Merton once observed, "We have what we seek. It is there all the time, and if we give it time, it will make itself known to us."

Through meditation you come to understand that you are indeed "in the world but not of it." Your incarnation will pass, but you—the true you, the you that is made in the image of

God, the you that is connected to all life—will not pass. Once you know you are not the roles you play, an interesting phenomenon occurs: You begin to play them with greater love and skill. Your spirit is certainly "heavenly," but your assignment is planet Earth. And we need you.

We do not value the world less because we see its transitory nature. If anything, we come to value it more, but in a different way—as the holy expression of life. A rain forest being destroyed is not just one more dire ecological statistic—it's a cathedral being desecrated. Wolves and tigers, egrets and whales are not merely lower species, whose worth can be arrogantly debated—they are valued participants in Earth life. And the extravagant diversity of human creativity is not to be feared; it is to be celebrated, protected, honored.

The question then becomes not how do I save the world, but how do I serve it? I have a friend who said she was worried about saving the world and went into a meditation. In her words, "God said to me, 'You just teach the people I send to you; I'll save the world.'"

Early in our spiritual journey, we think we just want to finish what we have to do and leave. But by the time we've done it, we are so filled with love, we wouldn't think of leaving as long as we can be of help to those still in the dark. It's sort of like a cosmic Catch-22. Of course—22 is a master number.

The story goes that Abraham Lincoln ordered his buggy driver to stop so that he could remove a thorn from the foot of a pig he saw limping down the road. The driver was much impressed, but Lincoln told him, "The thorn was in my heart."

During this intense time of purification on the Earth, we have to learn to use our commitment with great care. No spiritual tradition suggests that we be naive. My Indian friend tells me, "Wear your moccasins." Middle Easterners suggest, "Trust God and tie your camel." And the Bible advises us to be "wary as a serpent and harmless as a dove."

Some of Yogananda's devotees used to resist his advice that they lock their cars when they were attending services at the Self-Realization Center in Los Angeles. One night every car in the parking lot was burglarized, and everyone complained to Yogananda. "How could this happen?" they protested. "Everyone is God."

"Yes," was his answer, "but not everyone knows that he is God."

A Master was teaching all the animals in the jungle to be nonviolent. The snake was trying very hard to become conscious, so he took the advice to heart. When the other animals figured out that the snake was nonviolent, they began to give him a hard time. The poor snake returned to the Master all bruised and hurting. "I don't understand, Master. I really was nonviolent like you said and just look at what has happened to me." To which the Master responded. "I told you to stop biting; I didn't tell you to stop hissing."

It takes a lot of poise to create an environment of new possibilities. It takes patience to redirect the forces that have fueled ancient routings in our brains about war and competition and about seeing "the other" as enemy.

It takes poise to remain, as someone has said, "as steady as a seagull in a storm" during the turmoil of planetary change.

EXERCISE: CLAIMING YOUR POWER TO CREATE

I usually call this exercise "Making Yourself at Home." To achieve something, you have to be very clear about what you want to create and very, very consistent with the images and feelings you are feeding your subconscious. Getting clear does not mean vague, wishful daydreaming. Rather it's very specific and involves all of your senses—seeing your vision, tasting it, embracing it in every way, and last but far from least, having total faith in your ability to create it.

When you have decided exactly what it is you want to create, then ask yourself some basic questions. Be very honest with your answers.

• Am I willing to give up the payoffs, negative though they may have been (such as remaining a victim)?

• Will this choice I am making be harmful to anyone else? (The question is not whether others will like it or not, but whether it will create harm.)

• Am I willing to commit to this with my thoughts, my feelings, and my physical choices?

• Have I examined and accepted the foreseeable consequences of what I am about to create?

When you have satisfied yourself that you've answered these questions to the best of your ability, then make yourself at home with your vision by writing the experience as if it already exists. Use the present tense. How does it look, feel, taste in every way? Make it as alive and vital as you possibly can.

For example, suppose you want to lose weight. Not only do you want to have an image of yourself—perhaps in a skinny little dress or participating in sports you couldn't do before—but you want to feel slim too. You actually want to experience the emotions and attitudes of being the size you want to be. You might begin by writing, "Today I'm hopping out of bed feeling really good. I catch a glimpse of myself in my teddy and think, Girl, you are looking good! I do my exercises easy as pie. It's so good to feel my muscles responding. I do five extra knee bends with no problem. Breakfast is delicious—I now actually prefer healthy food. I can feel my body's appreciation, and my energy stays really high all day. I slip into my new outfit, which (you might want to describe in detail) I had a great time shopping for and having so much to choose from because so many things fit! I head for work. I get a giggle over all the people flirting with me now, but to tell the truth, I really don't need that. I just like the fact that I'm in charge of my own life. I'm actively creating what I want, not just reacting."

A note of warning: Be careful how you use your power to create, because there's a good chance you'll get what you ask for. When you're practicing how to manifest what you want, it's important to go over every detail and possibility carefully. For example, when you begin to lose weight, you'll have to deal with all the emotional and self-image issues that created the weight in the first place. If the weight was tied to family myth, or self-protection, or avoidance of your sexuality—whatever the reason—it will have to be addressed. Otherwise you might find yourself sending ambivalent messages to the subconscious. Then the messages will cancel each other out and frustrate you. If you're going to change something, that change has to cover the motivations behind the original choices. Creating conscious change is about personal awareness at all levels.

EXERCISE: DEVELOPING LOVING DETACHMENT

I recommend that you commit yourself to six weeks of daily practice of this exercise for it takes a while to establish a new program in the subconscious. Altogether these practices take only a few minutes each day, but their effectiveness is cumulative.

1. The first step begins as soon as you wake up. While still in bed or as soon as you can function, close your eyes, take a few deep breaths of Light, and affirm the following:

I am a Being of Light, daughter (son) of the Mother-Father-God.
This day, only that which is for my highest good shall come to me.
Only that which is Light shall go out from me.
Thank you, Mother-Father-God.

This may seem simplistic, but it affirms many basic and powerful principles. To affirm that you are a Being of Light is to claim your true identity. In the purest state of Spirit, you are neither male nor female but a being that embraces both polarities. But in this life you are in either a female or a male body, and it is important to be proud of this incarnation, and equally important to claim that you are a son or daughter of the Divine.

When you decree that only that which is for your highest good will come to you, you are not announcing that nothing "bad" will happen. Rather you are acknowledging that—whether it is known or unknown to you—whatever happens is drawn to you for the best reasons, giving you an opportunity to learn. Affirming this helps eliminate any residual victim consciousness or the despairing sense that nothing has any purpose or meaning. It all does.

Next, you affirm that only Light shall leave from you. This means that you are taking responsibility for your own power to choose. The usual syndrome of automatic stimulus-response then becomes stimulus-attention-and-conscious-choice-of-response.

The last line—the acknowledgement of gratitude—is extremely important. Gratitude is an energy that unlocks the power of conscious change. Gratitude actually energizes your prayers and intentions.

2. Step 2 is about releasing people, one at a time, as you interact with them during the day. After an exchange has taken place with a person, mentally visualize that person in his or her own bubble of Light and you in yours as you state to yourself, "I release all energy connected to (the name of the person)." If the energy clings, that is, if you're nagging yourself about that person's problems or if the person is trying to hang onto you, go wash your hands and mentally make the affirmation again. This is not an unloving act. Rather it frees you to see more clearly the correct action to take in any given situation.

3. At the end of the day, shower. As you wash your body, imagine your entire auric field being cleansed of all the residue from the day. Just see all of it washing down the drain.

4. Finally when you get in bed, take the people,

events, and concerns of the day and, one at a time, place them on an Altar of Light. In this release you are giving them up to the highest part of your self to handle. To take them to bed with you is to claim them and tie them to you. Relationships, money, and work problems do not resolve themselves when we attempt to nag them into consciousness. Remember, worrying is praying for what you do not want.

If you will use this combination of steps for a few weeks, you will find that you are lighter, clearer, and more detached in the face of all challenges, and therefore more effective in your life.

STEP SIX:

The Purification

I must decide either to die authentically to my past or die unauthentically in a fixation on a past form that will make me stagnate.

—IRA PROGOFF

During purification all that went before seems like preparation. It is the time when all of the old is actually transformed. It is the letting go. It is different from resistance because it has less to do with being and more to do with confronting fragments of our psyche that haven't gotten with the new program yet. Issues of the old form are no longer being debated during purification; they are actually dissolved.

During this time, which can be the most painful and lonely part of the process, old issues and fears surface again and again to be fully cleansed. We find ourselves face-to-face with issues we were sure were completed. What we discover is that while we might have examined parts of the issues we were ready to handle during earlier stages of the process, now the psyche is fortified enough to transform them. We are often forced to learn nonresistance to the challenges we brought in to this life to resolve.

Purification demands total confrontation and transmutation. It is the time of dying to the old, of testing our faith in our new direction. When the fires of purification are trying us, it is well to remember they are holy fires that will burn away our past limitations.

GIVE IT UP, GAIN IT ALL

During an interview a writer was asked if he liked to write. He hesitated a moment and then answered, "I love to have written."

Most of us feel that way about this cycle of conscious change. We love to have been purified. The process itself is not fun. The important thing to remember is that purification is a natural, predictable, healthy, and necessary part of the process. And, again, it is a process; it is not who you are. You are the being experiencing the process.

In a vision I found myself looking into a cross-section of a mountain. Running like lightning all through the vast black mound was the rich glow of gold. But it was packed hard in the dirt, while all around lay fool's gold in careless abundance. This image dissolved, and another appeared. I saw the gold, mined free of the dirt, being tossed into a raging fire. Then I saw a third image, a lump of gold, now pure but unformed, placed on an altar. There, blow by blow, hammers and chisels took the unshapened mass and made it into a goblet that glowed like the sun.

As the images danced before my inner eye, a soft voice said, "Be still and I will tell you what this means.

"You have walked a stark mountain wailing for your wealth. All the while the Earth beneath your feet waited for you to leave the outer world and seek the inner realms. Always the wealth is within. There you find your essence running through the dark dirt of your own materialism as a bright vein of truth. The first task is to mine your vein and beware the fool's gold that would tempt you with easy counterfeit.

"Through God's perfect alchemy, the fires of purification will burn away the lies. Be patient. God's fire is mercy. So, too, is the discipline that will shape and mold you into a pure vessel for holding Spirit. Within you lies the Grail whose mystery is that, as you empty it into the world, it is filled again and again.

"Remember," counseled the Spirit gently, "you are the gold,

not the process. Your search, your fires, your discipline are simply the means through which you become that which you have always been. It is an ancient, sacred way. Do not be discouraged when the fires melt your masks or when your inner Spirit disciplines you again and again. Rejoice. It means you have submitted and the glorious transmutation is working. Be gentle with yourself; be gentle with others. The Grail you create cannot be destroyed, and its sweet wines will quench your thirst forever."

I've seen many committed people become extremely discouraged during the purification cycle because they could not separate what they were experiencing from who they were. "What am I doing wrong?" they cry.

Nothing! Being in the purification stage means we're doing it right. It means we've grown enough, our egos are secure enough, to tackle another piece of unconsciousness.

The moment we choose to challenge the authority of a belief, we set in motion the energy that will lead to its death. As soon as we commit to a higher truth, the same principle of magnetism that reinforced the old belief will now begin to attract new experience and information, and it will also demonstrate where and how the old illusions are still present in our lives.

At first glance the purification cycle looks like resistance, but it is actually a very different dynamic. During the resistance stage we got to see everything that was standing in the way of our making the change. We were being helped to recognize our conflicts. This made us a perfect study in ambivalence until we experienced the awakening that helped us make the critical choices that led to commitment.

At this point purification burns away the past entirely. It frees us from any danger that our old patterns can hook us in again, and it prepares us for the full surrender that is to follow.

THE DISSIPATIVE UNIVERSE

We can take encouragement from a principle in physics discovered by Ilya Prigogine, a Nobel Prize winner in chemistry. He calls it the theory of dissipative structures. Dr. Prigogine sees nature as an open system in which all the parts are experiencing a continuous exchange of energy with the environment. In describing this theory, Marilyn Ferguson writes in the *Aquarian Conspiracy* that an open system is maintained by a continuous dissipation—consumption—of energy, "much as water moves through a whirlpool and creates it at the same time. . . . A dissipative structure might well be described as a flowing wholeness . . . highly organized but always in process."

The more complex a system is, the more energy it needs to maintain all of its many connecting points. This, in turn, makes it both continually subject to change and also threatened by change. However, this also means that the system has something new built in.

As energy moves through a dissipative structure, it creates disturbances. If they are minor, the system throws them off. If they're not so minor, then the number of adjustments that have to be made within the system increases. A large number of adjustments can shake up the whole system. If this happens, then all the parts have to renegotiate their contracts with each other and come together in a new pattern. But the really interesting part is that when they regroup, they do so at a higher order of being. Further the more complex the system becomes, the more likely it is to transform again. Human beings are, by their very nature, complex systems. During the purification cycle of change we get completely shaken up. *But once we regroup after the purification, our whole system will be functioning at a higher level.*

But first comes destruction—the first step in creativity. If I want to build a new house on the site where another now exists, the first thing that has to go is the old house. If a person doesn't know what's going on, this looks like wanton destruction. But this is the same explosive force that creates new land from the lava spewed by an erupting volcano.

EMPTY TO BE FILLED

By fits and starts, piece by agonizing piece, we give up the prized ego possessions of our personality to our larger selves. We gradually learn to die to all that we once thought we were in order to claim all that we are. In the words of Reshad Field, in *Footprints in the Sand*: "You don't die until you live, and you don't live until you die. Once you have died to yourself there is only the present moment and you are born into Eternity."

On the heels of a major revelation life has a way of settling back into being very daily. During one of those "daily" periods in my life, I went on a spiritual retreat at a lovely Catholic convent. I arrived with all sorts of preconceived ideas: *Now* I would not be so busy; *now* my mind would be clear; *now* Spirit could speak to me. I had made an appointment!

With great anticipation, I went to the meditation room and sat down. And I began to cry. And cry. For two days I cried. They were strange tears, as there was no specific unhappiness I was mourning. I felt no sense of Presence, no overshadowing, nothing. Just tears.

Finally, by the second evening, I was cried out. Puffy-eyed and blank, I just sat in the meditation room. Then, gradually, I felt a growing warmth around me. Peace settled over me and I heard from Spirit the loving words "One whom I would fill, I must first empty."

A great deal of the process of remembering our wholeness, and then living it, is just about that—emptying, letting go, dying.

"I want the truth," we cry to God.

"Fine," says God, "first you have to die."

"Well, actually I had something a little less painful in mind," we reply.

Like the youthful Saint Augustine, we tend to pray, "Lord, make me chaste—but not just yet."

During all of our rites of passage we are celebrating funerals as well as births—or, as an Icelandic friend says, "futurals." A child first going to school is dying to an earlier way of living in order to be born to another. Young parents die to their own childhood. A move to another city, a promotion at work, a retirement—in each case, something is given up in order to gain.

Where there is death there is grief. No matter how much we may be committed to a new direction, part of us will grieve for that which must be left behind. One of the most intense griefs I have ever endured was when the teacher who had been with me in Spirit for the first seven years of my work "promoted" me and I no longer had his presence consciously with me. I was only able to change my perception that I had lost something invaluable when a friend reminded me, "He hasn't gone anywhere. Where is he going to go? There's only one universe."

It's not very trendy to talk about the dying part of change, even in New Consciousness circles. In the West we grow up believing in our ability to fix things instantly: "I see it, I've got it—what's next?" In the East students are taught to respect and accept the purification stage in transformation.

Theoretically, of course, instant transformation is possible. But most of us don't see a truth and become it in one move. Most of us tend to cling to our self-images and addictions pretty tenaciously.

As long as we are holding any need to feed an old addiction, the universe allows us to do so. It just continues to flow and fill up the patterns we have willed into place no matter how off the mark they are. However that ceaseless filling of our creations, good and bad, is a gift of love—not a withholding of Grace. Part of the Grace is being given the unconditional privilege of becoming conscious.

New wine does not go into old wineskins. The old wine-skins have to go—whether they are habits, mind-sets, or emotional patterns. And they don't usually go gracefully. And yet, loss by loss and death by death, we learn to strip away the lies we've accumulated about ourselves.

It all seemed so easy when we made the commitment. "Just do it," as the Nike ad said. But we usually have to go through a lot of complexity in order to arrive at simplicity. And it frequently gets worse before it gets better.

The emptying process can be grinding, tedious, and painful. It can go on for years and show up in a thousand unexpected ways. Difficult marriages, long-term illnesses, bankruptcy—these are the potential raw material of long-term initiation. Dr. Dianne Connelly says our pain is like a monastery bell that summons us again and again "until we attend to the old familiar with a new wonder. Our lostness demands we find our way home."

Scholar and Mystery school initiator Jean Houston writes that these "sacred wounds" are "an invitation to your renaissance." Citing Saint Paul's thorn in the side, Job's boils, and the crippled leg of Aesculapius, Greek demigod of healing, she calls such wounding "soulmaking."

Purification does not happen instantly because we've chanted a dozen mantras or recited three Hail Marys. It can become what C. G. Jung called "a passion of the ego." We do a serious disservice to each other when we don't acknowledge that purification is real and inevitable during change. We sentence each other to lonely and confused passages when we clobber each other with such clichés as "Never think a negative thought"; "You created this reality"; "It's just your karma coming down." However true these may be, they're not only insensitive responses to someone suffering a cleansing, they probably reveal one's own deep fear of the dying part of the transformation process. Part of the fear is that maybe we won't know who we are if we let go. And yet we often have to let go on one level in order to discover what it is we really need to let go of.

Often when we let go of something we discover what was in hiding and *really* needs to go. I know a well-educated, sophisticated woman whose spiritual life was at a standstill until she realized, much to her surprise, that she was holding on to a stern, patriarchal image of God. Her own father was a minister, and her unconscious fear was that if she let go of that constricting image of God, she would be abandoning her father.

An ancient Zen maxim advises, "Grab hold lightly; let go tightly."

One reason that the purification cycle is so painful is that we've already had the awakening that assured us the shift was right and during commitment we've worked hard to make it happen. Yet when the purification starts, it can seem as though we've failed. It's easy to get caught in frustration. "What do you want from me, God? Get off my back!"

Mystical traditions from around the world are full of stories of the "dark night of the soul," where the fully committed disciple feels abandoned in the battle with the inner enemies.

Once we commit to living a greater piece of our truth, we can't get away with the same things we did before. We are literally, not symbolically, shifting from one octave of energy to another, and all the stuff that was unruffled in the lower octave is upset in the higher. It simply won't vibrate there. Purification kills off anything from the old form that can't vibrate within the new, more complex structure. The energy around the old form has to be fully transformed. It has to be re-formed.

JOHN'S STORY

John is a doctor in his late thirties. He attended a workshop in which I was discussing this model. And this is how it came up for him in one of his changes.

His *form* had been that the purpose of women was to serve men. That's what all the women in his family did.

His *challenge* came when he started dating and realized that all the women that appealed to him were bright and creative and not at all interested in serving men.

The *resistance* came when he realized that even though he was attracted to women whom he felt were his intellectual equals, he was intimidated by them. After a few dates with a liberated woman he would hurry back to the safety of a woman who said "Yes, sir" to his every request.

His *awakening* came when he met Susan and fell in love. Susan was studying to be a doctor and she had every intention of fulfilling that goal.

His *commitment* came when he married Susan.

His *purification* came through the daily life of marriage. Even though he was totally dedicated to Susan, he had to face the fact that he still had a lot of assumptions about what a wife should or should not do. He told me that most of them were unconscious. Sometimes they would show up when major decisions had to be made, such as career moves, investment choices, and other areas he'd grown up believing were male choices. Other times the old attitudes were more subtle and insidious—resentments over her working late, having to share chores around the house, not having, as he put it, "the last word on everything."

It took several years in therapy to work through the purification passage. He said that many times he wanted to quit and that if either of them had been less committed to each other, they would never have made it through the purification. But they did, and when he reported this, he said that now he couldn't imagine being in the intimacy of marriage without an equal partner. All of his beingness, his new form, is now surrendered to his current belief in an equal relationship.

After purification we actually become the new belief. It becomes our outbreath, a "given" in our view of the world. At an earlier stage, while we might have recognized our inner "enemies"—those habits that keep our old forms intact—they probably just went into retreat when we transferred authority to another belief. During purification these old habits have to be routed out. More than that, in order to transform they have to die.

But it must not be an act of violence. An old addictive pattern isn't transformed by brutalizing it. In fact that only energizes it. When we grit our teeth and swear we'll never have anything more to do with gambling, our mother's prejudices, people who are bad for us, then all we can think about is gambling, our mother's prejudices, and people who are bad for us. The more fiercely we need to insist that we won't ever do a thing again, the greater the likelihood it's still inside, waiting. Until these habits are transformed, one way or another they'll keep on resurfacing. Sometimes they show up in strong likes and dislikes.

One of the ways you'll know a habit is still there is when you find yourself getting very emotional when you see your "old" behavior in others. You may not be showing it, but you've still got it. The energy that has locked in those addictions and keeps them in place hasn't shifted at all. You may elect to get rid of the symptoms, but if you don't go fully into the causes, they'll just wait to express themselves in other, more devious, ways.

THE BODY IS A PRINTOUT
OF OUR BELIEFS

Years ago I recognized that if I was frustrated when things weren't moving fast enough to suit me, I would accept the delays on the surface very well. But my body told the truth—I held the tension in my thighs, buttocks, and lower calfs. I didn't understand why my body would express in that particular way, but I did know that the body prints out emotional and mental habits. Over a period of time—during sessions with a body therapist and in personal meditations—I sent my subconscious the message that I would really like to understand this tendency.

Several random memories came together to form the pattern. I recalled a remark my father had made about the woman who baby-sat me during the day for the first eighteen months of my life. He said, in an offhand manner, that he'd felt she was too strict. Then I recalled an image that I had dreamed. In the dream I was on a carpet and frustrated because every time I would go to the edge, I would be pulled back. When I told my mother, she was quite surprised. She said that this woman who cared for me trained me not to go beyond the edge of the carpet. When I put that together with my knowledge of my Sagittarian fire energy that wants to explore, the pattern became clear.

I began to work with that information, first of all by seeking to understand the pattern. As a baby I'd had no understanding of limits and was very frustrated by the ones imposed upon me. The tension held in my crawling muscles was the symbol of this frustration—I'd encoded that emotional response right into my physical body. But the habit of holding tension in these muscles didn't stop just because I recognized it.

So the next step was to pay careful attention to the stimuli that triggered the old response. The second I would feel frustration, I would stop whatever I was doing and breathe deeply into those muscles. Then I reprogrammed the crawling stage by visualizing the whole scene, only this time seeing myself crawling all over the room.

The most important step was forgiving the woman who had baby-sat me, as I knew I'd probably internalized my frustration with her as well. It took a couple of years of paying attention and reprogramming to change the pattern. But I no longer find those muscles tightening in response to frustration.

It is good to remind ourselves that our spirit, our mind, our emotions, and our body all function along one continuum. There are different frequencies on this continuum—from the very high rates of the Spirit to the slower wave patterns of the physical—but they all operate on one continuum. Anything that shocks or traumatizes us at any point along the frequency range, is felt up and down the whole continuum. It is experienced instantaneously without regard to whether the shock was "real" or not. What matters is that you believe it is real.

When a trauma—either real or imaginary—occurs, we tend to lock that trauma into a reacting pattern at the age at which it occurred. That part of us can't grow. It's blocked. When something happens years later that reminds us of the original experience, we react the way we did at the age the shock originally occurred. So at thirty-five we can suddenly find ourselves reacting to a threat like a three-year-old.

I think of all the "good people" I've seen who are sick with their own repressed rages and frustrations: seventy-year-old Martha, whose artistic talents found no channel into the world, the blocked energy pooling into painful crystals in her shoulders, wrists, and elbows; forty-six-year-old Alan, who believed "big boys don't cry" and whose body suffers from chronic sinus headaches because he still grieves for a mother lost in childhood; thirty-year-old Barbara, who eats her way into obesity in a futile attempt to get the nurturing she never had.

Eileen requested healing work on a ulcer. As I worked with her, I saw a pattern of jealousy that originated in childhood. She had an older sister who was very beautiful. She was reprimanded for having jealous feelings in childhood and instead of dealing with them, swallowed them. Her storage place for denied feelings was her stomach. She grew up to project those feelings onto all beautiful women. As the world is full of lovely women, she was constantly feeding her fear. The result was an ulcer.

There's an interesting corollary to this story. I didn't hear from her for months. And then she called with the accusation "My ulcer is back!" When I asked, Had she gone into therapy?

Had she forgiven herself, her sister, her family? Was she using any of the techniques and affirmations we'd discussed, there was silence, then she admitted she had done nothing. Of course the ulcer was back. She had not been willing to clear out, to purify, the old belief that had led to the ulcer in the first place.

I want to be clear that while my experience has taught me that all beliefs will, in time, manifest in the body, we don't know exactly where and how this will occur. I don't think we can generalize beyond a certain point; people are too complex for that. As in all aspects of growth, we have to know ourselves and our own predispositions.

When the old patterns are being released, it can upset familiar physical habits and rhythms. It's a good rule of thumb to assume that when we're releasing in our mind and emotions, our body is going to act out. Drinking lots of water, eating high-fiber foods, cleansing with saunas or steam, sweating through exercise—all this helps keep your organs of elimination in top shape, and this facilitates the process that can help get us through this trying period without getting sick.

LOVING OUR DARKNESS

The path of conscious change embraces all of our experiences, both good and bad. The more we expand toward our fullness, the more acutely we feel the parts of self that are in fear. When the sun is bright at high noon, the shadows are deeper, more clearly defined.

Jung heightened our awareness of the shadow side of our nature that we often deny. In *The Archetypes and the Collective Unconscious* he said, "The shadow personifies everything that the subject refuses to acknowledge about himself and yet is always thrusting itself upon him directly or indirectly—for instance in inferior traits of character and other incompatible tendencies."

He later comments in his autobiography, *Memories, Dreams, Reflections*, that "the conflict between the opposites can strain our psyche to the breaking point, if we take them seriously or if they take us seriously. . . . If all goes well, the solution, seemingly of its own accord, appears out of nature. Then and then only is it convincing. It is felt as 'grace.' "

Every time we accept another part of ourselves, we open ourselves to receiving more Grace. It is an ever-present fountain of light flowing unconditionally. The problem is, thirsty and wanting, we often sit with beggars' cups beside sacred waters and judge ourselves and others unworthy of partaking.

Transformation is not possible with denial. Denial is a choice to remain unconscious. But it doesn't change the magnetizing effect of the old beliefs. Whether we admit to them or not, our beliefs about reality are shaping the reality we experience. They set up our expectations. All of the Twelve Step programs for dealing with alcohol and drug addictions have as a primary step admitting that the addiction exists. Naming the "demon" is the first step in liberating ourselves from it.

Anna was a lovely young woman who came to counseling with one question: She felt blocked in her spiritual life and had no idea why. As I attuned to her, I became aware that she was newly pregnant. She giggled and confirmed that it was true. Then I was overwhelmed with the message that she was holding tightly onto guilt about an abortion she'd had when she was young. That was the block in her subconscious. Even though she was happily pregnant at this point, she had not let go of the aborted pregnancy. She unconsciously felt she had committed a great offense against Spirit. Until she faced and eliminated the guilt, all of her spiritual exercises were like pressing the accelerator with the brakes on.

In Dr. Elisabeth Kübler-Ross's pioneering work on death and dying, her model of progression toward conscious dying begins with the state of denial. She maintains that one cannot work through the other states—anger, depression, bargaining, and finally acceptance—until denial that one is dying has been met and overcome. Further, she says, we don't really begin to live until we've faced our own mortality. Until we face death, all we're doing is spending a lot of energy avoiding it.

It takes a lot of energy to hold our defenses against the death of a shadow as well. There's a very big difference between denying a shadow and denying its authority over us. When we're denying the shadow, we might say, "I'm not afraid of being abandoned." But the fear of being abandoned is still operating unconsciously, perhaps sabotaging relationships in an I'll-do-it-to-you-before-you-can-do-it-to-me maneuver. Denying the authority of the shadow admits to its existence and defuses its power.

When identity has shifted from ego to Spirit, shadows become aspects of the self that need loving, not judgment. When we run from a shadow, we're giving it power over us. When we face and embrace it, we take back that power; we deny it authority. We learn, as novelist Nikos Kazantzakis said, "to gaze with undimmed eyes on all darkness."

Many times people in our environment are stand-ins for our own shadow. If we can't accept our own prejudices, it's a good bet we'll see them exemplified by the people around us. If you want to find out how skilled the ego is in justifying itself, try this exercise in self-honesty.

Make a list of every person you dislike, pinpoint what you don't like about them, and then for the sake of the exercise pretend that it's a quality within yourself. Suppose it is not their selfishness, rudeness, boorishness, or prejudices you can't tolerate but your own that you haven't accepted. (You might want to use the exercise "Meeting the Committee" (see page 184) for discovering who is assigned to be the villain in your drama.)

In Tibetan Buddhism, students are taught that a shadow can be dealt with in one of three ways: The student can transmute a lower vibrating energy (the problem) by generating enough intense higher energy to force change. Or the student can ennoble the problem, treating it as necessary. The third way is to move directly into the problem and allow the shadow to run its course. This allows the student to develop a part of self that just observes the whole thing with a higher and more expanded awareness.

HONESTY AND PATIENCE

The very act of accepting a shadow defuses its power; it no longer has the charge of an unknown force. The goal is to integrate our shadows, not to just make them go away. As a shadow returns to us in new and different forms, we grow familiar with it and eventually exhaust all it has to teach us.

A reasonably healthy human ego has a built-in defense system. If it tried to take on the full impact of some of our deepest fears at one time, it would self-destruct in terror. So the ego takes on only as much as it can integrate at any one time. When an old pattern reappears, it doesn't necessarily mean we've been avoiding it or that we're failing; it could mean we're ready to bite off another piece of it. This is the time to be very patient with ourselves. Patience is an affirmation of self-love. And self-love is a light to take into the darkness of fears—your fears and mine. I know that you're not going to be patient with my terrors if you're not patient with your own. Patience means that we consciously choose to release judgments of ourselves and others. Patience goes beyond admitting that change cannot be imposed from the outside. It releases the judgment that one can know what's right for another person in the first place. It gives birth to the detached compassion that says: "I am empathetic with your pain, and I release my judgments about why you are experiencing it."

Things are not what they seem. What seems tragic in appearance may actually be an important purification rite or an act of sacrifice for the larger good. Who would presume to judge the larger design of the sacrifice of a Martin Luther King, Jr., or a Mahatma Gandhi?

GRATITUDE AND RESTRICTION

Even the most restricting circumstance is grist for the mill. The restrictions we experience force us to pay attention to the refinements that need to happen before we grow any further. It is the protective control of the higher self.

In astrological symbology the planet Saturn represents the energy of restriction and form. Most people consider Saturn passages, which recur every twenty-eight years, to be tough and sobering. But Saturn is recognized by the spiritual student as both teacher and angel. It's through limitations that we are forced to experience our spiritual realities on the Earth plane. They hold the classroom in place until the lesson is fully learned.

The nervous system cannot handle higher energies until it has been prepared to do so. It would be like trying to bring 220 energy through 110 wiring. The equipment has to be refined, and that happens during purification. The restrictions we experience force our attention on the refinements that need to occur before we progress and stretch our systems any further. They provide the protective controls of the higher self.

I worked with two men who had had heart attacks within a few days of each other. One accepted what had happened. Naturally he didn't like it, but by surrendering to it—with an attitude not of futility but of nonresistance—he was able to use his will to support the healing process. He steadily improved. The second man couldn't let go of his resentment that this had happened to him. He continually argued with the reality his life brought. He was still mad when he died.

One of the keys that unlocks the purification process is grat-
tude. We should really thank all of the irritating people in our
lives. We need them. They show us clearly where the work lies.
Without them we would coast along in perfect self-deception.
Gandhi once said that the ally you must always seek is the part
of your enemy that knows what is right.

More than that, we should thank all of the people suffering
for us. As astrologer Liz Green put it in *The Outer Planets &
Their Cycles*, "At the moment all our family scapegoats, the
schizophrenics and the anorexics and the depressives, act out all
our collective pain while the rest of us get on blandly and free
of conflict. Look at those suffering AIDS, the child who is
abused, etc. and say thank-you thank-you for giving us the opportunity to see where we're off the mark, what's out of balance,
needs fixing."

On the surface being grateful for every shadow, limitation,
and negative person seems to be the prerogative of saints. But
it isn't. Gratitude is a choice that becomes a habit. It is a major
ingredient in the alchemy of transformation and is closely related
to love. Macrobiotic master George Ohsawa names seven levels
of happiness, and the highest level is named gratitude.

Gratitude creates a combustion of energy that powers our
living cells. That's why all spiritual traditions teach the importance of gratitude. It certainly isn't because the deity needs any
reassuring. Rather it's because when we're in a state of gratitude,
we're affirming our faith in our own highest good and denying
authority to the paralyzing, constricting energy of fear.

In his 1918 diary Herman Hesse tells of hearing two voices
in a dream. The first voice, which he perceived as that of parents
and teachers, encouraged him to avoid suffering. The second
voice, which seemed farther away, more like a "primal cause,"
reminded him that suffering only hurt because he feared it. "You
know quite well, deep within you that there is only a single
magic, a single power, a single salvation . . . and that is called
loving. Well, then, love your suffering. Do not resist it, do not

flee from it. Give yourself to it. It is only your aversion that hurts, nothing else."

COLLECTIVE SHADOWS

Pool all our shadows, and we populate the collective unconscious with all sorts of rejected bogeymen—rage, fear, hate, racial, and sexual prejudices. But your truth, fully lived, is a beacon in the collective shadow, like a lighthouse guiding us through a dark and stormy night. But first we have to obey the ancient adage: "One who would bear the light must first endure the burning."

The turmoil we're experiencing now on Earth has stirred up our shadows. We seem to be accelerating up another rung in the evolutionary spiral, and many of the old pieces of our shadow simply won't vibrate where we're going. We can't claim unity with exceptions; we can't honor the Earth and still allow it to be polluted; we can't talk about the Family of Man and disregard abuses to human rights.

Many prophecies tell us we are moving toward a Golden Age. And we are. But first we have to live through the purification that will prepare the way. In the 1990s and even into the second decade of the twenty-first century we will continue to experience the overlapping of two major states in our collective journey. Even as we are stretching toward the golden Aquarian vision, we will be pulled down into the unresolved and dying shadows of Pisces.

Astrologer Liz Green said in a lecture, "It may be that Aquarius will bring us the awareness that we are indeed part of a vast, interconnected life entity, both biologically and psychologically. But the awareness is going to force up everything in us which obstructs us from living our vision."

Living the vision and living in a dying age feel dangerous at times. Therefore now is when we have to keep reminding ourselves that we're in this passage together. And it's not who we are, it's what we're moving through.

FORGIVE AND BE FREE

There are very few rules that underpin all spiritual training. Forgiveness is one of them. It is not a luxury; it is a necessity.

We really know this. So why is it so hard to give up all those prejudices? To forgive all those people? I mean, after all, God, I'll forgive these ten, but that one—you know, I'm entitled! Do you really want me to forgive myself, wholly and completely? To accept Grace and not think I have to earn it? To just let it all go and accept what is?

Yes, yes, and yes!

The unforgiven people in our lives are living with us as intimately as our next breath. Moreover we're sharing this incarnation with them and will carry them with us into future incarnations. A teacher in Spirit once said to me, "Who you do not love says nothing about the other person. It only defines the boundaries of your understanding."

After years of counseling I realized how imperative forgiveness was and instructed my subconscious that I wanted anything and everything that needed to be forgiven to reveal itself to my outer mind. By this time I'd already been through personal therapy and was experienced in all kinds of growth processes, both spiritual and psychological. I knew I'd done my homework with the usual "biggies."

I couldn't believe what came out over the next few weeks after I made this request to clean house. One day I was washing dishes and, seemingly out of nowhere, I recalled my third-grade teacher. I had imagined that she didn't like me, and there was that old feeling again, just as strong as it had been when I was eight years old. A few days later I remembered a group of girls from the sixth grade and an incident when I was sure they were gossiping about me. That unhappy feeling returned with the memory.

This went on for weeks—random, completely forgotten incidents that seemed to be of no importance. Yet they were all unreleased bits and pieces from the past.

One at a time I took them through a process of forgiveness. Now I keep current. If I have so much as a testy moment with the car mechanic, I take him into a forgiveness process that same night.

The law of attraction is always working, and an unforgiven experience is a sure setup to attract more of the same. It takes a tremendous amount of energy to hold tight to an unforgiven act. Walking away from situations isn't enough. Oh, you can get away with avoidance, smoke screens, and rationalizations for a long time. But the unforgiven person comes back again and again, wearing a different name or personality, but demanding that you deal with the unresolved issues.

Although David is in his forties, he won't forgive the childhood absence of his father. He continues to attract and argue with nonsupportive male authorities in every job he's had to date. Sharon had a healthy sex life—until she was raped. Several therapists and much insight later, she is still bitter about her nightmare experience and continues to fuel it with her anger, seeing all men as potential threats. The Vietnam war is as alive for Mark now as the day he was shipped home, leaving an arm behind. When the memorial was built in Washington, he sneered at it, saying, "I'll never forget and I'll never forgive." He has decreed his own prison.

People caught in devastating circumstances seem to be victims, pure and simple. And if we are reading only one chapter of their book—they are. But we do not know the whole story; we cannot judge. We do not know what piece of the collective madness they have taken on for all of us. We can only be compassionate and support them in the difficult turnings in their paths and do what we can to change the environment for all of us.

But support is not the same thing as rescue. A rescue mentality makes a judgment. It says, in effect, "I know more than your soul does about what you need." Support offers compassionate help. It encourages those who have experienced passages to face them, to own their feelings, and to be patient with the healing until forgiveness is possible.

Anything unforgiven is held in the body, the emotions, the mind, and even the soul. Unreleased, it crystallizes, forming obstructions in the very pathways along which energy must flow. Given enough time to harden, it will result in sickness. I know one highly respected healer who begins his treatments with the question "Who or what haven't you forgiven?"

In time we will grow into an understanding of the role pain and disappointment have played in our lives. In the meantime, our capacity to break chains through forgiveness is not limited to just this lifetime. In the realm of consciousness everything is the present.

If a fear from another life is being fiercely held in consciousness, it might as well have happened this morning. In real time it did. One doesn't have to recall the specific incidents or people that set the fear in motion. The specifics have simply constellated around a core magnet. Eliminate the magnet—the fear—and there's nothing to hold the memories, and they disperse as night shadows do before the rising sun.

It can be difficult to see purpose with the rational mind, especially those events that we share as part of the larger human drama, such as war and famine. The ego perceives with a limited perspective and creates categories: This act can be forgiven; this one can't. Degrees of guilt are set on a sliding scale—a number-one sin, not too bad—a number-ten, unforgivable. Of course the scale changes. The sin of yesterday might be quite tolerable today.

Sam is a man in his mid-thirties who came to counseling

because he was constantly blocking his own success. The father of several children, he was a very hardworking person who truly aspired to live, in his words, "a life that counts."

As I attuned to him, I began to suspect that he had either had a homosexual experience or really wanted to have one, and this issue had to be addressed first. When I mentioned it, he very reluctantly admitted that he'd had such an experience, and he began to cry. He felt he had sinned and didn't deserve happiness.

As I prayed for guidance to help him, I began to see scene after scene of devastating horrors—war, tortures, refugee camps, disease, starvation. Yet everywhere I looked there was love offered in great waves of golden Light—love moving through the war, through the diseases, through all of it.

And then I saw scene after scene of life expressing its joy—new life being born, friends laughing, the green fields of summer. Everywhere I looked in the beauty, there was the same golden light of love.

And then I saw Sam standing there with his lover, and there was the same golden Light of love. The message was clear: There is nowhere that love does not exist.

Forgiveness isn't doled out like gold stars as rewards for obedience to a human interpretation of God's moral code. It was never withheld in the first place. Ask the universe to forgive you and the answer will probably be silence—you will receive the same golden Light of love that has always surrounded you. But once you're able to forgive yourself, you'll recognize this Light and accept it at last.

All of us experience guilt and shame over choices we have made. Much of it comes from having internalized the punishing voices of others. When we are off the mark (a good, simple definition for *sin*), the still, quiet voice of our own guidance will lead us—not judge us, just lead us. Shame can be used as a mirror for perceiving what needs purifying, and that usually means what needs forgiving.

An ancient Egyptian poet said it well in a poem entitled

"*Nuk Pe Nuk* (I Am That I Am)": "and Hell itself is but a dam that I did put in my own stream when in a nightmare."

The first step in forgiveness is to be clear about what and who needs forgiving. That may seem obvious, but it is sometimes very subtle. For example, you may have dealt with your grief but not with your anger over a parent leaving you in childhood. The subconscious may be keeping feelings of abandonment intact along with the energy of anger. Forgiveness can be just as easily given to one who has died as to one who is alive. Or maybe you had a "good" parent, and the child within you still resents him or her for not protecting you from the "bad" parent.

The next step in forgiveness is to examine the implications of the original hurt—milk the experience for all it's worth. How did it effect your life, attitudes, relationships, self-image? If you find that knot hard to untangle, love yourself enough to get a professional therapist or counselor to help. Whatever you do, don't give yourself a hard time if you are still brooding over petty events. Gentleness with yourself is part of the tincture of forgiveness.

Finally the decision has to be made to let it go. Awareness is a first step, but it is not forgiveness. I've known many people who could articulate very clearly the many reasons why they hated this or that, but they still hated. Anger and hurt do emerge during the analytical part of the process and must of course be owned. The next step is to completely dissolve all the energy around the pain with forgiveness.

EXERCISE: VISUALIZATION—THE STAIRWAY OF GOLDEN LIGHT

If you are having difficulty shifting your perspective, you might try the following imaging exercise:

Create a beautiful meadow in your mind and see yourself there with someone you're having difficulty forgiving. Don't deny your feelings. Just let them be whatever they are. As you look at the person, you might want to review all the unhappy circumstances of your relationship.

Now, turn around. See the golden stairway right behind you. Slowly begin mounting the first of seven steps. Be deliberate and conscious with each step. Feel the warmth that is enveloping you. As you move up each stair, the warmth grows.

Now, look up. At the top of the stairs see the radiant being whose hands are outstretched to you. As you near the top, this being reaches out to help you up the last part of the climb. As you stand there hand and hand, the being looks deeply into your eyes and then embraces you. You realize that everything you have ever done is known to this being and completely accepted. You are loved unconditionally. Allow yourself to accept this fully. Recognize the healing taking place.

As you step back from the embrace, see that you, too, are aglow with the golden Light. Now, turn and look down the stairs to the unforgiven person standing at the bottom. What does the person look like from here? Can you see the humanness, the vulnerability of this person?

Are you willing to share the healing that has just

been given to you? Then walk down the stairs, take the person's hands in yours, look into his or her eyes and, seeing everything, choose love with the simple words "I forgive you."

Such an exercise, sincerely done, is no fantasy. You are actually beginning to alter the energy between you and the other person.

Event by event, person by person, disappointment by disappointment, we set the alchemy of conscious change in motion. In the beginning we make the choice to release personal injustices. By practicing our spiritual crafts, we will in time be able to release the shadows in the collective mind until one day we, too, can say with total clarity, "Forgive them, they know not what they do."

In the meantime, leave them to heaven. Universal law will bring all things into balance in time.

EXERCISE: ALTAR OF FORGIVENESS

1. Select a place and time when you can be alone and quiet.

2. Sit comfortably, preferably with your spine straight, uncrossing your arms and legs to help create a free flow of energy. Relax your neck and shoulders. Breathe slowly and deeply into your abdomen until you feel yourself becoming very relaxed. Simply breathe away the tension on the exhale, and breathe in golden Light on the inhale.

3. Move your attention to your heart and begin breathing through your heart. Breathe in love . . . and breathe out love. Then mentally direct the next breaths to any part of your body that needs balancing. Next direct breaths of love to your emotional body, feeling them like cool, soothing breezes. Then to your mental self, sensing added clarity with each new breath.

4. Surround yourself with pure Light and tell yourself that all that follows is blessed by the Universal Christ and is for your highest good.

5. In your mind's eye create an Altar made of Light. Design this altar any way you like, knowing that it is made of the highest, purest substance in the universe. Your subconscious mind knows that an altar means sacrifice and release. The symbol is quickly communicated to your inner mind.

6. Place the person you have chosen to forgive on the Altar of Light. Visualize light moving into every cell in his or her form. Direct light from your heart to surround this person as you say:

"I forgive you for all transgressions, real or imagined, remembered or unremembered, from this lifetime or any other."

Now dissolve the total image in light.

7. Place yourself on the Altar of Light, seeing yourself bathed in light that you direct from your heart center. And say to yourself:

"I forgive myself for any negative energy I have held against [name of person you are in process of forgiving], real or imagined, remembered or unremembered, from this lifetime or any other."

Now dissolve the image of yourself completely in Light.

8. The last step is very important, for it is here that you express gratitude—the energy of empowerment. Say aloud or to yourself. "Thank you, Mother-Father-God."

9. And it is done. Gently bring your attention back to an alert state.

STEP SEVEN

The Surrender

*Since my house burned down, I now own a better view of the
rising moon.*

—MASAHIDE

*W*hen we die to the old, we create a vacuum for the new.
Nothing can be added to a space that is full. In the vacuum lies
the potential for all things. As one moves deeply into the last
stage of the Seven Steps of Conscious Change, the process of
integration begins. Through the alchemy of synthesis, the new
becomes one with our whole being. We no longer theorize,
anticipate, struggle, or debate. We know for a fact that we
have become what we aspired to. Within surrender lies completion, and with completion comes peace. The old form seems
as distant as another lifetime. There is a growing sense of detachment.

The surrender is the passage that teaches us to trust the Divine within, to have faith that we are being guided. The lower
will—my will—is given to the Higher will—Thy will. The Inner
Grail has been made ready for new wine, and the deeper purposes of our lifewalk are revealed. Knowledge becomes wisdom;
insight leads to enlightenment. It is the season of the winged
butterfly, the soaring phoenix.

Beyond the Enemy

I poked through the hand-me-down opinions of others.
Reshuffled the phantoms of battles won and lost.
Where is it? Do you know?
A string of shiny words, another book.
　A pilgrim's tale retold.
Another's promise, another's way
Each a child's bubble, clear, iridescent
　—in a moment, gone.
"I give up," I screamed into the pale, silent sky.
Had I known the power my cry unleashed
I would have made it the mantra of my heart—
I give up. I give up. I give up.

There is the sacred place within each of us where the two
worlds touch—the world of Spirit and the world of matter—
where the inner and the outer are recognized as one. It is a place
beyond the enemy.

Who and what is the enemy? The enemy is the lie that says
you are anything less than creative Spirit. The enemy is the illusion that wears a thousand faces, some terrifying, some thrill-
ing, all of them seducing us into believing that we are the role
we are playing. Instead of realizing that "I am *experiencing* sickness, wealth, or confinement," we believe, in effect, "I *am* sick,
wealthy, or confined." The enemy keeps punching our ticket for
the karmic wheel and we keep buying it.

But no matter how fascinated and identified we become with
our creations, or how well we play the parts, or how many
myths we construct to support them, they all eventually die. We
don't.

Surrendering brings us closer and closer to the shift from *I
do* to *I am*. When we focus on false identities, most of our energies are invested in supporting these illusions. But once the
inner shift is made to *I am*, we can then "do" with greater imag-

ination, boundless energy, and a lighter touch. Poised in the place where our God self and our human self fuse, we are able to identify with Spirit and begin to create with a conscious awareness in the physical world. We have learned how to be in the world, but not of it.

Once we are beyond the enemy of illusory appearances, we know that our true identity is Spirit, essence; we know that we are neither male nor female, neither rich nor poor. No matter what happens in the outer world from this point on, the inner self is undisturbed. With each surrender we acquire more of that steady calm.

To live beyond the enemy is to accept Grace. It is a small step from there to becoming an expression of Grace in all the roles we play in the human drama. Every time a false identity is surrendered, the vacuum it leaves is filled with Grace. When we consciously move into harmonious alignment, at-one-ment, with Grace, we become self-realized, enlightened—saved, in the words of Lord Krishna, "from the endless ocean of death and rebirth." We begin to live unconditional love on Earth. No longer invested in appearances, we breathe love—and therefore Light—into even the densest congestions of confusion and hate. We are free to choose how and where to apply energy.

As Spirit penetrates every level and frequency of energy, we are free to use the laws of creation that govern the mental level or to direct energy at the emotional or physical levels. Because we are no longer locked into identifying with any one level, we are free to create on all of them. As long as we are being whipped about by the capricious dictates of the enemy, we look at the wounded world and think, It's too much. But once we are freed of the illusions, we can look at the world with the eyes of the incarnated Christ and say, "The burden is light."

It doesn't feel so light when we are still being held prisoner by our illusions. So we practice surrendering our limitations a bit at a time. And every change that we allow to go full cycle teaches us a bit more about letting go. Every purification we endure prepares us for the release and enables the new container, the new form we are creating, to hold a bit more Grace.

Purification demands that we die to the past. Surrender calls us to live in the present. During purification we are backed up to the edge of the cliff. And when we surrender, we jump.

A story is told of a famous Rabbi much sought for his spiritual wisdom. When a young man entered the Rabbi's home after making the arduous journey, he was quite astonished to see that it was only a simple room filled with books. The only furniture was a table and a bench.

"Where is your furniture?" asked the young man.

"Where is yours?" said the Rabbi.

"Mine?" said the young man. "But I'm only a visitor here."

"So am I," said the Rabbi.

We tend to speak of surrendering—or "the surrender"—as though we finally make one choice to let it happen. Actually it's more a choice to keep choosing. Usually along the way we are saying, "Thy Will, O God," but continue to whisper, "And a little bit of mine." We let a piece go, then rearrange and integrate what's left into new combinations. Then we live out of the new setting until we are ready to release yet another piece and then another.

Surrender gives up more than a compulsion; it gives up the desire that fuels the compulsion. The wisdom of the Buddha teaches that it is our desires that hold us prisoner. Before an old form is purified, it desires to fulfill itself. As long as there is anything left, it will continue to say, "I need, I want." It is learning the slow releasing of desire that frequently keeps us in the pain of purification. It is really a blessing that we are not released from purification before the desire itself is given up. Otherwise the desire would settle into the subconscious and continue to be part of the creative magnet that pulls people and situations to us without our having any idea why.

Desire is about the last bit of the illusion the ego-self is surrendering. Until the end it keeps insisting, "If I just get this or achieve that, I'll be happy." We think that once we get what we desire, we'll be safe. As Helen Keller once said, "Security is mostly a superstition. Avoiding danger is no safer in the long run than outright experience. Life is either a daring adventure or nothing."

INHABITING THE MYSTERY

Life cannot be controlled. It is a mystery inviting us to participate, to risk, to trust fate, to accept the blank rune stone, the unknown. Surrender teaches us not so much to understand as to "inhabit the mystery," as Ray Bradbury once said. Once we can accept the larger mystery of Life, we can consciously create within it.

The empty womb contains all possibilities. Lao-tzu once said, "It's the nothing that makes it possible." It is a place of maximum creative possibilities. In that moment of nothingness, we are free from the polarizations that dictate so many choices. "I am a mother, therefore I have to do the following twelve things," or "I am a doctor, and this is what is required." Empty of the roles, we dance with Spirit.

The diaries of mystics from all traditions speak of the necessity of emptying oneself in order to be filled. They echo Brother Lawrence, a seventeenth-century mystic who said, "I know that for the right practice of it, the heart must be empty of all else because God wills to possess the heart alone, and as He cannot possess it alone unless it is empty of all else, so He cannot work in it what He would unless it be left vacant for Him."

I have discovered in my own journey that all of my major points of change involved a giving up of preconceived ideas about myself and the world. Early in my work I had to surrender my fear of being in the public eye, and I learned to surrender that by being more public. When I feared for my financial security, I was forced to take more and more risks until I finally literally put my money where my mouth was and trusted the universe. I regularly had to confront my limited knowledge of how the universe worked in order even to be teachable. The more I dedicated myself, the more the illusions surfaced in order to be faced and surrendered.

I would love to report that I gave up all those attachments, especially the fearsome ones, with graceful ease. Or in one ecstatic moment. But I didn't. I discovered that the ego-will fights every step of the way to preserve the status quo.

One of the most significant surrenders I have ever experienced came when I was hospitalized with severe pain and a series of undiagnosed symptoms that puzzled the doctors. Test after test—blood workups, bone scans, X rays, and spinal taps—all came back normal. Yet the pain and symptoms persisted. My personal doctor had decided not to put me through the MRI (Magnetic Resonance Imaging) test because I had a history of claustrophobia. The MRI machine is very much like a big coffin—a tube about six feet long and just wide enough for one person. However, when the symptoms persisted, my doctor decided to call in a specialist, who insisted that the MRI be done.

I was nervous the Friday morning of the test, but I was as prepared in my mind as I could be. Not only that, the doctor had prescribed a heavy tranquilizer to help me overcome my anxiety (which had zero effect, by the way). Even though I had wonderful support from the doctors, the radiologist, the nurses, and my friends, once I was physically in front of the machine, my heart began to race, my body trembled, and I simply couldn't enter it. I wanted to do it; I willed to do it. But my body simply would not do it. Never before in my life had I reached the limits of my own will. I could not will myself to do it. I would not will myself free of a fear that had no logic yet was totally pervasive.

When I returned to my room after this failure, the consulting doctor called. He was very empathetic, reassuring me that claustrophobia could not be controlled. Nevertheless he still needed the information he could only get from that test, so I would have to try again the following Monday.

I really hit bottom that evening. I knew that I didn't have anything in me that could do it. So when everyone left, I went to God and gave up. If God wanted me to have the test, God would have to do it. My will couldn't.

As I finally relaxed into a deep meditation, I was told in Spirit that I had been correct in my earlier conclusion that my own breech birth had encoded the fear of tight places into my cells. The fear I held was below my mind; it was cellular memory. I was told that it originated in a lifetime in which I had been buried alive and that it had been reactivated in this lifetime by the breech birth. I was guided to spend the weekend blessing the MRI machine and collecting energy from all my subtle bodies into forming a fetus that I was to take into my heart and that when I entered the machine, I would in fact be entering the "heart of the lotus." There I would meet the Christ.

And that is what happened. On Friday I could not will myself in any way to enter that machine. On Monday I spent a blissful hour and a half in it resting in the Christ. The medical personnel were amazed. One just doesn't cure claustrophobia over a weekend. But "I" didn't do it. I only surrendered my will to a higher will. It became for me an initiatory chamber, and the experience changed my inner life.

Of course the results of the test were perfectly normal. The experience had never really been about finding a disorder. It was the way the universe used the material on hand to bring me to a deeper surrender. When I look back now over the many events that preceded that moment, I know that I was carefully setting myself up to give up. If I had not been so exhausted from weeks of pain and fear of the unknown, I might not have been able to surrender my will. Had I felt strong in my own will, I probably would have refused to do the test, and I would have delayed a significant point of surrender.

When I returned home from the hospital, I received a card on the front of which was a lotus painted by a friend of mine from Switzerland. Inside he wrote, "When I meditated on you, I saw that when you are finished with this powerful transformative process, there will be flowers growing out of 'the heart of the lotus.' " He had mailed the card a week before I took the test. It was as though God was synchronistically underlining the point in red lest my human brain try to deny what had happened.

In surrendering we discover the power of *I don't know* and even of *I can't*. It is then that we become teachable. I suspect that we cling to rigid, definitive ideas about the nature of reality because to let them go is to strip away the protective coverings and stare with naked eyes into an unending expanse of possibilities.

Surrender frees us to accept that we might not have any idea what the universe has in mind. I remember doing a long-distance session with a woman who lives several states away on a problem with her hearing. As I was experiencing the work being done through me, I heard in my mind, "Twenty-one days." She later reported that she had felt a lot of warmth and tingling in her ears for the first few days after the healing, but that she couldn't hear clearly. However at the end of twenty-one days she received a call from someone who had heard about her work and wanted to meet her. That someone turned out to be an ear surgeon. To make a long story short, the surgeon did the work that was needed to complete the healing on the physical plane. The spiritual healing had eliminated the obstructions and prepared the ground. But there's more. She and the surgeon became friends and went on to do several projects together. How could any of us have known such events would develop? When we surrender, we just do the job in front of us and release the ego's tendency to manipulate results according to its expectations.

SURRENDER TO NATURAL KNOWING

When we give up our conclusions about how things should work and what is successful and what isn't, we offer ourselves the gift of the Zen Buddhist "beginner's mind," allowing ourselves to see life in fresh, new ways. Without bias, we can see our world with the eyes Emmet Fox calls "the wonder child," and C. G. Jung "the Divine child." Perhaps this is what the incarnated Christ meant when he suggested that one had to become "as a little child" to enter the state of consciousness called heaven.

Perhaps this returns us to what biologist Lyall Watson calls natural knowing. We know—we just forget that we know. Surrender moves us toward remembering.

Natural knowing is intuitive knowing. It's not figuring everything out with the information on hand, which only takes us around and around, rearranging the known facts in preconceived packaging. The natural knower understands by receiving knowledge from his or her total beingness as it interacts with all other beingness. How else do we intuit the presence of God?

Intuition is a higher form of mind than what we call thinking. It embraces the functions of both the left and the right brains. It includes the wisdom of the heart as well as logic. It includes both the knowledge of the "masculine" specific and the "feminine" connective. It asks both what a thing is in itself and what its relationship is to the whole. Natural knowing doesn't have to choose between the two. The analytical mind says, "Here is a room, there is the ceiling, the floor, the desk, the lamp." The intuitive mind says, "I see that. Now, how are they related, and what does it mean?"

Spirit once told me that a developed intuition was the mark of an integrated intelligence in which all aspects of the mind—the reptilian and limbic brain, the imaginative right brain, and the analytical left brain—interact with the world at a level of understanding impossible for only one portion alone. Intuition is a higher expression of psychic knowing because it doesn't have to separate itself from the total self in order to understand. In natural knowing we don't have to perform split-brain surgery on ourselves and choose which way of thinking is right.

The intuitive mind changes our perception. Through it we are more likely to recognize the "I" behind everything we go through. As we experience conscious change, we begin to see that no matter how difficult a challenge has been, somewhere behind it all is the observing self that not only created it but is experiencing it and that will continue to exist after the challenge has passed. As a friend told me after enduring an almost unbearable passage, "Mainly I learned that I'm still here. I'm still me."

Natural knowing is an organic recognition of rightness. When a surrender has taken place in our change cycle, we know it. Without any conscious effort the components of our psyche rearrange themselves, and suddenly we feel different, see with new eyes, understand without stretching for it.

We can find ourselves looking back at an experience before the surrender almost as though it happened in another lifetime. "Did I really think like that?" we ask ourselves. "How could I not have known what I know now?" When we think of a past hurt, it's like reading an obituary. It has none of the emotion-filled energy that recharges and keeps the pain alive. We know that it happened, hopefully we honor the part it played in our life, but now we feel increasingly detached from it.

A woman I know was thrown into a major change in her life when her husband left her for another woman. For several years she really used this experience for personal growth, working through various cycles of the growth, including a lot of rage and grief. She realized that she had truly surrendered to her own process when one evening she took her parents to the theater and unexpectedly ran into the "other woman." Without having to think about it at all, she realized that the only feeling she had was sincere compassion for the discomfort of this woman whom she'd all but hated a few months before. The compassion came spontaneously and with no effort.

As long as we have to grit our teeth to make ourselves do anything, we can be sure that the old energy is still in there working. Most of us have to bite the bullet and keep committing in a particular way during the purification, but in the surrender it becomes an instinctive and natural response.

The sudden "knowing" in surrender is similar to the awakening cycle. The difference is that during awakening we see it; during surrender we become it.

Knowing doesn't follow an orderly, linear process. We circle around our ambivalence while the new idea teases us and seems to elude us. Then it's like seeing the hidden picture in a child's puzzle—one minute you can't see the rabbits and foxes, and the next you can't not see them. Before you learned to read, the alphabet was made up of jumbled fragments. After you learned, it was impossible not to read.

Mystical traditions all over the world are filled with stories of people whose lives changed in a sudden flash or insight. Before such a flash we tend to arrive at a realization piecemeal. Sometimes that can be like trying to hear music one note at a time. During a leap in perception you hear all of the music at once.

I once had a dream in which I was suddenly consumed by a big pink fish. I was estatic for weeks feeling the aliveness one does on falling in love. Even though the symbolism was clear to me—the fish being the ancient symbol for Christianity and pink the color of universal love—I did not become high on the intellectual process. It was the total experience of being surrendered in that moment to pure love, and that love consumed all of me in one bite.

My experience has been that when we are ready to shift our perception about even the most ordinary things, we draw to us the stimulus that provides the "click" that locks in the larger realization. During a period when I was examining my own materialism closely, I was at the Guggenheim Museum in New York. An elderly gentleman and I were admiring the same painting. In my enthusiasm I said to him, "Wouldn't you just love to own this?" He smiled, pointed to his head, and said, "But I do, my dear, I do." Suddenly I understood something—not only about that painting but about "owning" all beautiful things: Once you've taken them into your mind, there's no need to grasp them at the physical level. His simple remark was a gift to me that I've never forgotten.

A new perception is for keeps—it's a major paradigm shift. We don't really have a word in English that describes that leap very well. Our language tends to be too linear to catch the wholeness of cause-and-effect in one word. Some other languages come closer. For example, Hopi Indians say *reh-pi* which means both "light" and "flash" in one. We say, "The light flashed." *Reh-pi* is closer to what we experience during a quantum leap in perception.

We never know when someone around us is at a flash point. That's one reason it is important that we tell each other our experiences in Spirit. At any point someone could make a leap because you are living and speaking a truth that person is ready to grasp.

GIVING UP THE CONTROLS, NOT SKILLS

Surrender is about letting go of the controls. But that does not mean becoming passively irresponsible. We don't give up our skills. What we give up is using them to manipulate the world. Skills are to be carefully managed, not put in charge of our incarnation.

The skilled sailor or windsurfer knows that you don't learn how to control the sea. You learn the basics of the sport and then integrate them so well that you can trust your responses as you surrender to the wind and waves. A good ride is a subtle blend of control and letting go.

No one can tell us exactly what it feels like to have control and no control at the same time. It's like learning to sky dive. We can learn everything possible about equipment, safety, and technique. But we'll never become a diver by observing others or reading a manual even if we become an expert in theoretical skydiving. At some point we have to jump out of the plane, trusting both our own readiness and the winds over which we have no control.

It's a bit ironic, but to get to the point of surrender, we have to take back control of our life from other people. As long as we're directed by the internalized voices and dictates of others, we're not in touch with our own will; we're not in control. It's more like coping, imaginatively done perhaps, but nonetheless a reaction rather than an action.

However, no sooner do we move into the creative force of our own will than we're faced with giving up that will to a still higher directive—the One Will. At that level of attunement our place in the higher plan is revealed to us.

Giving up control comes inch by inch for most of us. "I'll give up my talent, God, but I'm keeping control over my relationships." "I'll trust you this far, but I had better worry about these other things myself." It sounds foolish, but it is a testimony both to the power of our individual wills and to the deeply held beliefs we have in separation.

Letting go is not giving up. Giving up usually means that a way can't be found to work the old form, but the desire is still alive. Letting go is being through with even the desire for the old form. Sometimes it's tricky to distinguish the difference.

Amy's rite of passage centered around her intense desire to write. She was a bright child and grew up in an educated family that valued scholarship above most things. She developed a desire to write while she was young, but she also developed a secret *form* that went something like this: "Being a writer proves I am a worthy person."

She grew up to be accomplished in many areas, teaching and being a lay minister, as well as writing. But her secret belief was never addressed until she told God she wanted to get fully conscious. It was at that point that she met the *challenge*. No matter how much she tried to manipulate her world so that she could write, the demands of her life allowed little time or energy for it. Her maturing spiritual self knew that her work was valuable, but she wasn't at peace with herself. Underneath all her success lay the old belief that anything less than full-time writing was not good enough. She was in deep *resistance*—an ambivalent struggle between the growing evidence in the outer world and the long-held assumption in her inner world.

Her *awakening* came when she realized she could no longer say to God, "Thy will—as long as it means writing." When she began to suspect that she was qualifying the conditions of her discipleship, she made the *commitment* to "Thy Will" and meant it. Soon she began to see her students and her opportunities in a new light.

However, the conditions she needed still didn't open up. It took her a long time to figure out that she was going through *purification* because she was secretly holding on to the old belief. Her *surrender* came when she willingly accepted the fact that her place in the plan might not be as a writer but that she was still a worthy person, writer or not. She was willing to let it all go and to serve in the ways she was directed by inner guidance and outer circumstance. It was a genuine surrender, a letting go in love and acceptance, not a giving up in despair.

Within weeks a book she had written earlier was bought by a publisher, and the university staff where she taught offered to help rearrange her schedule to allow her time for writing. She wasn't "rewarded" with a publisher and a cooperative staff—she simply got out of her own way. As long as she had the unpurified "holdout" in her subconscious, the universe couldn't move. It was like the plug that held an old pattern in place. Writing per se was never what the whole thing was about. It was about personal identity and worthiness. Writing was merely the symbol. Once she eliminated the qualifiers to her spirit, her life arranged itself to allow for the writing that itself was not the problem.

WALKING IN TOTAL FAITH

There are several ways of getting things accomplished on Earth. We can just say, "I'll do it myself." That's like practicing with the will, and there is nothing wrong about that. But it is limited because we can't move outside our own present understanding.

The second way of getting things done is to listen carefully to our inner guidance and say, "Okay, God, I've got it. Now I'll take it from here. You go back to running the universe." However while we're moving in greater harmony with our deeper intuition, we're *still* seeing ourselves as separate from God.

Then there's a third and better way: allowing the universe to act through us every moment. That's an entirely different way to live. We don't cease making decisions and taking action. We're simply making them from a different perspective.

We give up waiting to live our life. Attention and passion

are pulled into the now as we say to ourselves, "This person in front of me is the one to serve, the one to love. This meeting is my divine appointment. There is no greater opportunity than the one in front of me right now."

We learn to walk in total faith. If projects are delayed, we just do our job, recognizing that there are unknown forces at work and trust that all is in perfect timing.

Faith is a moment-by-moment commitment. At the point of surrender we are connected to the whole of life, not to just one part. Each surrender, no matter how small, is a significant step in learning how to allow the universe to work through us. At first it seems almost impossible. Our ego-will has a great deal invested in our belief that we need to control people and events in order to survive. Not only is it a great relief to give up all that control, but every time we do, the universe rushes in to support us in ways far greater than anything we could have manipulated into being. The very act of surrender lets loose powerful forces within us.

The Taoist sage Chuang-tzu put it this way: "Nonaction does not mean doing nothing and keeping silent. Let everything be allowed to do what it naturally does, so that its nature will be satisfied."

When we surrender to our essence which is connected to the whole universe, we resonate with the whole and pull to us all that is needed.

LIVING OUR JOY

One of the delightful discoveries in surrendering to your highest will is that rather than being assigned to do things we can't stand, we find that God calls us to live our joy to the fullest. We feel a sense of rightness when we're doing what we're supposed to do. Buckminster Fuller once said that it's "kind of mystical.

The minute you begin to do what you want to do, it's really a different kind of life." Look to your joy. Live your joy. "Follow your bliss," said Joseph Campbell. The word enthusiastic means to be filled with God.

Biologist James Lovelock suggests that evolution teaches us that to be true to who we are is essentially noble and that, in the long run, it serves all of us. In *Gaia: A New Look At Life on Earth* he describes a hypothetical planet with black and white daisies. The black daisies absorb heat and provide warmth. The white daisies reflect heat and provide coolness. When the planetary temperature needs cooling, there will be a preponderance of white daisies. When the temperature needs warming, the black daisies will predominate. Even though the whole planet benefits by the regulated temperature, the daisies are just being true to themselves.

No one's purpose in the scheme of things is any higher or lower than another's. None of us can do all that has to be done. And no one of us is expected to accomplish our mission alone. Native American cultures teach us that every action should be evaluated for its effects for at least seven generations. Today's breakthrough in physics may have happened because a first-grade teacher redirected a learning problem thirty years earlier for a child, who became the scientist, and therefore that teacher's energy is part of the breakthrough. The violin maker is present in every virtuoso's concert.

We must not confuse human smallness with divine effectiveness. Each of us is potentially the difference in the world. Who can say which blow is the one that cracks the stone?

Surrender teaches us to let go of jealousy, which is a byproduct of being out of touch with the value and point of our own life and of seeing ourselves as lacking. Surrender allows us to say, "You have painted that canvas. That means I don't have to do it. You have discovered that vaccine. Terrific. That's one less thing the rest of us have to do. You have marched on Washington, taken care of that homeless person, cleaned up that neighborhood. Great. We thank you. Now, thank me because I'm doing my thing, and my thing is our thing."

The assignment you carry may seem humble by your own evaluation—but that's more a matter of perception than of reality. If you can't change the reality, change the perspective.

Three people were chipping identical blocks of stone. A stranger came by and asked what they were doing. The first said, "I'm chipping a stone block." The second responded, "I'm earning a living for my family." The third said, "I'm building a great cathedral."

As Akshara Noar said beautifully, "There are no more maps, no more creeds, no more philosophies. From here on in, the direction comes straight from the universe. The curriculum is being revealed millisecond by millisecond—inevitably, spontaneously, lovingly."

In surrender we can both give and receive. Relationships take on a different meaning. We learn to be in someone's life without being in their dance. A relationship becomes important not because it satisfies personality needs but because it's the pathway to wholeness.

The trade-off is to give up the addictive highs and lows of the Ferris wheel that is going nowhere. Addictions carry high expectations and devastating disappointments. Surrender teaches us to let go of all preconceived ideas about what we think we must have to be happy. Even happiness is redefined.

Part of giving up control is giving up expectations. God speaks to us according to our readiness. Like a photographic negative slowly emerging in cosmic chemicals, the truth becomes clearer and clearer—as long as we don't pull the picture out prematurely.

DETACHMENT, NOT INDIFFERENCE

Letting go moves us gradually toward detachment. This may well be the single most misunderstood concept in spiritual development. *Detachment* sounds like "indifference to others." But nothing could be further from the truth.

Indifference is the offspring of denial, fear, selfishness, and judgment—a them-versus-us perception of the world.

True detachment acknowledges the problem, then releases the ego's need to interpret the purposes behind the suffering. Detachment is a surrender to the mystery of the universe as it moves through any person. Detachment allows people to unfold in their own time. It is a higher form of love because it loves the being behind the problem and doesn't get stuck in the problem.

Detachment opens the possibility of achieving the goal of the Serenity Prayer associated with Alcoholics Anonymous: "God, grant me the serenity to accept the things I cannot change, the courage to change the things I can, and the wisdom to know the difference."

In a detached state of mind, perception is heightened and discrimination is keener. We are more likely to become an open conduit through which love can pour into any situation.

As a counselor I have listened to a lot of problems. I have learned that when I am lovingly detached, I am able to perceive, touch, and, hopefully, empower the Spirit within the person to deal with their problems. When I am not detached—when I get hooked into "ain't it awful"—it is usually because something in me is resonating with that problem. When that happens there are two of us buying into a limitation.

In training healers I discovered that it was predictable that at a certain point they would come to me concerned that perhaps they didn't care anymore about their work. However, if I queried them closely, it would be clear that they were proceeding according to perfect Divine Plan.

The more people they worked with, the more they realized that some would accept healing, while others wouldn't. They were growing in their understanding of the more subtle purposes of illness. As they loved and served more, they became less and less ego-involved with the results. But somewhere along the way, they had quit bleeding and crying about all the pain, and they feared that it meant they didn't care anymore.

At this point I would tell them the story of the monkey who tried to pull a fish out of the water to save it from drowning. The "attached" monkey is always trying to rescue people. Rescue assumes that it knows what is best for someone. Support is willing and skilled and empowering—it honors a person's path and his or her right to choose.

GIVING UP THE STRUGGLE

During surrender we eventually give up the struggle itself. That may be the hardest release of all. We known how to struggle, how to survive by forcing ourselves to cope, and push through odds. What we don't know is how to relax, to trust, to allow the universe to carry us.

The temptation is to be like the prisoner who yearns to be out of jail and then immediately breaks a law as soon as he's released in order to return to the hated, but known, limitations.

I recall working with a dynamic man who became quite disoriented when he was told that he really didn't need to struggle so much anymore. He runs motivational seminars and is an excellent teacher. In order to become so, he had spent many challenging years working on his own issues and refining his skills in motivating others to claim their power. Having counseled with him for several years, I knew how sincere he was and how responsible he felt toward others.

As we started the consultation on this particular day, I saw a symbolic image of him gradually climbing a very rugged mountain. In the beginning he was heavily burdened with all the equipment he needed to make the first ascent. Periodically he would establish camps higher and higher on the mountain, assess what was needed, discard the unnecessary equipment, and keep going. He developed an ability to bite the bullet no matter how many surprises the mountain gave him.

But when I saw him at the top of the mountain, he was clearly confused. He knew how to struggle up to the top, but he didn't know what to do once he had arrived. All he had to do was be there. But he saw himself as one who climbs mountains. Now he had to take an entirely new look at what he was.

I'm not suggesting that he won't in time have other mountains to climb. To master one turn of the spiral of conscious change is to be at the foot of the next. But at some point in our growth we can surrender all the struggle and meet our new challenges with less stress and more trust in the support of the universe.

AFFIRMATION

Remember the old test-pilot movies when the time and sound barriers were whipping by and the ship was vibrating just at the point of breaking apart? Mach 1, Mach 11—accelerating tension—and then suddenly, silence. Surrender can sometimes be like that, unbearable struggle and tension released to silence. The poet Emily Dickinson once wrote, "After great pain a formal feeling comes."

No matter how well-intentioned we are, there can be times during a change when we feel we might lose our nerve and give in to the lines of least resistance, regress back into old, worn-out but familiar ways. The simple affirmation that follows seems innocent enough, but done sincerely it is very powerful.

Sit in front of a mirror, close your eyes, and breathe deeply until the brain slows down its monologues. Now open your eyes, look deeply into your own eyes, and say,

"I am a Being of Light, son (or daughter) of the Mother-Father-God. I see that I am whole and deserving of abundance in every area of my life. I know that I am drawing to me now all that I need. I accept fully the support of the universe and know that good things will flow through me. I release all anxieties around this passage into the Light. For this remembrance I give thanks."

INTEGRATION: REPATTERNING THE MANDALA

During surrender a re-formation period begins a time when the new must by synthesized and integrated. This is an extremely important part of completing the Seven Steps of Conscious Change. In a reasonably healthy psyche there is an early-warning device that sounds the alarm when we're taking in more than we can integrate. It's wise to listen to it and allow for a reality check now and then. To "blow your mind" symbolically is one thing. To do it literally can be dangerous. Remember, take a step and integrate.

During integration the components that make up our subconscious begin regrouping into new combinations. Like threads in a fabric we've unraveled, they can now begin to be woven together in a new way, even adding new colors.

We are creating a new living mandala in which we are the center. The symbols, colors, and patterns are composed of everything that we believe, and they depict what we're holding in our personal or racial memory, all that we think ourselves to be. That mandala is in constant motion, vibrating its message to the world. As we go through changes, the mandala begins to change,

like the patterns in a kaleidoscope. At the point of a major surrender, the old mandala dissolves and another pattern begins to
emerge.

At each new level of our unfolding we experience a blending
of the intentionality of will and heart, and we decree, "This is
what I desire to bring into the physical plane." Once those words
are spoken, the new mandala is locked into the brain.

When such a powerful synthesis takes place, not even the
hysteria of a world in change can pull us off center. But we must
be clear and persistent about what we want in our new mandala.
Everything that no longer vibrates in harmony with our highest
goal must go. The degree to which we remain confused, longing
for the new but looking back to the old, is the degree to which
we keep ourselves in a spiritual purgatory.

Once the new mandala is in full focus, it is often symbolized
on the physical plane by movement—a new job, a new relationship, or a redefining of old attitudes. People comment that we
seem different. They may not be able to see how we're different,
but they feel it. And of course we are. We're transmitting a new
pattern into the world.

During the integration part of surrender we become the
embodiment of our new truth. It is present in everything we
do—going to work, vacationing with friends, disciplining our
children. That's where the change is made manifest—an ordinary
life become extraordinary.

In our culture the spiritual and the material, the mundane
and the sacred, have been sharply divided. This makes it more
challenging for us to see the profound significance of our daily
lives. Jean Houston tells of a tribe in West Africa that has no
wars, no neuroses as we define them, and women elders. She
says that they solve their problems by talking about them, then
dancing them, then singing them, then talking some more.

Anthropologists researching unusual longevity among the
Hunza found that in addition to healthy diets and lots of exercise, one of the characteristics of their lives was that work and

271

play were not separated. In the midst of the working day they might stop in the fields and have a party.

One can't help but wonder what a terrible price we paid when we quit dancing and worshiping in our bodies and locked spirit up in theologies and buildings.

EXERCISE: RELEASING TO HIGH SELF FOR ANSWERS

We have all the answers inside us—the trick is to access them. We tend to be very much invested in our rational, left brain. Sometimes we mentally nag a challenge to death and end up turning our ideas over and over and getting nowhere. This exercise in visualization calls on your left brain for some new input.

1. First, get clear about what you're asking. Write down all the ideas and insights you now have about the issue—all the pros and cons, confusions, and opinions. When you find you are beginning to retrace the old arguments, you'll know you've just run out of rational feedback.

2. Now write the situation in the form of a clear-cut question.

3. Take a deep breath and, on the exhale, release the question. Imagine that there is a big balloon in your lap. Put the question in the balloon, tie it off, and set it free. Watch as the wind lifts it higher and higher until it disappears.

4. Now return your attention to your breathing, just watching yourself breathe in and out. In a few minutes notice that the balloon drifts back down into your lap. Open it up and you will find new information. It may come as a memory, a symbol, a story, or a statement. Don't put limits on it—the right brain is very imaginative.

Your logical mind is only one way to get information, often not even the best way. Your intuitive mind is plugged into realms of reality usually not even recognized by the logical mind, which is struck with processing the information that education, environment, and experience have put there.

EXERCISE: GUIDED IMAGERY— THE RIVER JOURNEY

This is a trip into your imagination that will carry you through the 7 Steps of Conscious Change. You might want to play some soft music in the background. After you have thoroughly read this through and feel that you know all the landmarks on the journey, you can do the exercise alone. Or you might prefer to read it into a tape recorder. It is also very effective if you do it with another person, one of you reading while the other takes the trip.

Begin in a quiet place where you won't be disturbed for a while. I suggest that you sit up—comfortably of course—and be sure to uncross your arms and legs; it facilitates the flow of energy.

Very gently begin to focus your attention on your breathing. Take slow, even breaths. On the exhale release all tension and everything that's concerning you about the drama of your life. As you inhale, breathe in the pure, revitalizing energy of the universe. Now, surround yourself with the protective light of the Universal Christ and ask for only that which is for your highest good to come to you.

In your mind's eye imagine yourself in a very lush, green mountain forest. This is a sacred place, untouched by civilization, alive with natural life. Be sensitive to the good Earth beneath your feet, the towering trees reaching for heaven. Smell the clean air, fragrant with the breath of leaves and wildflowers. Feel the peace of this forest and know that you belong here. You are part of this creation, one with everything here.

Listen carefully and you will hear the melody of a

brook. It sings an invitation to you: "Come, friend, share my refreshing waters." Take off your shoes and step easily into these waters, feeling the coolness curl around your feet. Begin to walk in the brook, following its path, feeling the water rise around your ankles. As it widens and deepens, it invites you to sit down in the water and bathe yourself—to share more fully in its power to restore you.

"Come," sings the brook, "come share my journey." And easily and naturally you lie down in the water and float, feeling it support and rock you as it moves through the forest. So at one are you now with the water that you relax the borders of your physical reality. You are experiencing becoming the water. Feel yourself expand to meet the banks on either side. Feel the life force pulsing [through] you, knowing that it is a current that will direct your course. Let go of all your concerns.

Relax into it. Become sensitive to the banks on either side setting your boundaries. Observe the trees and brush passing you by, the blue canopy of the sky overhead, the birds riding the currents of air.

Your inner rhythm begins to quicken. You become aware that there are other tiny brooks emptying into you. You are not the same—you are growing. Overhead, storm clouds appear, and soon their waters are pouring into you, churning up your own waters. But the storm soon passes, and you can sense that you are moving more quickly now, more surely. You always feel the current within you, directing your course. As you feel it, you also begin to trust it.

Ahead you can see that you are approaching massive jutting rocks. The force of your momentum carries you crashing into them. Accept the impact. Part of you seeks paths around the rocks; part of you splashes back onto yourself. But in spite of the fury, you find that you still exist, you are. The impact forces little pebbles and stones to surface from your depths and tosses them around. These pebbles and stones have traveled with you all along, but until now they had gone unnoticed.

A part of you, frightened by the mad, swirling waters that seem to have no direction, rushes toward a cul-de-sac in the riverbank, seeking comfort away from the mainstream. At first it is sweet relief. It is quiet here. You feel protected.

But as time passes and there is no movement, you begin to feel sluggish. You can't seem to muster the energy to get out of this backwater that now feels less like a safe haven and more like a trap. Everything feels dead. The sunlight itself grows dimmer as you become aware of a filmy haze that dulls the light. Gently allow yourself to be here for a moment.

Finally from deep within your waters an urge arises to get out of this trap—a distantly remembered call, a search for the current. And a tiny bit of you, only a trickle, begins to move once more.

It's a small stream at first, with only your determination forcing its way through the dense undergrowth. It takes great effort to keep going. Often you feel unsure. But that small stream has a destination, and you know it. So you persist, a tiny part of self seeking to find a pathway.

And very gradually you begin to sense that the banks are receding. There is more room. You can breathe deeply again, see the sun again. You are stronger now.

The old force is back. You feel yourself picking up speed, growing wilder, moving steadily along, passing mountains, valleys, and cities. The inner pulse is very strong now, and you feel a sure direction within you.

In the distance you hear a roar that grows louder by the second. You are moving very quickly now, and a torrent of feelings rise inside you. There is a waterfall ahead, and you cannot avoid pouring over it. Will it mean death to all you've known? Will all that inner force you worked so hard to develop be lost as you surrender to this plunge? The banks fall away. You are swept toward the brink. Exciting. Irresistible. Terrifying.

You are falling. Falling. All awareness is lost in the roar of water cascading down, down, down. For a time all is disoriented. Then, impact.

In the clear silence there comes fresh awareness. You are still there, still flowing with that undercurrent of will directing your course. Now you truly know it. Around you gathering waters will join your own as you begin moving toward the Source.

Soon you find yourself part of a great river. You are now in a flow that cannot be stopped. Its course is sure and even. As the banks grow ever wider, there is more and more room to express yourself. Sunlight dances across you, pure light. Storms come and go. Many life-forms find a home within you. And still you move. The journey is joyous now, energized.

And there, just ahead of you, beckoning—the wondrous sea: "Come home, come quickly now."

The movement swells within you as the loving, mothering sea rushes to welcome you home. In the exquisite reunion you are absorbed. You become one with the mother sea, one with All That Is. And the great secret is yours: You have not been lost. You have not disappeared into the vast waters. The sea has been absorbed into you.

Now rest in your vastness. Rest in your freedom.

Your journey began in a high and holy place. No matter how many limitations have bound you; no matter how much confusion has tossed you around; no matter how much escape you have sought or how difficult the struggle has been to find your path again, even when the mandate to surrender seemed to mean death; ever and always your course has been set toward home.

Now, very gently, prepare to bring your attention back to an awakened state. Take a deep breath. Breathe into your arms and legs, your trunk, your head. As you open your eyes, know that you are balanced, attuned, and harmonized. So be it.

PART III

*From Form
to Surrender:
Living with
Conscious
Change*

Working the 7-Step Model

A HIDDEN AGENDA: FEAR OF DEATH

*S*am was an achievement-driven doctor in his mid-forties when he entered the most significant change in his life: He discovered that he had cancer.

At the time the diagnosis was made, Sam was totally invested in what he perceived to be hard science. If you couldn't see it or measure it, it didn't exist. That was his outer *form*. He had little patience with emotions and no interest in Spirit. His strong, controlling ego was the mechanism that kept the real issue hidden: He was terrified of the unknown; he was afraid of death. That was the hidden *form*.

The *challenge* came with the diagnosis of cancer and the failure of his cancer to respond to the chemotherapy. That put him face-to-face with his own fear of death. His faith in a mechanistic science was failing him. So he sought out a cancer-support group, in which, for the first time in his life, he was encouraged to examine his attitudes, feelings, and life-style.

For a long time the *resistance* dominated as he vacillated. Part of him believed and therefore energized the new self-awareness techniques he was learning—using the mind to image health and taking responsibility for his feelings. However another part of him was still invested in the old programmed belief that if medicine couldn't fix it, it couldn't be fixed. He was really on the horns of the proverbial dilemma—but he was so afraid of dying that he was willing to try anything.

The *awakening* came when he began to have real breakthroughs about those things in his life that had led to the cancer. At this point the cancer went into remission.

Now convinced that his thoughts and emotions did count, he entered the *commitment* phase of his process. He began to see a counselor regularly and participated fully in the support group. He seriously began to explore his own Spirit, something his original form had disallowed. Even though he was stabilizing during the commitment phase of the change, he was still haunted by his own fear of death. But he persisted in the search for his own truth.

The *purification* cycle forced him over and over again to confront his ambivalent attitudes toward what he perceived as the split between Spirit and matter. He had to look at all the many ways his original form was embedded in the fabric of his life— in his relationships as well as in his work and self-image. But he stayed with it and began several spiritual processes.

One of these took him to a Native American sweat lodge, where he experienced a deep *surrender*. As he began the ceremony, he was consciously praying for a healing from the cancer. But the healing that came was not what he had expected. In the course of the ceremony the leader said, "It's a good day to die." Sam was now ready to really hear this. Every bit of the work he had done had strengthened him to take on the real fear, the hidden agenda that needed to go—his fear of death. Those words penetrated his fear of dying like a beacon in the dark. He surrendered to his fear of dying and he let it go. In that surrender he began to live his life more fully.

FROM PERSONAL IMPOTENCE
TO PERSONAL POWER

Sandra's *form* was that she was powerless to do anything about her sexual attraction to abusive men. She had been raised in a dysfunctional family with a sexually abusive, alcoholic father and a mother who had assumed a codependent, passive role. She lived daily with trauma and stress. Her early relationships with men were as predictably abusive as the one with her father had been. She didn't know she had a choice.

Her *challenge* came when she went to college and met and interacted with men who did not view her as a potential victim. An intelligent woman, she quickly realized that there were other ways for people to relate to one another than the way she had been raised.

One of the ways *resistance* expressed itself was that even though she began to date men who were not abusive to her, she wasn't sexually attracted to them. She liked them and wanted to be in a serious, healthy relationship. But because of her old form she could only feel validated when she was being victimized by a man. After several painful relationships she turned down the man who might have been good for her and chose to marry one who wasn't.

Her *awakening* came when, following a divorce, her ambivalence led to her becoming almost frigid. She had been in so much conflict that she had literally frozen her sexual energies. In time she developed a very serious problem in her reproductive system that required surgery. It was during this time that she fully recognized how deeply she had somatized her powerlessness over this issue. And she made up her mind to get to the source of the problem.

She took charge of her life for the first time. She made the *commitment* to herself. She joined the Adult Children of Alcoholics program and began to move toward recovery. She also went into personal therapy and began practicing Yoga. She grew stronger by the month, gaining more and more insight into the programs she had internalized from her family and the self-fulfilling prophecies she had created.

But she was not purged of her past through study. She drew situation after situation into her life during the *purification* that made it increasingly clear which magnets were still operating in her life. Often it came in the guise of men she would try to rescue who would end up abusing her either physically or emotionally. But because she was fully committed to taking charge of her own life, she learned to recognize the symptoms and apply the new understandings and techniques she had learned. It took a long time for her to eliminate the subconscious triggers. But, one by one, they died.

Her *surrender* came more as a process than as a result of any one event. Each time she decreed her own choices and took responsibility for them, she died to her self-image of impotency. When she found that she was responding sexually to men who were kind and gentle, she knew she had surrendered to the truth that she deserved to be treated well and that she always had a choice. She was no longer powerless.

FROM OPPOSITE ENDS
TO THE MIDDLE

Bob and Charlotte are a couple married not only to each other but to the vision of a new world. However, they arrived at this dual commitment through diametrically opposed routes.

Bob's *form* was one of superindependence. It began in the cradle with a neglectful mother who routinely left him alone in hotel rooms in New York. By the time he was a teenager, he was a confirmed loner. He excelled in school and established a reputation for academic excellence. When he attended college, he was so accustomed to "going it alone" that he preferred to live by himself in an apartment off campus. His academic success continued throughout college and his master's degree program.

His *challenge* came through the career field he chose to enter. When he went for an interview with a consulting firm, they made it clear that in order to do the job well, he would have to draw upon the opinions and skills of other people. He was hired, but his magnets attracted a difficult supervisor, and things didn't turn out well.

The *resistance* came when he literally couldn't see the problem. He had always succeeded, and the fact that he wasn't successful now must be somebody else's fault. He was on the verge of quitting. Along the way he had also married a very dependent woman, and the marriage ended in divorce.

But then a man appeared in his professional life who became his mentor. His message was direct: Don't quit. The *awakening* arrived as he took Bob under his wing and began to teach him how to cooperate with others while still remaining faithful to his own ideas.

Bob's main task during *purification* was just to "hang in there" while the old tapes played themselves out. He had to learn not to overreact, to listen to others, and to respect their ideas. He had to acquire understanding and experience and accept rejection of some of his independently conceived ideas.

But it worked. His *surrender* to cooperation and interdependence with others has taken him to the top of his field, where he heads a consulting company of several hundred employees. His success is due not only to his singular brilliance but also to his ability to work with and enhance the skills of others.

By contrast . . .

Charlotte, Bob's second wife, was raised in a highly dependent environment, where she was not encouraged to be herself. The message was just to be a "good little girl" and mind her mother and the Catholic church. That was her *form*. Her authorities for living her life were completely outside herself—just the opposite of Bob's.

Her *challenge* occurred when she began to realize that her mother didn't live what she preached. When she went to college, she began to doubt that the Church did either. So she quit going to church.

As the *resistance* moved in, she felt guilty about her mother and leaving the Church. She was quite young and hadn't developed the skills for making choices for herself; in fact she didn't believe she had the right. Afraid of being alone, she married and transferred authority in her life to a husband who became abusive.

Once again education became the catalyst for Charlotte's growth. Eight years later she went back to graduate school and experienced her *awakening*. Now she felt empowered to make the choice to leave the unhappy marriage and seek answers for herself.

Her *commitment* was to become independent. For the first time she lived alone. She started therapy and began to work on her blocks to self-actualization.

During *purification* she experienced a great deal of physical stress. In her words, she had to learn how to "recycle the body." She used several body therapies to help her, including hatha-yoga and Rolfing. She became a serious spiritual student, began to meditate, and learned techniques for releasing her guilt and resentment toward her mother. Mainly she learned to love herself. And she found her own way back to her God, not someone else's.

As she opened her consciousness to full expression as a healer, she knew she was in a process of *surrender*. She was able not only to forgive her mother, but she was also allowed to help her through the transition of dying.

Bob and Charlotte found each other after both had arrived at the point of *surrender*—from opposite directions.

YOU CAN'T CHANGE OTHERS

Mary grew up in a chaotic household with an overworked mother and an alternately disappearing and tyrannical father. She learned early that surviving emotionally in her home depended on her correctly psyching out the atmosphere and adjusting accordingly. She worked very hard at everything she did and received a great deal of ego reinforcement through her achievements. She also took it upon herself to "fix" crises and people. Both of these patterns were an outgrowth of the total family myth. By the time Mary grew up, her *form* was that you would be rewarded if you were good and that you could change other people by your behavior.

After a very successful college career, Mary began to move up the career ladder quickly. She was in her element in a profession where crisis was daily fare. But as her form was still intact, she fully expected to be rewarded by her boss for all her hard work.

It didn't happen that way, and the *challenge* was set up. Not only did he not reward her, he lied to her and even took credit for her work. Still believing she could change people, Mary tried to manipulate things—but it didn't work. However, by this time she was becoming more conscious of her own family patterns and she began to understand her part in the drama. As a result she began to withdraw her expectations and her attempts to change her boss.

But old ways die hard, and Mary found herself in the middle of the *resistance* cycle, alternately detaching and getting hooked again. She would accept the situation and then fight it. Although she deeply resented her boss, she was slowly perceiving that this was his personality flaw. Yet, she couldn't quit trying to manipulate him into fairness. Because she had so much energy tied up in fighting the reality, she wasn't yet able to see creative ways of working within the situation.

The *awakening* came when Mary took full responsibility for

her own attitudes and faced the fact that she was in her own way perpetuating the drama by continually feeding it energy. Through her work with Adult Children of Alcoholics, she began her own recovery from the crisis-manipulating *form* she learned as a child. She finally realized that she could not change or take responsibility for another. She could only change herself.

Now, fully aware of the dynamics involved, Mary had to reeducate herself. This called for *commitment* and a new contract with herself. She couldn't act as long as she was seeing her boss as the villain. That simply fed her original form. She reinforced what she was learning through weekly support meetings and daily reading material that would remind her of her new goals. She used affirmations, prayer, and nightly reviews to identify those places where she was still giving authority to the old form.

One of the important gifts she gave herself was patience, and it was needed during the *purification*. Because Mary was seeking to make this change a conscious one, she was honest with herself about having created a perfect classroom for herself with this boss. It was hard, but she realized that if she avoided learning with him she would only have to learn the lesson in another way. He was still very difficult, so she had to pay close attention to her reactions on a daily, sometimes hourly, basis. There were days when she found that in spite of herself she was still trying to manipulate her boss into being something that he wasn't and then making herself miserable because he'd acted out of his own nature. But slowly the energy diffused, and in time she was able to see him objectively and not react.

With *surrender*, Mary was finally able to let her boss be who he was. She no longer parroted the words, "You can only change yourself," as an idealistic truism. It became a powerful truth for her. She no longer had any emotional investment in making him do anything. As a result, she could begin to make more rational decisions about how to protect herself in her business. As she integrated this knowledge during the final part of the cycle, she realized that she had not just given up remaking her boss; she had given up remaking anyone.

Mary is still working on letting go of her old patterns of creating and then proving herself through crisis. She reports that she is in *purification* on that one. While this is a more complex issue, letting go of trying to change people has helped her take a giant step in this direction.

STRONG MEN DON'T CRY— THEY GET SICK

As with most of us, Darrell's strongest *form* was set in child-hood. As he put it, "The message was to be cool, macho, and strictly objective. I didn't feel good with that ever, but I did feel safe." Any emotional expression was questioned, denied, or rid-iculed. He also learned to distrust, even fear, women because they were too preoccupied with feelings and emotions.

This *form* was overlaid with a sense of additional masculine responsibility, since Darrell came of age during the civil rights movement and was the third son in a powerful, high-achieving black family. He was also a very, very sensitive child.

His strong programming, which led him directly to a sci-entific career, stayed intact until a health crisis brought him to *challenge*. "A bleeding ulcer is definitely not fun," he reported. "It was a clear signal that I wasn't doing something right." The doctors were emphatic with him. He had to come to terms with his inner feelings—or else.

Resistance was very intense for Darrell. His analytical self knew that the doctors were right, that he would die if he didn't change. But he was terribly afraid. He reported that he was ter-rified that he would become out of control if he got into his feelings, so he tried to read his way into an understanding of feelings—the self-help books buffered him from personal reality.

One evening, during this period of cautious intellectual investigation of emotions, Darrell attended a lecture. There, his *awakening* came as a sudden *Aha*! He couldn't remember exactly what the speaker had said that finally broke through his *resistance*, but when he left, he knew he had to begin to work with his own emotions, not keep hiding behind theories. It was Darrell's willingness to stay with the *resistance* cycle that set up his readiness to hear the right words at the right time.

He made the *commitment* to explore his feelings. This part of the cycle was unusually difficult for Darrell because he was totally unequipped to cope with this. Not only that, but he had no support from his family. Calling up the same determination that had aided him in his scientific pursuits, he turned to self-knowledge. He started therapy, first with a man—women were still too scary. He learned a lot with this therapist, but then he really began taking risks when he shifted to a second therapist—a woman. She was bright and objective enough for him to accept intellectually, but she was also loving and gentle. She totally respected his anger and tears as they came and helped him to begin accepting them. Gradually, he began to trust both her and his own emotional responses.

Purification came when Darrell felt strong enough to take his new insights into the world. True it meant he had to take more risks, often painful ones.

Although on the one hand he was a successful scientist; on the other hand, he was untried and inexperienced in relationships. Now he learned to really cry and to really laugh. By trial and error, he learned to be irrational on occasion and to accept it. When I asked him to sum up what this cycle was like for him, he said, "I would give myself permission to get angry, and then I would stay up all night worrying about it."

But Darrell withstood the fires of his purification. Then during *surrender*, he discovered that he could safely explore the full range of his emotions. He has found that he likes women, and he's now in a healthy relationship. He no longer represses what he feels—and he no longer has an ulcer.

THE SPIRIT ISN'T HANDICAPPED

Alan had been handicapped by a muscle disease from the time he was seven. He was the eldest son in a wealthy family that could afford the best in specialists and therapists. And all of them agreed that Alan could do more for himself than he did. But Alan had an additional handicap—parents whose misguided love spoiled him. He went into rages that lasted for hours, and he patently refused to do anything for himself. His parents acquiesced to his unreasonable demands and hired more and more people to serve him. The result was that Alan didn't learn to do anything for himself. He would walk only with assistance. He had no hobbies and was disinterested in intellectual studies. He became more and more powerless. That was his *form*: "I'm helpless."

The *challenge* came when Alan was fourteen and his parents, on the strong recommendation of his supervising doctor, sent him to a camp for handicapped children for the summer. The camp staff received the medical reports that said there was no reason whatsoever that Alan could not walk on his own. They decided they would help him realize that over the summer.

The attitude of the camp personnel was entirely new to Alan. They treated him as though he were a person, not a handicap. During physical-therapy sessions he was told over and over that he could do all kinds of things for himself—including walking without help. But he didn't want to hear that. In the early weeks Alan didn't get to do a lot of things because he wouldn't make the effort, and no one would help him. In the meantime, Alan was observing other young people who had similar or more challenging handicaps doing all kinds of things he couldn't do. So he began making tentative efforts to try new things. But as soon as he got frustrated, he'd go into a rage and refuse to try anything new for days. Eventually, he'd try again. And every time he made an effort, he got full support of the staff; but his rages were either ignored or severely criticized. This was "tough love" in action. His *resistance* was in full force.

The *awakening* was sparked one evening when the young people were out playing in a meadow before dinner. When the dinner bell rang, everyone started for the dining hall. Alan looked around for a staff member to lean on for the walk, but no one was there. He yelled for help, but they called back to him that if he wanted dinner, he'd have to walk to it.

At first Alan was livid. Then he was frightened. And then he started taking his first steps on his own. He fell. He got up. This was repeated several times. Staff members called encouragement to him from the dining porch. The children began yelling "A-lan . . . A-lan. Go for it! Go for it." It took thirty minutes for him to make it, but he did, and there wasn't a dry eye when he did.

After that, he was unstoppable. He had discovered a new power within himself, and he made a *commitment* to it. For the next few weeks Alan was relentless in his efforts to try to do everything for himself. At times, the staff even had to slow him down. But it was as if a dam had broken in him, and he now had access to a self determination that he'd never known before.

Alan's parents were stunned when they arrived to take him home. Their "helpless" son walked, albeit awkwardly, to meet them. He showed them carvings he'd done, a swim merit he'd won, and introduced them to his many new friends. They were thrilled and amazed. But they had not seen the process that Alan had experienced. And when they took him home, they tried to go back to business as usual. This is when Alan's *purification* began.

Now he was back in the environment that had supported the helplessness. The exaggerated cautiousness, the too-quick assistance, and the isolation threw Alan back into his rages and often back into impotence. But he had tasted personal liberation one summer and it was sweet. So he fought for it—and won. Fortunately he had all the doctors and therapists supporting him. The entire family had to go into family counseling to untangle the complicated dynamics that had been holding him prisoner to his handicap. But once his family members released their own issues around his body challenges, he was able to work through his adjustments fairly rapidly.

Surrender brought a new life for Alan. He no longer perceived himself as helpless. He had the dignity of his selfhood. Pushing his independence to the limit, he became skilled with his hands, read voraciously, and looked forward to college, where he planned to study to become a history professor. He had many friends who loved his sharp sense of humor and were consistently inspired in their own goals by his modeling. They grew accustomed to hearing him say, "If I can do it—you can do it!"

GIRL CHILD: DAUGHTER OF EVE

The story of Margaret's change began on the day she was born— a girl child and therefore automatically a "daughter of Eve." It took her half a century of experience, two marriages, many affairs, and much work on herself to uncover the power this *form* had in shaping her life.

Margaret was born into an extremely strict religious family in the Midwest. Her father, a solid figure in his church, was rigid and opinionated, and the "sin" he was the most verbal about was sex. He condemned all women as seducers and corrupters of men. Margaret's mother, as frightened of the father as the children were, coped in silence through the verbal harangues and the beatings.

Margaret grew into an extraordinary beauty, which only fed the *form*. Men were very attracted to her, not only for her beauty, but also for her supportive nature. True, she was supportive, but not of herself. She had little self-esteem. She always needed a man to ensure her identity. Margaret went to college, became a teacher, and married. But behind the facade of the dutiful, obedient housewife lay her image of herself as a corrupter of men. In time, she began to act out that prophecy. She would have affairs and follow them with a round of serious depressions. She was in the grips of an unconscious but very real double bind. Her two marriages were to men who were ambivalent about females. Their criticism reinforced her secret fear that she was fundamentally bad. Various therapies took her as far as she was ready to go, and they surely laid the groundwork for her later work. But she had not yet built enough ego strength to really tackle that original *form*.

When the *challenge* did come, she moved through the next six stages in only five years. The blow came during a time when she was in her second difficult, nonsupportive marriage. Again her old self-image surfaced, and she acted out her anxiety by getting involved with another man. This time she was caught. But now she was ready to go to the source of her problem.

Once Margaret decided to look squarely at the myth she'd internalized since infancy, many buried memories returned, and old patterns began to fall into place. Her marriage was already weak, and the discovery of her affair dealt its death blow. It was a very trying time for Margaret, as separation and divorce are not easy even when desired. But it was also a fruitful time.

Then came the *resistance*, and the struggle began again. As she moved into new relationships with men, Margaret was still facing her old patterns. She knew how to seduce in order to fulfill the prophecy; she didn't know how to relate in a way that

was good for her. But she was learning. Even though she reported that she would go unconscious for a while, she would
quickly wake up and realize what she was doing.

By this time Margaret had found her own spiritual path, and
it began yielding insights through meditations and prayers. Her
therapy was also proving effective—she was no longer diving
into depressions following affairs or in frustration over failed
relationships. But some major piece of the puzzle was still missing.

Margaret's *awakening* came during a guided visualization. She
suddenly recalled being sexually molested by her father. This
was the ultimate insight that would break the pattern, for it was
this abuse that had locked the *form* into place.

Once she recovered from the shock, Margaret made the *commitment* to use that information from her subconscious for self-
understanding. This meant she had to accept all of the feelings
that came welling up. She had to relive the powerlessness, the
rage, and the shame.

Part of Margaret's *commitment* was to invest her energy in
herself, and not just in relationships. She learned to recognize
right from the beginning relationships that would not be good
for her. She learned to say No. She left her job for a new career
in something she'd always wanted to do. She was learning to
really love herself.

But the form was very deep, and it wouldn't let go without
a fight. During *purification* Margaret found herself riding emotional extremes—high and optimistic one day, depressed to the
point of suicide the next. This was the time in which she was
actually transforming the energy she'd been holding in her body.
As she worked with her issues, Margaret was able to forgive her
father. This in turn, led to her being able to let go of the abuse.
Lastly, she had to forgive the weakness of a mother who couldn't
protect her.

During *purification*, Margaret struggled with the temptation
to return to a pattern of sexual relationships that, however

harmful, was familiar and certainly easier than the hard work of birthing a new form.

But finally she reached the point of *surrender*. She knew she was there because her emotions stabilized. Now, when Margaret is in crisis or has a bad day, she doesn't get depressed. Her priorities have rearranged themselves so that now she chooses only those things that are good for her. She has become assertive for the first time in her life. Having forgiven her aging parents, she views them with compassion. The abuse is no longer alive inside of her; it's history. She doesn't have to tell herself not to get involved with the wrong men because she's no longer even attracted to them or they to her. Margaret likes and respects herself now, and she's attracting sensitive and caring relationships.

THE TRUTH OF YOU IS INSIDE YOU

Not all of our life shaping *forms* come from family or religious myths. Many of them originate in the powerful thought forms of our peers. Ned is a good example of this.

When Ned was a small boy, he wanted to be a dancer. His family didn't discourage it. It was a little offbeat for a child in a small southern town, but it was okay. No one could figure where this preoccupation with dance came from, but they proudly clapped when he performed as a small child. His dad even cleared the garage when eight-year-old Ned insisted that he had to have "a studio." He begged to take dance lessons, and they found a teacher for him. And for two years Ned and fifteen little girls went to dance class every week. We can assume Ned had an affirmative *form* on this subject from his family.

But when he was ten, things changed. Ned's brother began to tease him, then his friends. Dance was for "girls and for queers," they said. Ned didn't really know what a "queer" was, but he knew he didn't want to be one. He began to be self-conscious about dancing. His parents were fairly indifferent during this period. After all, children change their minds. But the new *form* was taking shape, and by the time he was twelve it was clearly defined: Real men don't dance.

Ned said he felt as if he had a shameful secret because he'd still go into his makeshift studio, put on a record, and dance the lead in a ballet. But he told no one. Instead, he poured his energies into those values that his peers taught him counted: playing sports, getting a car, dating girls, and making money. Ned was well-coordinated, so he did fairly well in competitive sports, and he received a lot of positive feedback from his friends. He liked that of course. By 16, he rarely danced in private. But he says that he never felt as free in his life as he did when he danced. Even as a teenager, he was aware that something important had gone out of his life.

Years went by and Ned continued to get his satisfaction from the praise of his friends. He graduated from a local college with a business degree and no idea of what he wanted to do with his life. But like everyone else he valued money, so he began to put time and all his energy into making money. And he made a lot of it. He married, had a family, made more money. But Ned wasn't happy. Like most of his friends, he followed sports, played a few, and focused on his business. By thirty-five he had a big house, membership in several clubs, a divorce, a new wife, a new baby, and a growing alcohol problem. He defined himself at that time as "a man's man."

Ned didn't know he was drinking to cover up the sadness of his inner self that was not being honored. But he didn't know that his life wasn't working. Because the drinking was threatening both his second marriage and his business, he committed himself to a treatment program for alcoholism.

What he didn't know then was that this step was a real *challenge* to the form he was living. Drying out was only one part of the program Ned was in; getting honest with himself and taking responsibility for himself was the emphasis. Through group sessions and private therapy, he began tracing his life choices and realized how many of them had been based on other people's values. The *challenge* did its work fully the day Ned broke down and sobbed in uncontrollable grief over the death of his beloved dancing when he was twelve.

When Ned returned to his hometown and resumed his life, he knew he couldn't begin a new career as a dancer. That was not realistic. He clearly understood that dance was symbolic at this point in his life, but now he had to face the *resistance*. No longer drinking, there was nothing to dull the messages from his inner self. And that self looked around and decided it didn't like the life he was leading. The problem was, Ned didn't know what he wanted instead. He was deeply involved in business and community affairs, and all his friends and colleagues related to him in terms of the values they all seemed to share—sport, money, success. He was lonely and totally bewildered as to which way to turn. One morning he'd wake up, look at his life and say, "Hey, this is okay. Who would want more?" And the next morning he'd wake up dreading what the day would bring.

Ned went back and forth for a couple of years with the *resistance*. However, during this period he really used the skills he had learned at the alcoholic treatment center, and he didn't deny or bury any of his conflicts.

Ned's *awakening* came as a total surprise to him. He was invited to participate in a state task force for business leaders. The object was to involve businesses in improving the cultural and artistic environment of communities throughout the state. As part of the entertainment program, there were performances of opera, ballet, and theater.

"I don't really know what happened," Ned says of those few days. "Maybe it was because I was away from my home-town. I don't like to admit it, but maybe I was influenced by the positive response of the other businessmen. Or maybe I was just ready." Whatever the trigger, something popped loose in

Ned, and he found himself joyously excited for the first time in years.

This experience became the vehicle for Ned's *commitment*. He worked so hard on the task force, that he was soon recognized as a leader. In that position he found himself interacting with people in the arts. And he made friends with other businesspeople throughout the state and region who cared about the cultural life of their communities.

The *purification* of Ned's old form was real but subtle. Although he still found himself trying to go along with his old buddies, pretending that a round of golf and a review of the stock market would satisfy him, he also began to admit to himself that he really didn't share the values of many people in his community. His view of himself, and of the world, had expanded, and he wanted more. For a long time Ned tried to build cultural fires under the other money powers in his town, but there just wasn't enough interest.

At this point he decided to leave his hometown. Fortunately he had the resources to do that, and his wife backed his decision. So he sold his business and moved to a large city where he could pursue his real interests.

The move itself was a *surrender*, for it represented Ned's choice of what he needed for fulfillment. After he settled in the city, he became involved in the business end of the arts—ballet in particular. In time his inner artist made it clear that he needed even more than that, and he began taking painting classes. Ned has no aspirations to be a professional painter, although many have encouraged him to submit his work to shows. But he has claimed his own creativity.

There's an interesting postscript to Ned's story. A couple of years ago he got involved in helping develop a project to keep kids off drugs and off the streets by bringing them into a dance program.

CYCLING TOGETHER
THROUGH CHANGE

Organizations, businesses, governments, even social attitudes progress through the 7 Stages of Conscious Change. Not every individual is ready to move through his or her next stage in group change gracefully. Not all of us will arrive at the next point together. In larger challenges the more people who are involved, the more resistance there will be and the slower the change. Major societal changes can take hundreds of years. But when a critical mass is formed by enough of us being ready to make a shift, the change occurs with lightning speed.

Let's look at the civil rights movement at the point at which change really began. Until the time of the Civil War we accepted a *form* that allowed the ownership of slaves. No doubt there was always a certain percentage of people who knew that to be wrong, but it was sufficiently acceptable to society at large for the practice to continue for centuries. That form was held in place in part by the supporting belief that black people were inferior.

The *challenge* to that form really had its roots in the fundamental tenet of American philosophy: All people are created equal. The moment we claimed to believe that, we set in motion the mechanism that would eventually purge away all that was not consistent with that belief. It took nearly a hundred years for a full-blown challenge to shape itself in the events that surrounded the Civil War. The symbol for the challenge was the Emancipation Proclamation. Although we still had a long way to go, change had been set in motion. Our old form had been mortally wounded.

In spite of the changes in laws that disallowed the legal owning of slaves, the *resistance* to the full acceptance of black people in the larger society was intense. For the next century we endured the backlash of the old form, a hierarchical model of reality that ran very deep in our collective psyche. Fear, with all of its henchmen—from the Ku Klux Klan and corrupt courts to the isolation in educational, residential, and social ghettos—kept the black population in economic, social, and psychological slavery.

The *awakening* stage of the cycle couldn't begin until enough of us—black and white—had endured the *resistance* and were ready to make a conscious change. The civil rights movement provided that awakening for thousands. People of all colors woke up from the illusion that America lived the philosophy that it espoused. Leaders like Martin Luther King, Jr., cut through the old form to touch the hearts and minds of millions.

The price of the awakening was dear. Hundreds paid with their lives. And we still had a long way to go. But after the awakening we began to feel the momentum of the change at work.

During the *commitment* cycle important laws were changed and put to work, not without many people still deeply acting out the resistance, of course, but the weight of public opinion had shifted. More and more people were dedicated to equality in all ways for black citizens. Integration opened up new possibilities. We began the process of reeducating black children to having pride in themselves and white children into a new understanding and acceptance. Blacks entered more deeply into schools, business, government, and all levels of their communities. The long and tedious process of resolving inequalities wherever they existed met with constant discouragement and frustration. Nothing less than a total commitment of time, money, talent, and sheer hard work could bring the dream of equality into physical reality.

And we have by no means completed this change. We are now in the *purification* stage. Every aspect of our society that does not fully accept blacks as equals will scream at us until we live what we say we believe. There is no place to hide prejudice and fear during purification. All of the hidden trash comes out. The change must be authentic.

When the day comes that being an Afro-American has no more to do with one's worth or potential or opportunities than to be of French origin or Scotch-Irish or Asian or whatever, we will know that our change is complete. Then we will move into *surrender*, the time of synthesis, when we truly have a society that lives out the principle that all people are created equal.

PROGRESS ISN'T WHAT WE THOUGHT IT WAS

Let's use another societal example and follow the rhythm of change through a typical issue facing communities today. We have lived with a *form* for a long time that says, "Progress is great." To this add the corollary "Progress means more and more of everything." Out of that form we have created a life-style undreamed of by our grandparents. For a long time, in spite of the warnings of early environmentalists, everyone simply accepted that.

Then Mother Nature began to discipline us. At first a few and now many of us are facing a serious *challenge*. Gradually the very science that we had depended upon to provide us with all these wonderful new "things" has begun to report that there are side effects to this progress. Our seas are getting sick, our food is filled with dangerous chemicals, and the very air we breathe is polluted. We are killing off whole species of animals and upsetting the balance of nature. We are endangering our life-support systems all over the planet.

Resistance to these reports runs high. We have a lot invested in our life-styles. We have also created industries that have provided millions of jobs that depend on the system continuing as it is. Progress-as-more is so deeply ingrained in our perception of reality that we've come to view money as our dominant symbol of success. We're finding ourselves to be very ambivalent. On the one hand we want a clean environment, but on the other hand we want the things "progress" has provided. Governments, from city councils to the nation's capital, are confronted with the high cost of changing systems.

But many more people have moved into the *awakening* stage over the past ten years. Books, magazines, newsletters, and television are telegraphing to us the devastating effects of perpetuating the status quo. We are realizing that we don't have the luxury to allow this change to take hundreds of years. We now have to redefine what progress means, or we won't have a planet at all in a very short time.

All over the globe people are beginning to make a serious *commitment* to change. They are banding together in groups of many sizes, picketing, protesting, writing letters, dispensing information, forming task forces, confronting offending industries, lobbying, and getting issues to the public and onto ballots. They are addressing local pollution problems. They are questioning the conveniences we have taken for granted, from plastics to aerosols. By thinking globally but acting locally they are demanding, and gradually getting, more environmental watchdogs on industry and more awareness in the general public.

Now we have to live through the *purification*. We are likely to see all of the manifestations of our old form run their courses. It will take time, patience, and clarity to clean the air, the land, and the seas. Wherever we continue to value money or things over all the life of this planet, we will suffer the consequences. Any remaining arrogance that we can outsmart nature rather than working with her will be severely corrected—and we'll all suffer.

During a purification cycle selfishness and indifference will surface in order to be cleared away. It is, and will be, a time that calls for brutal self-honesty on the part of individuals and communities alike. We'll have to make hard choices, but thanks to the commitment of so many people our choices are becoming clearer: Either put the brakes on progress as we have defined it or hand our children a terminally ill environment.

As with all conscious change, *surrender* will come when we fully change our consciousness. It is our birthright to be creative. We are fully capable of creating life solutions—and progressing—in harmony with nature. But we can't create anything higher than our own consciousness. Those who have already challenged the value of progress at any cost and have committed themselves to the change will arrive at surrender more quickly than the general population. They then become active agents of change.

THE BUDDHA

The life of the Buddha, partly the biography of a real man and partly another retelling of the One Story, offers us an ideal model for both the journey of the aspirant and the unfolding of the 7 Steps of Conscious Change.

The term *Buddha* is actually a title. It means "awakened one," just as "Christ" is a title meaning the "Anointed." In mystical teachings one first finds a path, then one travels the path, and finally one becomes the path. When a self-realized being is the path, that person is the embodiment of the title. As we popularly use the term, we know whom we are speaking of when we say "Buddha" or "Christ."

The lines between fact and legend blur when they have to do with beings who have become the path for millions. We must interpret the reported facts of their lives with the understanding that what we hear is partly legend. Nevertheless the story of the Buddha still follows the seven-stage cycle of change. Even if some of the facts are questionable, the continual telling of these stories makes clear how our own lives pass through these same stages on the way to self-realization.

The Buddha's *form* was to be a king and rule a physical kingdom. Born Gautama Siddhartha in 563 B.C., son of King Suddhodana (ruler of the city-state of Kapilavasta) and Queen Mahamaya, he was raised with every luxury imaginable and groomed for the role of king. Nevertheless several events surrounding his birth indicated that he would be a very high soul. His mother dreamed of a white elephant, a very auspicious symbol in the culture of India. Wise ones prophesied that he would become either a great monarch or a Buddha. At sixteen he was married and continued to live in splendor, protected from the harshness of the life outside the palace.

The story tells us that Siddhartha's *challenge* to this form came when he was twenty-nine (ages 28 to 29 are the years one experiences a Saturn return astrologically—the time when something important occurs in a life to utterly change it). On three different occasions he asked a devoted servant to take him outside the palace walls. On the first trip, he was confronted with the sight of a person stooped with "old age," on the second with a glimpse of someone suffering from disease, and on the third trip with a view of a dead body accompanied with a sudden awareness of death. It is highly unlikely that these experiences should be taken literally. Rather they indicate that it was during this period that Siddhartha really saw the true condition of humankind, and his protected world view was forever changed.

His *resistance* occurred when he had to choose between fulfilling the expectations of his parents and wife and his desire to seek understanding of the meaning of life for all humankind. We can assume that his decision to renounce marriage, luxury, and kingship did not occur without some ambivalence and struggle.

He began his search by becoming a wandering ascetic. This period in his life is recognized as the great renunciation. We could think of it as his *awakening*, for it resolved any remaining ambivalence over returning to his former way of life.

Siddhartha made a complete *commitment* to his search for enlightenment. He studied with Arada, a sage of great renown, mastering his path for enlightenment. It took him very far, yet not far enough to suit Siddhartha. He then studied with Udraka, a second great teacher, and was led into even higher mystical states of awareness. He later left to join a group of ascetics. It is told that he spent years practicing severe austerities and self-mortification, but even then he felt he had not achieved what he sought.

At this point Siddhartha finally left the ascetics and all other teachers and set off to seek his own path. The depth of his commitment is told to us in the story of his sitting under the sacred Bodhi tree, from which spot he declared he would not rise until he had attained enlightenment.

As he sat beneath the branches of the tree of awakening, the deepest *purification* occurred. We are told that he had to face Mara, king of death and lord of passions, and his vast band of tempters and demons (which is of course very similar to the temptations Jesus had to face in the desert). As Siddhartha held his own against these forces, he came to realize that these enemies lay within himself. Each confrontation brought him greater clarity and understanding.

When he rose at last, he was fully *surrendered*. He had become the Buddha, the enlightened one. He was thirty-five at the time, and for the next forty-five years in the physical body he became The Way for hundreds of disciples. Today he continues to be The Way for millions.

EXERCISE: WORKING
THE 7-STEP MODEL

One way to understand the change you are now experiencing is to review the rhythms of a change you've already experienced. Take a change that you are sure you've completed and use the process of the 7 Steps of Conscious Change to see how those steps were operating.

First make a list of the 7 Steps, and beside each step write down how that dynamic was expressed in your passage.

For example suppose you started out with a *form* inherited from your family that said women would be rewarded with a Prince Charming and happiness-ever-after if they were pretty and submissive. But now you no longer believe that.

• When did the *challenge* first come? Was it during college or further education? Was it a disappointing relationship?

• When you first started to break the pattern, what kind of *resistance* came up? Fear of breaking with tradition? Attraction to both an old form and a new way? What did that resistance feel and look like?

• What brought clarity and the *awakening*? Was it a sudden *aha*! or a gradual dawning? Was it triggered by one single event?

• What did you have to do to make a *commitment* to a new model? How did your list of resources change? Did you take classes, go to therapy, take risks?

• What kind of *purification* had to take place so that

the old form had no more pull on you? Did you pass through loneliness? Did you regress and rerun the old form for a while?

• When would you say you honestly *surrendered* to the new form? When did you know, no matter what the cost and where it took you, what it really meant to be a woman (or to relate to a woman) in a new way, from the inside out—no more talking yourself into it, no more ambivalences?

You may find that some of the steps were well defined by an event. Others may have consisted of several happenings and attitudinal shifts.

Once you have consciously examined the process of a change you have already completed, then take a shift that's in process and see where you are in that particular cycle of change. Experience and understanding can help you realize that "this too shall pass." Reread the section that concerns the stage you're in and see if you can find some hints for moving through it. Note the characteristics of the step you're currently experiencing—really think about the nature of this part of the change. See whether other characteristics of this aspect occur to you.

Above all, remember that you are in a passage. It is not who you are; it is what you are experiencing. You are the conscious being who is experiencing the change.

AGENTS OF CHANGE

Becoming World Servers

And it is still true, no matter how old you are, when you go out into the world, it is best to hold hands and stick together.

—ROBERT FULGHUM

*W*hen I was very young, a fellow worker and I would grumble about the bosses. "They" did this and "they" did that. Then he got promoted one day, and not long afterward he burst into my office with an astonished look on his face and cried, "Oh, my Lord, I just realized I've become a 'they.' "

That's what happens when we wake up. We realize it's all of us together—not some faceless "they"—who are creating our group realities, from our communities on up to planetary realities.

Before we can consciously begin to contribute to group change, we first have to challenge the old *form* within ourselves that assumes that somebody "out there" is in charge. This isn't always a comfortable confrontation. It's much easier to blame, deny, or ignore. Certainly the daily news can overwhelm us into paralysis. But not to challenge is itself a choice that becomes part of our total pattern.

Our group changes don't happen because some mythical "they" out there finally changes the rules. It happens through the actions of ordinary human beings. Often these people have first met their personal pains, losses, conflicts, and anger and have then converted those energies into something positive for all of us.

Nearly every week we hear someone being interviewed on a talk show who has started a group for support and public education that grew out of personal pain—from finding lost children to protecting abused wives to getting alcohol off the highways and drugs off the streets. Just as evidence that we are deeply involved in a planetary rite of purification is being telegraphed to us daily, so are we increasingly sharing information with each other about how to make creative changes in our lives.

All over the planet people are waking up to our total interdependence. My own understanding was sharpened through years of counseling numbers of people. As I psychically attuned to individuals to learn their personal patterns and promise, I would see how their lives were inseparable from the life of the planet. Their changes were tightly interwoven with the changes our whole species was experiencing. Their deepest longings were drawn toward participating creatively in the changes. Over and over again the guidance was to honor the piece of the whole they had undertaken to transform. I observed that those who were willing to work with their personal changes began to expand their desires to serve the whole. The more they grasped the principles of connectedness, the more they conquered their fear and their feelings of powerlessness.

It is the recognition of wholeness that provides the key for affecting it. It's the most important "aha" we can have. Until then idealism can seem isolated, Pollyannaish and impotent. Once we remember—and that's what it is, a remembrance of wholeness—then suddenly the implications of every word, every image and every action take on new meaning. We may realize that we can choose to go on an R and R for the rest of our lives, but once we're awake, we don't want to. Passion and purpose are alive again when we wake up.

The wake-up call for a lot of us came with the photos of our

Earth sent back from the moon by the astronauts. How foolish our preoccupation with national boundaries seemed when we actually saw the wholeness of the Earth for the first time.

For others this realization of oneness came when we witnessed the fallout from Chernobyl drifting from country to country completely indifferent to political boundaries. Others watch the dollar, yen, or mark and know that a depression in any major economy affects all economies; just as a regional oil slick has ecological repercussions around the globe. The release of Nelson Mandela, the fall of the Berlin Wall, and liberation in Eastern Europe are victories for all of us.

From physics, biology, and ecology comes the same message: Our lives and destinies are irrevocably linked to each other. Our well-being, our very survival, depends on how well we cooperate, not how well we subjugate nature or each other. It is no longer just debatable whether or not we should adhere to a philosophy of isolation. At this point, we now realize, everyone is family.

AGENTS OF CHANGE

As children, we often sensed intuitively that all life is connected. With a deep and innocent wisdom we rejoiced in "saving the world." Cloaked in our chenille bedspreads, with our broken broomsticks magically transformed into swords of light, we swore to defend the downtrodden. We battled the bad guys and rescued the good—simply for the joy of saving the world.

As we grew older and our dreams began to seem a bit embarrassing, we announced our intention to go to Africa or Latin America. There we would feed the hungry, house the homeless, and free the oppressed.

Our elders smiled indulgently at our proclamations and went

right on planning the serious stuff of our lives—the right colleges, good marriages, and secure jobs—a litany of priorities that slowly dulled our noble impulses.

Even so, for many of us those impulses to save the world never completely died out. As we matured, our desire to save the world matured into "serving the world." We became world servers disguised in three-piece suits, silk blouses, and blue jeans. We began to discover that everywhere there are growing numbers of people who hold the vision that peace is not only possible, it is our destiny.

Thirty years ago when the vision of a possible new world began to go public, those who were heavily invested in maintaining dying forms yelled "peacenik" as a sort of umbrella insult against any attitudes that didn't suit the status quo. And certainly flower children, Vietnam war protestors, and coffeehouse ballad singers seemed lightweight warriors against the powers that seemed to be.

When the challenges to the status quo in society became visible, the backlashes began: fear of the unknown, ridicule, denial, suspicion, counterfeiting, trivialization. That's all part of the inevitable cycling of change.

But the vision has matured now, and more and more people are moving into the commitment cycles of change. This phenomenon has rightly been called a leaderless revolution and with good reason. It is not a vision envisioned by any one individual or group. It is the simultaneous dream of our species.

Esoteric language says we are responding to the closing of the Aryan Age which is moving toward an epoch not yet named but whose beginning is the shift from the Piscean Age to the Aquarian Age. Others speak of a golden New Age soon to come. Some speak of a New Thought Movement or a Paradigm Shift making way for a Quantum Leap in human consciousness. Words like "rebirth" and "transformation" are no longer confined to religious literature but are used in the descriptive language of everything from studies in death and dying to personal psychotherapies.

Conscious Evolution is a phrase that seems to accurately define the dream of the new world servers. It is about evolution and becoming aware of our capacity to built a new and better world by changing consciousness.

A world server is anyone who first remembers and then actualizes the deep knowing that disease in the society, just like disease in the emotions, mind, or body is not to be accepted as natural. What is sick in the particular is out of harmony with the whole. A cancer of poverty, war, or cruelty is as ravaging a condition to our one planetary body—and as personal—as to our personal bodies.

The instruments of healing may be the boardroom, the guitar, the scalpel, or the computer. It's the consciousness that wields the instruments that identify these people. They have not lost that childhood instinct of serving–saving the world. It allows them to endure the unendurable. It sustains them through the tedium of long hours buried in law books or running laboratory experiments again and again to wrestle one more fact from the unknown. It pushes them to burrow through deadening bureaucracies to gain one more piece of equality, to feed or house one more person. It prods them to rewrite, repaint, and rehearse until the truth shines through their arts. The dream motivates them to doggedly resist the money-god and discover ways to make profit without exploitation.

World servers tend to be independent in their thinking and to defy labeling. They come from every religion and nationality, every age group, every economic and social status, every profession.

Within the network of world servers there's a sense of all-inclusiveness that celebrates exploration. They can seek without dogma or censure. The great majority that I know do not give up their religions and social causes. If anything, the passion they rediscover within themselves awakens the desire to contribute to the world. "How can I help?" is one of the most common declarations I hear, both in the counseling office and in teaching.

World servers create environments—intellectual, fiscal, political, emotional, and educational—in which life cán come to fruition. Simply by being in the world, far more than any philosophy they may espouse, world servers are doing their job. A person living a transformed life is a world server.

They are idealists, yes, but also highly practical dreamers who are living the vision, often passionately. They are agents of change, instruments through which evolution moves us toward tomorrow. Surrendered to a Higher will, they serve to redirect the will of humanity. Having taken on the work of transforming their own personal shadows, they are enabled to pour Light into humanity's shadows. They walk the line between intuitively knowing the promise of a better world and not knowing the outcome of their efforts.

World servers are showing up everywhere that change is in progress—both where it is obvious and in quiet places where it is not so easy to spot. Some are here to hold the hammer that cracks up the old forms; others are here with blueprints for the new. Most are builders working one-on-one and in groups. All of them are straddling two worlds—the one they envision and the one that is passing.

Marilyn Ferguson was describing this passage we are in to an interviewer and called those who are dedicated to it transitionists. She said that it was as though there was a huge wave coming. On the shore there are three groups of people. The hedonists are down on the beach saying that we might as well have a good time since we're going to die anyway. Then there are the philosophers on the top of the hill puzzling over the meaning of it all. And then there are the transitionists gathered on the back side of the island trying to figure out how to live under water.

World servers don't always choose to protest the old order.

This can be very puzzling to those who haven't caught the vision and are living and acting out of an old order that still makes one person's politics or religion right and somebody else's politics or religion wrong. World servers are frequently *for* something rather than *against* something.

For example they may not always "fight" apartheid by demonstrating or protesting. They just won't invest in companies that participate in it. They may not protest government propaganda about foreign governments; they simply send scientists, groups of private citizens, artists, athletes, and students back and forth as human bridges between countries to increase understanding. When they do choose to "fight," they are often found using the tools within the system, organizing a focus for protest and offering alternatives, and educating the public.

It can be risky being a world server. You may be led to take jobs that aren't "good career moves." You may be guided to jump off emotional and financial cliffs; to lead when you'd rather follow; to shut up when you want to speak up—and vice versa. You may find your personality all but overwhelmed with the tasks.

A world server I know started a greeting-card company. Rather than fighting the large companies that strip forests, he chose another way. His cards celebrate the natural world on recycled paper, and the company only does business with those who work cooperatively with the environment. They take the time to check the hiring and promoting policies of companies whose treatment of women and minorities are fair. Profits are used to support wildlife habitats. The idea, he says, is "for everyone involved to benefit, including Mother Earth."

John Graham and Anne Medlock are a couple from Whidbey Island, off the coast of Washington, who started the Giraffe Project. They were not wealthy when they started this, but they were concerned. The Giraffe Project is now a foundation whose sole purpose is to recognize people who "stick their necks out for the common good." Often that means that they make a commitment with much personal risk involved. In fact taking a risk is the major criterion for becoming a Giraffe. In August 1988, *Time* magazine reported that 252 Giraffes had been named, each receiving a commendation for creative actions.

Giraffes have ranged from people who collect farmers' discarded potatoes and deliver them to the hungry, to a man who brewed a recipe of sugar-beet pulp to give black bears so that they wouldn't strip the trees and have to be killed.

ONE + ONE + ONE = TRANSFORMATION

Self-knowledge is the primary step in conscious evolutionary change. When people confront and integrate their individual fears and limitations, they facilitate the confrontation and integration of our racial, national, and planetary fears.

Lasting social change is only possible when individual consciousness has first been changed.

Conscious change, both personal and planetary, is like a high swell that begins deep in the ocean and breaks into visible waves on many shores. Its impact will eventually touch every aspect of our lives.

Energy does not build on simple addition. It builds on exponential progression. Your thoughts added to mine are much bigger than the sum of our two thought forms. Who can say which addition to the dream finally makes the balance shift from the old to the new? We can't say.

It makes no difference where you live or what role you are playing. Your power to create is within you. Your thoughts matter; your desires for this planet matter; your words matter. You *are* needed.

In the realms where conscious change begins, there is no hierarchy of importance. Not only does your place in the world offer you the perfect classroom for your own evolution, it is the place of your greatest opportunities to be a world server. If that corner of the world isn't lit up by you, who will do it?

As I write these words I am fully aware of how idealistic they sound. They are intentionally, and not innocently, offered to you in hopes that your own idealism resonates with them. We cannot create any higher than we are willing to conceive is possible. There is nothing naive in the demanding path of love.

To be a world server is to be a lover. It means that you love the truth behind appearances. The full force of evolution is behind every act of love and infuses us as we live our deepest intentions.

Love is the point of power within each of us where our God-self and our human-self fuse. It is the place where the two worlds touch and become one. There all polarizations vanish. Matter is perceived as Spirit revealed, the created is seen as the extension of the Creator. And change is understood to be the alchemical process through which God takes our divided self and makes of it a sacred whole.

I have put duality away and seen the two worlds as one.

—JELALUDDIN RUMI

Bibliography

A Course In Miracles. New York: Foundation for Inner Peace, 1975.

Alder, Vera S. *Finding of the Third Eye.* 1938. Reprint. New York: Samuel Weiser, 1978.

Berry, Thomas, *The Dream of the Earth.* San Francisco: Sierra Club Books, 1988.

Besant, Annie. *Esoteric Christianity.* 1901. Reprint, Wheaton, Ill.: Quest-Theosophical Publishing House, 1971.

Blair, Lawrence. *Rhythms of Vision.* New York: Shocken Books, 1975.

Blofeld, John. *Bodhisattva of Compassion: The Mystical Tradition of Kuan Yin.* Boulder: Shambhala, 1988.

Bohm, David, and F. David Peat. *Science, Order, Creativity.* New York: New Age Bantam, 1987.

Campbell, Joseph. *Hero with a Thousand Faces.* Princeton: Princeton University Press, 1968.

Capra, Fritzof. *The Tao of Physics.* 1976. New York: Bantam, 1984.

Care, Ken. *Terra Christa: The Global Spiritual Awakening.* Kansas City: Uni-Sun, 1985.

Carter, Forrest. *The Education of Little Tree.* Albuquerque: University of New Mexico Press, 1986.

Chitrabhanu, Gurudev Shree. *Realize What You Are: The Dynamics of Jain Meditation.* New York: Dodd, Mead, 1975.

Coates, Gary. *Resettling America: Energy, Ecology, and Community.* Acton, Mass.: Brick House Publishers, 1981.

Cohen, Alan. *The Healing of Planet Earth: Personal Power and Planetary Transformation.* Somerset, N.J.: A. Cohen, 1987.

Colegrave, Sukie. *The Spirit of the Valley.* Los Angeles: J. P. Tarcher, 1979.

Connelly, Diane M. *All Sickness Is Home Sickness.* Columbia, Md.: Center for Traditional Acupuncture, 1987.

Dass, Ram and Paul Gorman. *How Can I Help? Stories and Reflections on Service.* New York: Alfred A. Knopf, 1985.

Dass, Ram and Stephen Levine. *Grist for the Mill.* 1977. Reprint, Berkeley: Celestial Arts, 1987.

Daumal, Rene. *Mount Analogue.* Boulder: Shambhala, 1986.

DeMello, Anthony, *Song of the Bird.* New York: Doubleday, 1984.

Eisler, Riane. *The Chalice and the Blade: Our History, Our Future.* New York: Harper & Row, 1987.

Feinstein, David and Stanley Krippner. *Personal Mythology: The Psychology of Your Evolving Self.* Los Angeles: J. P. Tarcher, 1988.

Ferguson, Marilyn. *The Aquarian Conspiracy: Personal and Social Transformation in the 1980's.* Los Angeles: J. P. Tarcher, 1980.

Feild, Reshad. *The Invisible Way.* San Francisco: Harper & Row, 1979.

———. *Steps to Freedom.* Putney, Vermont: Threshold Books, 1983.

Fillmore, Charles. *Twelve Powers of Man.* Unity Village, Mo.: Unity School, 1985.

Fox, Matthew. *A Spirituality Named Compassion, and the Healing of the Global Village, Humpty Dumpty, and Us.* New York: Harper & Row, 1979.

Frankl, Viktor E. *Man's Search for Meaning.* 1939. Reprint, New York: Pocket Books, 1963.

Gawain, Shakti and Laurel King. *Living in the Light.* San Rafael, Calif.: New York Library, 1986.

Greene, Liz. *The Outer Planets and Their Cycles: The Astrology of the Collective.* Reno, Nevada: CRCS Publications, 1983.

Griscom, Chris. *Ecstasy Is a New Frequency: Teachings of the Light Institute.* Santa Fe: Bear & Co., 1987.

Haich, Elizabeth. *Initiation.* 1965. Reprint. Palo Alto: Seed Center, 1976.

Hall, Manley P. *The Secret Teachings of All Ages: An Encyclopedia Outline of Masonic, Hermetic, Quabbalistic and Rosicrucian Symbolical Philosophy.* Los Angeles: Philosophical Research Society, Inc., 1978.

Heinberg, Richard. *Memories and Visions of Paradise.* 1985. Los Angeles: J. P. Tarcher, 1989.

Hodson, Geoffrey. *The Hidden Wisdoms in the Holy Bible.* Wheaton, Ill. Quest-Theosophical Publishing House, 1967.

Houston, Jean. *God Seed.* Warwick, N.Y.: Mythos Amity House Inc., 1987.

———. *The Search for the Beloved.* Los Angeles: J. P. Tarcher, 1987.

Jampolsky, Gerald G., M.D. *Teach Only Love: The Seven Principles of Attitudinal Healing.* New York: Bantam, 1983.

Johnson, Robert A. *He: Understanding Masculine Psychology.* 1974. Reprint. New York: Perennial-Harper, 1986.

———. *She: Understanding Feminine Psychology.* 1976. Reprint. New York: Perennial-Harper, 1977.

———. *We: Understanding the Psychology of Romantic Love.* New York: Harper & Row, 1983.

Jones, Alan. *Soul Making: The Desert Way of Spirituality.* San Francisco: Harper & Row, 1985.

Joy, W. Brugh, M.D. *Joy's Way.* Los Angeles: J.P. Tarcher, 1979.

Jung, C.G. *Collected Works: Archetypes in the Collective Unconscious,* Volume 9, Part I., Second Edition, Princeton: Princeton University Press, 1968.

———. *Memories, Dreams, Reflections.* 1961. Reprint. New York: Vintage, 1965.

Keyes, Ken, Jr. *A Handbook to Higher Consciousness.* Berkeley: Living Love Center, 1975.

Kubler-Ross, Elizabeth. *On Death and Dying.* New York: Macmillan, 1969.

L'Engle, Madeline. *The Irrational Season.* New York: Harper & Row, 1977.

Leonard, George. *The Silent Pulse: The Search for the Rhythm that Exists in Each of Us.* New York: Bantam, 1981.

Levi. *The Aquarian Gospel of Jesus the Christ.* 1907. Reprint. Marina del Rey, Calif.: DeVorss, 1972.

Lovelock, James. *Gaia: A New Look at Life on Earth.* New York: Oxford University Press, 1987.

MacGregor, Geddes. *Reincarnation in Christianity.* Wheaton, Ill.: Theosophical Publishing House, 1978.

May, Rollo. *Love and Will.* New York: Norton, 1969.

Mishlove, Jeffrey. *The Roots of Consciousness.* New York: Random House, 1975.

Moss, Richard. *The Black Butterfly: An Invitation to Radical Aliveness.* Berkeley: Celestial Arts, 1986.

Moyne, John, and Coleman Barks, trans. *Open Secret: Versions of Rumi.* Putney, Vt.: Threshold Vt., 1984.

Pagels, Elaine. *The Gnostic Gospels.* New York: Random House, 1979.

Peat, F. David. *Synchronicity: The Bridge Between Matter and Mind.* New York: Bantam, 1987.

Progoff, Ira. *At a Journal Workshop: The Basic Text and Guide for Using the Intensive Journal Process.* New York: Dialogue House, 1975.

Rodegast, Pat and Judith Stanton. *Emmanuel's Book.* New York: Bantam, 1987.

Selye, Hans. *Stress Without Distress.* New York: Signet-NAL, 1975.

Sheldrake, Rupert. *A New Science of Life.* Los Angeles: J.P. Tarcher, 1983.

Siegel, Bernie S., M.D. *Love, Medicine, and Miracles.* New York: Harper & Row, 1986.

Singer, June. *Androgyny: The Opposite Within.* Boston: Sigo Press, 1987.

Spangler, David. *Reflections on the Christ.* Forres, Scotland: Findhorn Publishing, 1977.

――――. *Revelation: The Birth of New Age.* San Francisco: Rainbow Bridge, 1976.

Starhawk. *Dreaming the Dark: Magic, Sex, and Politics.* Boston: Beacon Press, 1989.

Steiner, Rudolf. *The Reappearance of Christ in the Etheric.* Hudson, New York: Anthroposophic Press, 1983.

Stone, Merlin. *When God Was a Woman.* San Diego: Harcourt, 1978.

Suzuki, Shumyer. *Zen Mind, Beginner's Mind.* New York: Weatherhill, 1970.

Swimme, Brian. *The Universe Is a Green Dragon: A Cosmic Creative Story.* Santa Fe: Bear & Co., 1984.

Targ, Russell, and Keith Harary. *The Mind Race: Understanding and Using Psychic Abilities.* New York: Ballantine, 1985.

Teilhard de Chardin, Pierre. *The Phenomenon of Man.* 1955. Reprint. New York: Harper & Row, 1965.

Trungpa, Chogyam. *Cutting Through Spiritual Materialism.* Boulder: Shambhala, 1987.

Unity School of Christianity Staff, ed. *Metaphysical Bible Dictionary.* Unity Village, Mo.: Unity School, 1931.

Watson, Lyall. *Gifts of Unknown Things.* New York: Simon & Schuster, 1976.

Whitfield, Charles L. *Healing the Child Within.* Deerfield Beach, Fla.: Health Communications, 1987.

Wilker, Ken, ed. *The Holographic Paradigm and Other Paradoxes: Exploring the Leading Edge of Science.* Boulder: Shambhala, 1982.

Williams, Jay G. *Yeshua Buddha.* Wheaton, Illinois: Quest-Theosophical Publishing House, 1978.

Woititz, Janet G. *Adult Children of Alcoholics.* Deerfield Beach, Fla.: Health Communications, 1983.

Wolf, Fred A. *Star Wave: Mind, Consciousness, and Quantum Physics.* New York: Collier-Macmillan, 1986.

Yogananda, Paramahansa. *Autobiography of a Yogi.* 1946. Los Angeles: Self Realization Fellowship, 1971.

Young, Meredith Lady. *Agartha: The Essential Guide to Personal Transformation in the New Era.* New York: Ballantine, 1989.

Ywahoo, Dhyani. *Voices of Our Ancestors: Cherokee Teachings from the Wisdom Fire.* Boulder: Shambhala, 1987.

Index

Change process
awakening, 159–89
of the Buddha, 304–6
case examples of 7-step
model, 281–300
challenge, 124–42
commitment, 190–220
exercise to work 7-step
model, 307–8
form, 73–87
purification, 221–48
resistance, 143–58
societal examples of, 300–
304
surrender, 249–78
See also individual topics.
Channeling, 177–82
cautions related to, 179,
181
historical view, 178
inner-plane teachers,
180–82
low order spirits and,
180–81
making contact with
higher energy, 180
mediums, role of, 177–
78
purest form of, 178–79
use of term, 178
Chetwynd, Tom, 165
Children, past-life memories,
115–16
Chitrabhanu, Guruder, 21
Choice, 34–35
Christianity, feminine aspect
in, 55

Chuang-Tzu, 264
Clairvoyance, 129
Claustrophobia, 254–55
Coates, Gary, 27
Coincidences, 163, 164
Collective shadows, 239–
40
Commitment
to change, 7
characteristics of stage,
190, 192–93
clarity of intention and,
203–4
doubt and, 196–98
faith and, 198–203
meditation, use of, 212–
14
visualization, use of, 207–
11
Connelly, Dr. Dianne, 38,
227
Consciousness, change and,
64
Controls, letting go of, 261–
63
Creation, cycles of, 5
Crisis
change and, 3–4, 15
meaning of term, 15
Crystals, 99
Cynicism, 22–23

Daumal, Rene, 191
Death, 226
denial of, 234–35
fear of, 281–82
De Mello, Anthony, 21

Kelly, Walt, 77
Keyes, Ken, Jr., 130
Kierkegaard, Søren, 196
Krippner, Stanley, 131
Krishna, 41, 251
Kübler-Ross, Elisabeth, 234

Lao-Tzu, 41, 253
Laurence, Brother, 253
L'Engle, Madeleine, 19
Lessons
    exercise related to, 142
    learning of, 17, 19
Light, 66
    Pure Light, 178–79
Limitations, handling of, 238
Lincoln, Abraham, 213
Love
    forgiveness and, 115
    pure love, 52
    unconditional love, 108
Lovelock, James, 265
Lower will, 35, 36–37

Machu Picchu, 128–29
Macoy, Robert, 50
Magellan, Ferdinand, 82
Mahabharata, The, 197
Maharaj-ji, 176
Mandala, repatterning of, 270–71
Man's Search for Meaning (Frankl), 34
Masculine aspect
    characteristics of, 54

dominance of, 57
visualization, to meet
    male committee, 189
Masculine energy, 53
Masters, making contact
    with, 180
May, Rollo, 131
Meditation, 212–14
    effects of, 212–13
    learning methods of, 212
Medlock, Anne, 315
Memories, Dreams, Reflections (Jung), 234
Memory, past-life memories, 106–7
Mitchell, Dr. Edgar D., 160
Money, giving up addiction
    to, 204–5
Morphogenetic fields, theory
    of, 150–51
Moses, 196–97
Mother Goddess, 54, 55, 65
Mount Analogue (Daumal), 191
Mystery Schools, 49–51
    ancient precursors to, 50–51
    education of, 62–63
    entrance requirements, 51
    gender and, 53
    method of teaching, 49–50, 51–52
    Secret Doctrine, 49
    self-knowledge, training
        in, 52–53
    types of, 50, 51